The Handbook of
DOLL REPAIR
and
RESTORATION

BY MARTY WESTFALL

ROBERT HALE LTD.
LONDON

® *1979 by Marty Westfall*
Reprinted 1991
First published in Great Britain 1981
ISBN 0-7091-8857-9
Robert Hale Limited
Clerkenwell House
Clerkenwell Green
London, EC1

To Bud,
my husband, my sweetheart, and my best friend

Printed in the United States of America

The Handbook of
DOLL
REPAIR

and

R ESTORATION

Contents

ACKNOWLEDGMENTS

I am most grateful to Dena June Moore, who allowed me to photograph her antique dolls with my replicas.

And I am deeply indebted to Mrs. Kay Pinney, my editor, for the care and patience she showed in working with a most difficult book.

Introduction

Out of the dim shadows of antiquity she comes, into the light—it's daybreak for that beautiful old doll you have acquired. She has no memory to offer, only faded clothes and a dirty face. The clothes she is wearing, the condition she is in—they are an unwritten diary of the time when she was created, the time in which she existed. From these evidences of the dear departed past we can imagine the loving hands that held her, played with her, perhaps unknowingly preserved her, so that we today can look upon her with pride of ownership and with the certain knowledge that we, too, shall preserve her for generation upon generation.

A small percentage of collectors display any doll treasure "as is" or "as found." Never mind the chips, the hairline cracks, the decrepit rags she is wearing. Ignore the missing finger(s)—even a missing arm or leg is not important. What *is* important is that she is authentic. She has not been tampered with. And she has many stories to tell to the person who will "listen."

Hold such a doll close to you; put your cheek against hers, and in spite of the musty odor of age, you will almost feel the vibrations of those who have loved her. Close your eyes as you hold her and let your imagination go back through the years with her—chances are, the things you imagine may really have happened. If you belong to this category of collectors—those who love an old doll no matter what its condition—you are a member of a minority group, elite though it may be.

The majority of collectors who visit my studio fall into other very specific categories. Age and sex have nothing to do with the matter. Some of the most enthusiastic collectors I have encountered are men, but I find they have one thing in common with women collectors: they want damaged dolls restored as near to their original condition as possible.

Next come those who demand "prettiness" rather than authenticity. Some well-to-do collectors who spend time traveling around in search of old doll treasures rush their finds to me as soon as they get home. "Fix this broken finger," they demand, or "Make a new body—this one is dirty and patched." Or "Take these rags off her and make her a new costume." "Put her head on a new composition body—this old one is hideous." Or, when the body, arms, and legs are good but the head is damaged, "Make a new head."

Often, although I keep careful records of what was done in the restoration process, and offer clients not only this record but also all the old parts that have been replaced, they refuse to accept them. And though advised against unnecessary repairs, rarely can this type of collector be talked out of doing what he or she wants. So what, if such repairs are costly and time consuming? Money is no object—"I simple wouldn't display something that looks like *this* in *our* beautiful home." It's "Pretty her up, and hang the cost!"

I would be remiss if I did not warn that you should *never*—if avoidable—make or have made *unnecessary repairs* on valuable and rare old dolls. But don't pass up the opportunity to acquire a doll that captures your heart, just because it may have hairline cracks, small chips, worn areas, and other evidence of age and handling. These may reduce its value, but not greatly decrease your pleasure if you really admire the doll.

From the standpoint of investment, we all prefer to buy a doll in pristine condition, but they are as rare as a dog without fleas. If you are fortunate enough to find a doll that is a real artifact, do nothing more than clean it as best you can—and with the greatest of care—and if the body has a hole or two, put on a patch where necessary so that the stuffing will not leak out. Resist the urge to "fancy it up." Such a doll is highly desirable to the serious collector even if its clothes are faded, worn, or beginning to deteriorate, or other damage is apparent.

If an old doll looks as if it's ready for the junk pile, make an effort to salvage or reclaim it—but treat it just enough to prevent further deterioration. Don't try to make it look as though it just came from the factory.

It may seem contradictory for me to caution collectors against any restoration beyond that which will save a doll from discard or total disaster—and then write a book like this one. It really is not. You see, by far the majority of the collectors I deal with are people with limited incomes who cannot afford to buy complete dolls in mint condition. They come from every age group, from the young mother with a passionate love for dolls who cannot afford today's high prices, to older people who have raised their families and now have the time, if not the finances, to build a collection. These collectors do not have the money to travel extensively, and so they haunt flea markets, auctions, garage sales, and the like in search of doll parts. Never do they bid on a complete doll at an auction; instead, they bid on any heads, arms, legs, bodies, and related items that are put up for sale. Their reasons for such purchases are fairly obvious. They may be trying to build a personal collection at minimum cost, or perhaps they repair damaged dolls for resale, to augment their small incomes. In either case, they are just as serious about dolls as are the so-called elite collectors.

It is for these people that I have written this book, hoping to provide them with the basic information and the methods needed to turn out truly fine restoration work—for their own satisfaction and enjoyment and, perhaps, to make a small but honest profit if that is their aim. Everything such a person can learn to do will save the expense of high-priced professional repairs—and the savings can be used to buy more doll parts and supplies.

The value of belonging to one or more good doll clubs cannot be overemphasized. But belonging is not enough. You should attend their meetings, for the discussions will not only acquaint you with fellow members; through association with them you will learn much about antique dolls that might take you years to find out otherwise. The United Federation of Doll Clubs, Inc., is one of the oldest, and it has the largest membership of the doll clubs in operation today. Each year a national convention is held somewhere in the United States, one year on the East Coast, the next on the West, the next in Middle America—so members in all areas have an opportunity to attend one of these magnificent affairs at least once every three years (or every year, if they can afford transportation fees). On a smaller scale, the various regional U.F.D.C. clubs hold regional conventions that are patterned after the national one. Club meetings are held monthly, at which time visiting speakers often give lectures, demonstrations, slide programs, and other doll-related presentations.

I also cannot stress too emphatically the need to invest in fine books for study and research. Though I have a comprehensive library of doll books (and many not worth the price of shipping and handling), I highly recommend the two massive volumes written by the Colemans, *The Collector's Book of Dolls' Clothes* and *The Collector's Encyclopedia of Dolls*. Their cost may seem prohibitive to some, but the amount of information they contain is worth many times their price. If you're going into this business, or are already becoming established, you owe it to yourself and to your customers to become as knowledgeable as possible. The Colemans did years of research to provide you with just such information.

Unfortunately, for future generations who will tread the same paths that we now follow, research will be even more confusing than it is now. More and more collectors are "marrying" odds and ends together in order to make a so-called *complete* doll, either for their own collections or to sell. If these dolls are kept in private collections, sooner or later they will fall into other hands. It has always been so—and it will forever continue so, as long as there are those who love and collect dolls, or those who buy and sell dolls as a business proposition.

Within the pages of this book you will find chapters on repairing damaged bisques and chinas; setting sleep eyes; setting stationary (fixed) eyes; making new wigs and safely refurbishing old ones; repairing ball-jointed bodies; stringing bodies; repairing and cleaning kid bodies; making gusseted kid bodies as well as bodies for china-heads; taking patterns from old kid or cloth bodies without ripping them apart; and general instructions on the care and cleaning of old composition and wax dolls. The final two chapters, which I believe will prove two of the most important, deal with detecting repaired dolls and distinguishing reproductions and fakes from genuine antique dolls. The information they contain may shock the complacent—even those who think they cannot be fooled will become more wary of accepting without question what appears to be an antique doll in mint, or nearly mint, condition.

Lest there be confusion over the usage of the two words *replica* and *reproduction* in the text of this book, I want to make clear that this is simply a matter of semantics. I *choose* to call the dolls I create replicas, and that is the way they are listed in Dollspart Supply

Company's catalog. I have nothing to do with other dolls sold by them and labeled reproductions. Therefore, when you read the word *replica* it refers to my creations; *reproductions* as used in this book refers to dolls made by someone else.

Though I no longer do repair work, over the years I have handled and restored many beautiful antique dolls, studying them and researching them; and I have inspected many museum exhibits. I have also experimented with literally hundreds of repair materials until I finally found products that would work successfully. I know that the in-depth instructions and procedures described herein will produce satisfactory results. Among the various materials mentioned in this book, you will find many that are common enough to be bought locally. These are pointed out. Other items will have to be ordered, and an appendix provides the names and addresses of suppliers. I have used these materials and products successfully, but I cannot be held responsible if any of them are misused. I cannot predict how they will work or react unless they are handled precisely as specified in the directions.

1

Antique Dolls– How They Were Made

Many doll collectors, mostly beginners—but, strangely enough, some who have been collecting for several years—do not know the difference between chinas and bisques. A case in point: a "collector" came into my studio recently at closing time. Though she had been collecting dolls for five years, she had just acquired her first "glass-head" doll. Her collection before that had included only compositions, one tin-head Minerva, and a large number of the now collectible plastics. Of them all, she was proudest of her "glass-head" doll, which was, of course, an old china. It was one in the morning when she finally left, armed with (I hope) at least a basic working knowledge of collecting not only chinas but bisques.

Her love affair with these old beauties is representative of that of many collectors with whom I come in contact. They fall in love with old dolls at first sight, but are completely lacking in knowledge about them. Some of these collectors are people with limited incomes, and so they will find this book invaluable: it will explain how they can obtain damaged heads and restore them—as well as add missing fingers and make any other necessary repairs—and build a handsome collection of which they can be justifiably proud.

Damaged heads can often be found at flea markets, rummage sales, auctions—even stuck back in a corner of an antique shop. The price you pay in an antique shop is determined by how extensive the damage is. At flea markets and rummage sales, if the price is too high try making an offer more in keeping with your budget; quite often a fair offer will be accepted. It's at least worth a try. The only advice I can give about auctions is to get there at least an hour before sale time so that you have an opportunity to examine any boxes of so-called junk—quite often damaged old doll heads and parts of dolls are tossed in with other odds and ends that seem worthless. If you spot such a treasure, keep your eyes on that box. Someone else may notice the same thing that you did, and may remove what she wants when no one is watching. Thus, you may find yourself bidding on a box that no longer contains the objects that were originally in it. Another thing to watch for is a single doll head or several parts of dolls displayed separately on a table. The same type of person, thinking herself unobserved, may scoop up a few such items and hide them in the bottom of a box of obvious junk, bid that box in when it comes up for sale, and oftentimes get herself a dishonest bargain.

A bit of basic information on the manufacture of antique dolls will teach the collector to call a china doll a china (and not, as so many uninformed collectors do, a "glass head"), and to recognize a bisque doll when she sees one. It will also explain what processes the doll went through before it reached the hands of the consumer and how the collector can preserve its beauty. Most important, it will show why the repair methods described here will not damage a doll.

Parian, china, bisque—they are basically the same. All began with a mixed formula that included kaolin (china clay), ball clay, feldspar, and flint. Sometimes other "earth products" were added. If several women were to bake chocolate cakes, each using her own proportions of the basic ingredients, each cake would be slightly different. One might have a fine texture, another might be slightly coarser, and still another might be quite coarse indeed. This is a rather broad analogy, but easily understandable when one considers that each cook or dollmaker handles the ingredients in a different manner. Too, the origin of the porcelain ingredients had a great deal to do with the texture of the finished product. Each factory carefully guarded its formula, but the methods of firing and finishing were essentially the same.

Earlier dolls were made by rolling out the "clay dough" much as a cook rolls out piecrust. After it was rolled to the desired thickness, squares were cut out large enough to finger press into molds, one for the front half, the other for the back. If a collector is lucky enough to own such a doll, an examination of the inside of the head will reveal the finger-pressure marks of the person who made it. Sometimes you can actually see fingerprints. Poured doll heads are smooth inside, with no indentations like those made by the fingertips.

"Poured" heads came later, after dollmakers discovered how to convert the clay dough into a mixture thin enough to pour into molds, thereby cutting down on work time. This thin mixture (used exclusively today by dollmakers) is known as porcelain slip. It was poured into a plaster mold, and as the liquid part of the porcelain slip was absorbed by the porous plaster of the mold, a buildup of the solids from the slip began to accumulate on the mold walls and form the doll's head (or whatever part of the doll was being molded). As the liquid continued to be absorbed by the plaster, the level of slip in the mold naturally went down; so more slip had to be added, to keep the level up to the proper height.

When the buildup of porcelain on the mold walls eventually reached the desired thickness, the slip remaining in the mold was drained off, leaving the hollow doll's head (or other part) inside the mold. Then the mold was propped upside down and allowed to set undisturbed, until the newly molded piece reached the necessary degree of solidity.

Then, as today, it was impossible to set a specific limit on how long slip should be left in a mold, or to plan the exact time required for a piece to dry to the "greenware" stage, so that it could be removed from the mold. The humidity of the day, the dampness or dryness of the mold, even the density of the plaster from which the mold itself was made, affected the time it took not only for the proper thickness to develop on the walls of the mold, but for the material to dry to the greenware stage.

When a greenware head had been removed from the mold but was still damp, the mold lines were partly removed, the ears were pierced, and—when necessary—eye sockets were cut out if the doll was to have glass eyes. Then the head was placed on a "plaster bat," simply a large, flat plaster area on which porcelain greenware was put to draw out the dampness. Once the head reached the "leather-hard" stage, the remainder of the mold lines were removed, the holes for pierced earrings were enlarged, and any final carving and removing of flaws was completed. Finally, the entire piece was polished before it was put into the kiln. (In the old days, kilns were referred to as ovens.)

When the "firing" (sometimes called baking) was completed, a temperature of approximately 2,300° had been reached. This sometimes required as long as 30 hours. (The kitchen ovens in which some repairs are "fired" today cannot reach such a temperature. That is why the methods to be described later will not damage your doll *if* you follow the instructions.)

The fired product was white porcelain, or bisque. If the finished doll was to be the parian type, the "skin" was left in its dull-finished white. Cheeks, eyes, lips, brows, and hair were painted in the decorating room by artists skilled at china painting.

China paints, also called overglaze colors, are primarily oxides and carbonates of metals—in other words, mineral colors. The addition of fluxes to the finely ground mineral colors, combined with the heat of a kiln (approximately 1,300° F at this stage), caused the colors to fuse to the ware permanently. The colors were first ground in an oil medium, then applied, and finally fired lightly to the above temperature. The only purpose of the oil medium was to hold the colors on the doll until a temperature was reached that would burn out the oil and make the colors fuse permanently with the bisque.

If the doll was destined to be a bisque with a delicate flesh-tone "skin," the skin was painted prior to the addition of cheeks, lips, eyelashes, and brows. Because of the second light firing necessary to fuse the colors, the face, hands, and feet of a china, parian, or bisque doll can be washed. The color will not come off if only mild soap and water are used, but never use an abrasive cleaner. If soap and water do not do the job satisfactorily, use a soft cloth dipped in gasoline or denatured (wood) alcohol.

Chinas (sometimes, as already mentioned, erroneously called glass heads today) were made exactly like the dolls just described, but before the surface was painted, they were covered with liquid glaze that was allowed to dry. Then a second firing, to a temperature of approximately 2,150° F, melted the glaze and caused it to fuse permanently to the body of the ware.

There has been some debate among researchers and today's dollmakers as to whether the color on chinas was applied under the glaze (directly on the bisque, prior to covering the ware with liquid glaze) or *over* the fired glaze. Innumerable experiments carried on in my studio, using every product advertised as being "stable" through a cone 2 (2,150° F temperature), have been dismal failures as far as underglaze colors are concerned. Without exception, there was some "bleeding"—that is, color running under the glaze into areas where there should be no coloration. Examination of old china heads will almost always reveal signs of fading, even total lack of color, on the backs of the heads where, as dolls were handled and laid in a reclining position over the years, the color wore off. Sometimes dolls were picked up and put down so often that friction completely rubbed away the *overglaze* colors.

After the artists applied china paints, the dolls were given a third and final light firing.

In summation, only those dolls that have been glazed to give them a brilliant, shiny surface, a high gloss, are chinas. Those *without* a high gloss are referred to as bisques. Those described as parians have neither flesh tones nor gloss. Most chinas and parians have one thing in common—painted, molded hair. Rare ones have glass eyes and wigs.

Actually, dolls of all races—Negroes, Indians, Orientals among them—were made of porcelain bisque. Although these are rarer than their Caucasian counterparts—and command higher prices—the colored porcelains began exactly as those already described here. It was after the bisque firing that those meant to be Negroes, Indians, or Orientals were painted a "skin tone" representative of their race, be it black, brown, reddish-brown, or yellow-brown. There are still many of these beauties available.

Later, following the Civil War, manufacturers discovered methods of coloring the previously white porcelain slip; therefore some of the antique dolls are colored all the way through. The older ones, though, had their color painted on the white base.

2

Repairing Doll Heads

Judging from hundreds of letters received over the years, I believe there are as many reasons for wanting to do doll repair as there are products to use. Because there are many handicapped people with limited budgets wanting to learn, as well as other would-be doll repairers who must start out with as little investment as possible, the basic instructions that follow here will include filler recipes that can be made at home, along with suggestions for using materials to be found around the house at little or no cost.

The equipment I use in my studio is very expensive. So are the supplies, but I didn't start out with them. After all, one must learn to crawl before he can walk—and I really "crawled" for several years, saving to buy that next piece of equipment, to add better products to my inventory, to buy expensive books to study. I taught myself, and I believe I can teach you, and steer you clear of many of the pitfalls that plague the beginner, as well as help you avoid some of the disastrous experiments I resorted to.

If you have sufficient funds to start out with the best products, write to William Karl Klein of A. Ludwig Klein & Son, P.O. Box

245, Harleysville, Pa. 19438, and ask for a price list. Order also his book *Repairing and Restoring China and Glass: The Klein Method,* and study it before deciding what products to order. As this book progresses, you will be introduced to the specific Klein products I prefer. The only item recommended in the Klein book with which I disagree is the single-diaphragm air compressor. I did not find it practical for my work because, in spraying, occasionally the air brush would spit out globs of color and ruin my work.

I prefer a Craftsman, which provides a very steady source of air. It is equipped with an air storage tank and a pressure regulator gauge with controls from 0 to 125 PSI (pounds per square inch, the measure of air pressure delivered to the air brush). Not once in all the years I have used it has it ever behaved erratically.

REPAIRING DOLL HEADS, SHOULDER PLATES, AND SHOULDER HEADS

Where I felt it was important, in various chapters throughout this book I have recommended specific glues used in repairing dolls. Of course there may be other kinds that will also give good results. Ordinary waterproof household cements that dry transparent will hold broken edges together indefinitely.

In this section we will deal with the various types of damage to doll heads (socket heads), shoulder plates, or shoulder-head dolls. Since the aim of the mender is to make the doll look as nearly as possible as it did originally, the first consideration is to *repair* it, and the second is to make the repair as inconspicuous as possible. The main difficulty is that the doll is porcelain, but the mending materials, colors, and finishes are nonfireable—that is, they cannot be put through a *kiln* firing as the porcelain was. The best we can do is to simulate the porcelain, the glazes, and the colors. Except for the hardness and durability of the porcelain, we can do this very closely.

A broken shoulder plate (part of the swivel head and socket unit), a head broken off at the neck of a shoulder-head doll, and sometimes the doll head itself, broken into several pieces, are common problems in the business of restoration. If you have all the pieces and they have not previously been glued together, this type of restoration is relatively easy to make, though time consuming.

Cement will not bond to a soiled surface, and so the broken edges must be cleaned even though no glue has ever touched them. Scrub all breaks with a toothbrush dipped in soap and hot water, rinse thoroughly, and dry *before* attempting any repairs. This is a good time to clean the entire doll head or part, to remove the years of accumulated dirt and grime.

Before any glue can be applied successfully, all parts must also be absolutely dry. Drying can be speeded up by placing the just scrubbed and rinsed part inside a *cold* oven and turning the temperature no higher than 125° F. One hour at this temperature is adequate. Do not remove the part until it has cooled.

If the broken part has been badly glued together, it must first be taken apart and cleaned before attempting any repairs. This presents a few minor problems when working on a broken bisque head with glass eyes, a wig, and possibly a fabric tongue, for these too must be removed. Wigs are usually affixed to the pate with water-soluble glue. If you cannot peel off the wig a little at a time (but you usually can because glue deteriorates over the years), fill a Windex spray bottle with warm water and spray the water, a little at a time, *under* the wig base. After each spraying, peel that section of the wig loose. Try not to saturate the wig or its base. Should this method fail, use a single-edged razor blade to scrape carefully under the glue. If the old wig is to be discarded (heaven forbid), such care is not essential.

After the wig and pate have been removed, soak the head in warm water to remove the eyes. Soaking allows water to permeate the plaster holding the eyes in place. Fifteen minutes is usually ample time. Using a pointed tool (a nut pick is good for this), dig out the plaster, being careful not to break the eyes. If the eyes were set stationary (fixed in position), dig out one eye at a time. If they were sleep eyes, the unit must be removed intact, and that requires a lot more care. As you dig and scrape at the plaster on *both* sides of the eye rocker (alternately), place your forefinger on the rocker at the center point between the eyes and hold it firmly. Be sure to clean all the remaining plaster from around the eye sockets. If there is a cloth tongue, remove it and let it dry while you're working on the head.

If you're restoring a reglued bonnet head, or any head with molded hair or other decorated, uneven surfaces, the following procedure applies to it, as well as to the others mentioned thus far: badly glued breaks must be taken apart and cleaned before attempting any repairs. Place the head (or whatever part you're working on) in a large pan, fill it with *cold* water to a height of two to three inches *above* the parts, and slowly bring the water to a boil. Do not be afraid of this procedure. Remember, during its manufacture the head withstood firing to approximately 2,300° F. The boiling point of water is only 212° F at sea level, and although that figure varies with the altitude, at no time will the temperature be high

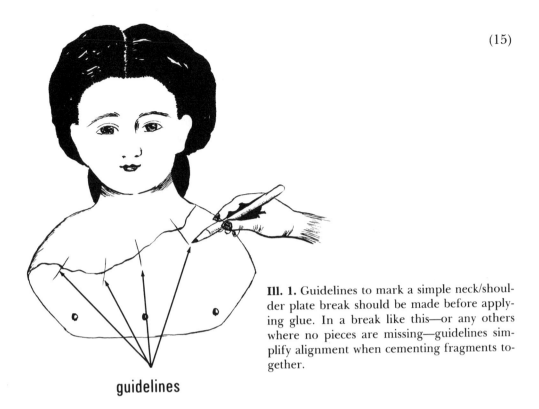

guidelines

enough to damage the doll head, unless it is cracked already. After 10 minutes, remove the head to a thickly folded towel. Metal serving tongs are ideal for lifting the head, but hold the tong jaws in hot water a few seconds before touching them to the hot doll part. *Never* grasp an area near a broken or damaged surface with the tongs.

Place the head gently on the folded towel. Glued pieces can easily be pulled apart while the porcelain is hot. Then the broken edges can be scraped clean, using a sharp knife with nonserrated blade. If the head cools too quickly, repeat the process of starting the pieces in a pan of cold water and slowly bringing it to a boil again.

After all broken edges are absolutely clean and dry, plan the reassembly and mark out guidelines (Ill. 1). Guidelines are essential because once you have applied the cement, you must work fast. Without guidelines you would have to slide the pieces back and forth seeking correct alignment, and chances are that small pieces of porcelain would chip off. Filling these in would make extra work later. With the guidelines premarked, it is simple to match them up and press the two pieces firmly together, to squeeze out excess adhesive. Do *not* remove the excess until after the repair has dried. To do so would push the pieces out of alignment.

Pieces may be held together while drying in several ways, the safest of which is by means of a sandbox (Ill. 2). Other materials

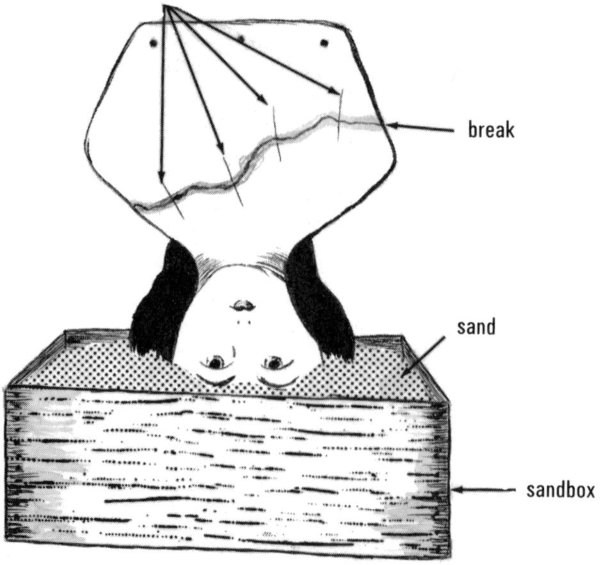

guidelines

break

sand

sandbox

Ill. 2. After broken sections have been marked with guidelines and cemented together, place the head in sandbox deeply enough to obtain a perfect balance. Let dry undisturbed 24 hours. If further drying is needed, put box and head (being careful not to disturb the balance) into a *cold* oven, turn the heat to 125° F., and leave for two hours. Then turn off oven but leave box and head inside until they are completely cool. *(Never use a cardboard box in the oven.* Lacking a wooden box for the sand, use a rectangular metal cake pan or any glass or metal container of appropriate size.)

used for the same purpose include masking tape, nonhardening modeling clay, and Mortite, a product available at most hardware stores. Mortite is actually a weatherproofing substance, used for sealing cracks around doors and windows. Although it is much cheaper than hobby clays, it has the same properties. In using any of these materials, do not apply excess pressure to the glued area or you may push the pieces out of alignment.

After a thin coating of glue has been applied to *both* broken edges, press the pieces tightly together. *Feel* the joining with a fingernail to locate any unevenness, and if any is found, correct it at once.

In pressing the pieces tightly together, the pressure forces out any trapped air and prevents air from getting back into the joint. It also makes the cement coating *skin thin* by forcing out any excess, thus making a perfect cohesion. The weight of the top piece in balance in the sandbox is all that is required for pressure during

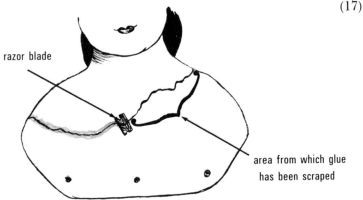

razor blade

area from which glue
has been scraped

Ill 3. Sketch above shows correct way to hold a single-edge razor blade (as flat as possible) for scraping off excess glue, which is represented by shaded area on both sides of break. Before removing outside glue, reinforce inside of break with outing flannel saturated in Elmer's Glue. Strip off excess glue and put flannel in place. Let dry overnight. *Then* scrape off dried outside glue, represented here by shaded area at left.

drying. Complete setting of the cement can be hurried by force-drying (if the glue container directions so specify), but first allow 24 hours of *un*disturbed air drying. Then place the sandbox in a *cold* oven and heat it at 125° F for the length of time given in the directions. Turn off the oven and let the contents cool before removing them.

Clean all excess cement from the surface with a single-edged razor blade. The way you hold the blade is important. It must be held in such a position that it will not dig *into* the cemented joint (Ill. 3); unless you hold it nearly parallel with the surface, you may gouge into—or cut out—some of the cement *in* the joint. Do not make any careless motions with the blade.

Check the repaired area for nicks or small chips on the edges or along the cemented joint. *Inside* nicks or chips (those that don't show) can be filled with epoxy glue, making the repair stronger than ever. On the outside a filler is required, one that can be sanded down later to make the repair as invisible as possible.

If you are repairing a doll head broken in several pieces—and this applies to *all* kinds, particularly those with molded hair, bonnet heads, and so on—the techniques just described are followed; only the procedure for glueing is different. *Always* begin with the *front* breaks (the face). Do not cement *all* pieces at the same time. Join one or two with hand pressure and leave them balanced in the sandbox until the cement hardens before adding more pieces. The final piece to be glued in should be in the area covered by a wig or molded hair, or a bonnet in the case of a bonnet doll.

Even the thinnest amount of glue adds some bulk to a repair area, and so the last piece to be added will never fit *exactly* into the space left for it. On this final piece, it will be necessary to grind down all the broken edges slightly. Lacking an electric grinder, you can use a carborundum stone. Any irregularities can be filled in with the same product or mixture used in repairing other damaged areas.

After the excess cement has been scraped off the repair with a single-edged razor blade, sand the bisque or china until every trace of adhesive is removed. Unfinished joints show slightly in spite of the tightest and most accurate alignment and glueing, but by carefully filling in any irregularities and following the directions given later, the repair will be hard to find.

Replacing Missing Parts of Shoulder Plates

The preliminary steps described earlier for preparing parts of a doll for mending—i.e., placing the head (or pieces) in a pan of cold water and bringing the water slowly to a boil, then scrubbing off any dirt or foreign material—must also be followed before attempting to replace any missing parts. All surfaces must be absolutely clean for perfect cohesion of the materials used.

To build up a missing part—on a shoulder plate, for example—glue cardboard *under* the damaged area, shaping it as nearly as possible to the way the original was. If the cardboard cannot be pushed into shape, soak porous-type gray cardboard in warm water until it's pliable. It can then be easily shaped by hand *under* the damaged area. Or the softened cardboard can be forced into shape by putting it over a similarly shaped area, binding it against that area, and letting it dry into the proper shape. Use string, or wrap tape around and around, to hold the cardboard in place while it dries.

Remove this shaped cardboard and glue it inside the broken place. After the glue has dried thoroughly, fill in *over* the cardboard with a creamy mixture of Durham's Water Putty mixed with just enough water to bring it to the right consistency for spreading. Apply the Durham mixture thinly, and allow each layer to dry enough to change from its shiny, just-applied look to a dull appearance; then add another thin layer. It should take no more than three layers to bring up the level to *just below* the surface of the part being mended.

Because Durham's, when dry, is a yellowish color, a final coat of white filler must be applied over it, thickly enough so that the final sanding will not expose any part of the top coat of Durham's.

It is difficult to get a replacement part as smooth as the rest of the object, but—correctly made—a replacement part is extremely strong. When dry, it can be further smoothed by sanding. Any low places can be made level with fillers.

When repairs are completed, they can be made more durable by reinforcement on the inside. Dip heavy strips of fabric, such as outing flannel, into glue, and work the strips, *inside,* over the repair, extending them onto the unbroken area in all directions.

REPLACING TEETH AND TONGUES

Three types of doll mouths will be discussed in this section: the open-closed mouth, the open-closed mouth with molded teeth and tongue, and the open mouth with teeth and tongue separate. All three came from molds—in the greenware stage—with *solid* mouths. The first two remained that way; the third type required cutting a hole in the mouth, as well as some carving and shaping to prepare it for receiving teeth and tongue, glued separately, to give the doll a more realistic look.

After an open-closed mouth doll was bisque fired, its upper and lower lips were painted separately; the small area between the lips was left white, or tinted pink to represent a slightly open mouth. After a doll with open-closed mouth and molded teeth and tongue was bisque fired, its "inner mouth and tongue" were painted a slightly darker red (for contrast) than the upper and lower lips, and its teeth were left unpainted, or white. Usually dolls with these types of mouth had the outline of the two points of the upper lip, the outer edge of the bottom lip, and often the inner edges delicately accentuated with a darker lip color. One rarely finds any damage to the teeth or tongue because these features were very shallow, the porcelain (as stated earlier) was *solid,* and the mouth was *painted* to create an illusion of an open mouth or of one with teeth and tongue. There was no hole through which an eager young mother could jam an object in an attempt to "play-feed" her baby. Too, the projection of the lips afforded protection to the shallow lower portions of the mouth.

On the other hand, one often finds beautiful open-mouth bisque heads with one or all of the teeth missing. Frequently a red cloth tongue is also gone. In some cases, the tongue was made of what appears to be molded porcelain.

Make an effort to find a doll artist—one who works exclusively in porcelain—and have teeth custom made. If you're lucky, she may already have "press molds" made from patterns obtained either from old doll teeth, or the new plastic teeth, some of which are beautifully shaped (they come assorted—two on a peg, four on a peg, sometimes six on a peg). She may even have some already made up, in which case you can try them in your doll head to get a perfect fit.

If the doll artist has none of the above, perhaps she will hand carve teeth for you. In this case, you may have to pay a premium price.

If the tongue is missing from the head, the same doll artist will probably make one for you—if the original was in porcelain and you want the replacement to be of the same material.

Should you be tempted to order plastic teeth from a supplier— and I do not recommend the use of plastic with an old doll, in *any* capacity—most of them come in assorted sizes and are affixed to a small, bright red square of felt to represent a tongue. The gaudy red felt can be "toned down" by pulling the teeth loose and saturating the felt material with a solution of china paint (of the desired color) ground thoroughly in water. Allow the tongue to dry before glueing it in place. I will admit that once the plastic teeth are glued in place, it is almost impossible to tell the difference—most certainly a beginner would be fooled by them.

Other fabrics besides felt can be used to make a tongue—outing flannel and similar materials. If a shaped tongue is needed, cut a very small rectangle of heavy fabric, fold it in half, round off the corners, and, using tiny whip stitches, close the raw edges. Turn right side out. In the center of the fold, cut a very small opening, just large enough to push wisps of cotton through for slight padding. A round toothpick, broken off at one end, may be used as a "stuffer." When the tongue is as thick as you want it, cut a narrow strip of matching cloth long enough to fold across the back of the tongue (adding enough to the length so that small extensions will project on either side of the tongue). Fold the strip in half and glue the *center* of the fold over the opening in the tongue and across the back of the tongue. Let dry. This "creation" should now resemble a tiny apron with strings.

Next, place the unit on a square of waxed paper so that the "apron strings" are positioned straight out from the tongue. Squeeze out enough Elmer's glue onto the strings, from one end to the other, to cover them completely. Work the glue into the cloth, all the way across and if necessary add more. This is one instance where an *excess* of glue is necessary because when the cloth has dried, it must be stiff enough to remain stable when glued inside the mouth. When the glue has become "tacky," remove the unit and place it in position inside the head and behind the teeth. At this point, once the back of the tongue and its extensions are properly seated, add a bit more glue to each extension to give the tongue more rigidity when it is dry. Lay the head face down and let glue dry thoroughly.

REBUILDING FINGERS AND TOES

To rebuild a finger on a porcelain doll, drill a small hole into the area of the missing digit. For instance, if the little finger is missing— whether broken off at the point where it extends from the hand, or lower down, near where a knuckle would be—drill a small hole into the surface at the spot where the break occurred. The same procedure applies to the rebuilding of a toe.

This type of repair is almost impossible to do without a hand grinder (see list of suppliers). If you purchase one, be sure to buy a pair of safety goggles as well, for in drilling or cutting into porcelain, almost invisible tiny flakes are thrown into the air, and these are best kept out of one's eyes.

For rebuilding fingers or toes on a very small doll, it is almost impossible to drill a hole. Instead, anchor grooves must be cut by using diamond-cutting discs. Directions for this procedure are given in Ill. 4.

Whether a hole is drilled or anchor grooves are cut, the following procedures are applicable:

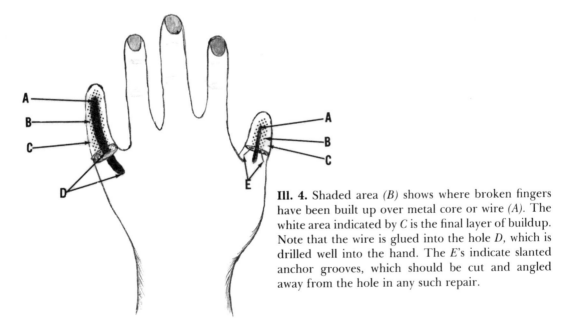

Ill. 4. Shaded area *(B)* shows where broken fingers have been built up over metal core or wire *(A)*. The white area indicated by *C* is the final layer of buildup. Note that the wire is glued into the hole *D*, which is drilled well into the hand. The *E*'s indicate slanted anchor grooves, which should be cut and angled away from the hole in any such repair.

First, measure the same finger (toe) on the other hand (foot). Cut the wire—paperclips are a good source for this wire—short enough so that when one end is placed in the groove or hole, the other end is not too long to have mending material applied at the tip end to cover it. If the wire is cut too long, when the end is covered that finger or toe will be longer than the corresponding one on the opposite hand or foot. Before glueing the wire in place, bend it slightly so that the finger will look more natural.

Next, fill the anchor grooves or hole with epoxy glue mixed with Durham's Water Putty. Add only enough glue to make the combination workable. Stick one end of the precut wire (Ill. 4) into the groove or hole. Let dry.

Durham's water putty is the material I also use for rebuilding fingers or toes, but for this it is mixed with Elmer's Glue. Mix a small amount at a time: using a palette knife, remove only the amount that can be lifted out of the can on the rounded tip of the knife. Place the powder on a saucer and add two drops of Elmer's Glue and two drops of water. Mix with the palette knife. If the mixture is too thin, add a bit more powder. It should have the consistency of *heavy* pancake batter.

Using an inexpensive brush, about ⅜ size, with a pointed tip, apply the mixture to the anchored wire. Start with only a thin coating at first, being sure to cover the end where the tip of the finger will be. Let this coat dry thoroughly.

Usually only one more coat is necessary. In mixing the second batch, *if you're repairing a bisque,* omit the glue and add just enough water to make a workable solution. (In repairing china, add the glue.) Try to complete the missing part with this second batch.

A small jar of clean water is needed to complete the final shaping. Do not "walk away" from this—you must stay with it, or all your work to this point will be wasted. After the last coat has been applied with the brush and smoothed as much as possible, watch it closely. As the mixture dries, it begins losing its shine. When it begins to look dull, dip the brush into the water, shake off any excess, and start manipulating the mixture in whatever direction seems necessary. The wet brush will enable you to achieve the final shaping and smoothing. If they are done correctly, little or no sanding will be necessary when the repair is dry.

3

Fillers, Sealers, and Colors

FILLERS

No doll repair can be made without glue, and no glued area can ever be made inconspicuous *without* the use of fillers, either those purchased commercially or those mixed at home.

If you want to avoid the mess of making your own filler, and want to get the best commercial ones available, order these two from A. Ludwig Klein & Son: No. 20 White Molding Powder; No. 53 Hard Paste Powder and Liquid. Directions for the use of these products are furnished with them.

The five following fillers are easily mixed at home from readily available products. Quantities can be changed by halving or doubling the formulas:

    1. Mix together 2 tablespoons of molding plaster (available at a lumberyard) or plaster of Paris (from a drugstore), 1 tablespoon of wallpaper paste, and 4 tablespoons of finely sifted sawdust. Add enough water

to produce a claylike mixture to use for modeling parts; thin it down with more water to use it as a filler.

2. Mix together 1 cup flour and 1 cup finely sifted sawdust. Add boiling water and stir until very thick. Add ¾ cup powdered glue (available at drugstores). Continue stirring and adding boiling water until the mixture has the consistency of modeling clay.*

3. Add enough Elmer's Glue to 1 cup of finely sifted sawdust to make the mixture workable.

4. Put 1 tablespoon of liquid sodium silicate (water glass, available at drugstores) in a small container, and add enough powdered chalk (whiting) to give the mixture the desired thickness.

5. Mix 1 tablespoon of dental plaster (your dentist will sell you a small amount) with enough water to make it workable. Mixed thin, this is one of the best fillers and is also excellent for building up missing parts. Dental plaster comes in white, pink, and yellow.

When you have decided which filler you are going to use, examine the repaired area closely. (A magnifying glass will reveal irregularities you cannot see with the naked eye.)

Whether you use a commercial product or one you've made, an artist's flexible palette knife is ideal for mixing and for packing the filler into the repaired area. After the filler has thoroughly dried, sand the joint smooth with fine sandpaper (size ⅔). Apply a *diluted* coat of filler next. This will be thinner than the first coat, and will fill in tiny holes that may have appeared on the thicker first coat as it dried. Again sand lightly, this time using size ⅝ sandpaper.

Even light sanding, however, sometimes uncovers tiny air holes in your repair. Dental plaster, mixed thin with water and brushed over the repaired surface as many times as necessary, with light sanding between the coats, is the ideal finishing filler.

At this stage, it is important to use your sense of touch rather than depend only on eyesight and a magnifying glass. Close your eyes and run your fingertips over the repaired area. You will feel irregularities if there are any. And you must have a smooth, flawless surface before proceeding. Otherwise the flaws will be glaringly obvious in the finished restoration. A careless *basic* repair cannot be covered up with paint and glaze.

Among other products that you may find helpful is porcelain

---

*Most fillers must be rather thin to seep into pinholes and flow into irregularities; therefore, when using any of these formulas, add enough of the recommended liquid to thin it down.

filler, available in local stores, packaged in a small bottle. This is often used for filling in nicks and chips on porcelain tubs and sinks. It can be easily colored by "grinding" china paint into it (information on china paints is given elsewhere in this chapter under "Coloring a Repaired Area"). Porcelain filler dries to a high gloss unsuitable for bisque but ideal for china repairs. It can be used for the final coat over a built-up part on chinas, or for filling nicks and cracks in chinas.

Dental plaster tinted with *high-gloss* interior enamel, which is available at paint stores or hobby shops, is good for filling cracks or nicks in *china*, but has no place in bisque repairs.

Gesso, a mixture of glues and plaster, is another commercial product that has its place in doll repairs. It can be found in most art supply stores.

It would be impossible for any one person to know about all the new glues and fillers. Each manufacturer extolls every new product as the best, the strongest, the easiest to use. My advice is to beware of trying any new product without experimenting first. Try a new product on something of your own— *never* on a customer's doll.

Be curious, be innovative, but be cautious. Expect many disappointments and failures, but know that some of your experiments will be successful.

SEALERS

After fillers are used, still a second product must be applied— sealers or sizing liquids—before a truly fine coloring job can be accomplished. No matter what type of filler you have used in your repair, or how much sanding you have done, you still have what I call a "raw repair." It is porous, and if you attempt to color it at this point, the filler will suck up the paint the minute it hits the surface, whether it is applied with an air brush, an artist's brush, a "polly puff" (fine sponge on a stick), or any other applicator. A raw repair is impossible to finish in a professional manner.

A "sealer" does just what its name implies. It seals the filler and prepares the surface for decorating. It prevents color from soaking into the porous filler and creating light and dark areas.

If you're using Klein products, order No. 18 Heavy White Sizing Liquid and No. 18 White Sizing Thinner. Use this on white and light-colored surfaces. An added advantage of using No. 18 is that it not only seals (or sizes) the surface, but also fills tiny holes you may have missed in your earlier examination. (Full instructions come with all Klein products.)

Several coats of white shellac thinned with denatured alcohol also make a good sealer. Both of these are available at lumberyards.

Clear spray-on sealers cost a little more, but are easily applied. They can be purchased at lumberyards, art supply stores, and ceramic supply houses. Always buy the best, and *always*, when working with spray-on materials, wear a safety mask and, if possible, work in a well-ventilated area or outdoors on a windless day.

Never try to do it all with one coat, if you're using a spray. Avoid pointing the nozzle directly at the area and then depressing the button. Instead, aim the spray at empty air *near* the repaired area, depress the button, and when the spray has started, use a rotating motion. Continue that motion over the repair *briefly*. A quick "spritz" is all that's needed for each coat. Don't wait until the sealer starts to run before stopping the motion.

Note: After *each* spraying, turn the can upside down and depress the button until nothing but air comes out of the hole. Otherwise, next time you try to use the sealer, the hole will be clogged. If the hole does become clogged, sometimes you can take the button off another can and use it on the clogged one, but this does not always work, and it's unnecessary if you clear the hole after each use.

For working on a china doll, buy a high-gloss spray sealer. For work on bisque, ask for matte sealer. Little difficulty is encountered with high-gloss sprays, but sometimes the clear mattes, when dry, are not dull enough to match the surface of the doll. Should this happen—if the sealer dries with too much sheen—dip a damp cloth into powdered pumice stone (available at drugstores) and lightly rub the area until the desired matte finish is attained.

COLORING A REPAIRED AREA

An invisible repair depends, finally, not only on how well the basic repair blends in with the original surface, but also on the perfect matching of colors. Some specialists use tube showcard colors, tempera, or casein tempera. Others prefer the tube-type oil colors used by artists. Interior high-gloss household enamels are often used because they dry with a hard, natural gloss simulating the glaze of china. The beginner should experiment with all of them to learn their advantages and limitations.

I use china paints and balsam of copaiba (an oil medium) exclusively. I do not recommend the premixed ones available in hobby or ceramic shops and sold in small jars. They have been ground in oil, and there are many times when it is necessary to grind the *powdered* mineral colors in water, something you cannot do if you buy them premixed. At other times, the water-china paint mixture is added to fillers for light coloring prior to the final decorating. Rynne China Company (see list of suppliers) is my source. Not only do they carry a fine line of imported German quills and other decorating brushes; their German Dresden overglaze colors (china paints) are unsurpassed. After you obtain Rynne's catalog—when you have decided on the colors you need—order *vials* only. These are tiny glass tubes of powdered mineral colors, and even if they seem to hold barely enough for one small job, a tube will last six months to a year, depending on how busy you are. Do not order "Matte Paints." Stay with colors listed simply as "Overglaze Paints." These are much easier to grind.

Under "Imported Oils," the only two you'll need are balsam of copaiba, for use on bisque, and heavy balsam of copaiba, for use on china dolls. Order no more than 1 oz. of each.

I discovered, quite by accident, that the use of china paints in repairing antique dolls is the "icing on the cake." Being a professional doll artist and also somewhat of a perfectionist, I found that sometimes I could not get the mischievous curve of a lip I was striving for, the delicate lash lines, or the long, thin brow strokes. Late one evening when I was too tired to clean off a misaligned eyebrow I had been painting, I laid the doll head on a shelf, intending to remove the china paint/copaiba mixture next day and try again. My efforts the following morning were fruitless—the paint/copaiba mixture would not come off. But instead of throwing the doll head away, I finished putting on the cheeks and lips, the red dots at the inner eye corners, a red dot in each ear, and again let it dry; then I sprayed *over* the entire head with a matte sealer. It was when I viewed the finished head that I gained an entirely new perspective on decorating a repaired area. I discovered that although china paints are made to be fired in a kiln, they can also be used to decorate repaired areas—and with beautiful and predictable results. But if you make a mistake, clean it off immediately. Don't let it dry, as I did.

Grinding China Paints

In addition to the vials of powdered paints, you'll need a white tile (with glazed surface) or a china painter's palette. Both are available from Rynne's China Company, as are the needed palette knives. (Of course you can use a china plate instead of the tile or palette.)

Tap a very small amount of powdered china paint onto the glossy surface of the white tile. If it is to be used in coloring filler, add just enough water to dissolve the granules completely when you grind them with the tip of the palette knife. Hold the blade of the knife almost flat against the tile surface, mashing down on the grains of color and, at the same time, using a round-and-round motion. When no tiny specks of color remain, add the resulting mixture to the filler in whatever amount seems necessary.

If you're ready to decorate a repaired and sealed area, use the same procedure, substituting balsam of copaiba for water, if the repair is on bisque; if it's on china, use heavy balsam of copaiba.

The reason for using heavy oil when preparing colors to use on china is that when regular copaiba medium is padded (a procedure that will be described later) on glossy china dolls, it will not adhere satisfactorily. Heavy balsam of copaiba, on the other hand, is very sticky, and by proper manipulation of the silk-covered cotton pad, enough color adheres to make a beautiful decorating job.

The mixing of colors cannot be taught by the written word. Practice is the key to learning. The following guide for mixing paints will be of great help as long as you keep in mind that the proportions may need to be varied. Some of these may seem like odd colors to be used in doll repairs, but breaks often occur on dolls with molded yokes or other ornamental areas. It is good to have a working knowledge of color combinations to follow when repairing such dolls.

Yellow-green	2 parts yellow, 1 part blue
Green	1 part yellow, 1 part blue
Blue-green	1 part yellow, 2 parts blue
Blue-violet	2 parts blue, 1 part red
Violet	1 part red, 1 part blue
Red-violet	2 parts red, 1 part blue
Red-orange	2 parts red, 1 part yellow
Orange	1 part red, 1 part yellow
Yellow-orange	2 parts yellow, 1 part red
Citron	1 part orange, 1 part green
Olive	1 part green, 1 part violet
Russet	1 part orange, 1 part violet
Brown	1 part yellow, 1 part red, 1 part blue
Pink	1 part red, 1 part white
Charcoal	2 parts blue, 1 part red, 1 part yellow

White is added to make lighter shades of *any* color.

Red, yellow, and blue cannot be made by combining other colors; from them, however, you can produce other colors in various shades.

Flesh is the tint you will use most often. It requires a combination of white, yellow, red, brown, and sometimes blue. Start with a small amount of white mixed with oil medium (this applies to china paints) and add other colors sparingly. When using other kinds of liquid paints, fill a small glass jar half full of white. Add small amounts of red, yellow, and brown. Mix thoroughly as each color is added. You will eventually produce a flesh tone to match the surface of the old doll. Occasionally you will have to add a tiny bit of blue, particularly in working on a baby doll. Continue adding a small amount of needed color until you get a match as nearly perfect as possible.

Whether you're mixing flesh tones or color for other areas, when you think the shade is right, paint a small area on a piece of white paper and let it dry. Hold the paper against the original color on the doll. If it does *not* match, add whatever seems needed. Then repeat the test until the *dried* color on the white paper perfectly matches the repair area *when both are held in direct sunlight*. Artificial light always leads to inaccuracy of color matching.

WARNING: Never dip an unclean palette knife into the container of oil medium. Form the habit of cleaning the knife thoroughly by dipping the entire blade into gasoline and wiping it dry. Otherwise, you will contaminate the medium.

For applying color to a repaired area, you will need brushes ranging in size from 000000 (%), for all kinds of fine line work, to square shaders used in applying color to larger areas.

You will also need to keep a "pad" handy, for blending colors on large areas. Pads are made by enclosing a cotton ball inside a square of *china silk*. Only this type of fabric gives perfect results. Other materials leave texture marks in the china paint, but china silk is woven so tightly that it blends the colors without leaving evidence of its use. Older women will remember the filmy scarves they used to tie around their hair, only to have them slide off minutes later. These were made of china silk. Today I know of only one source for china silk other than the old scarves sometimes found at auctions and rummage sales. New china silk can be ordered from the China Silk House, Ala Moana Shopping Center, Honolulu, Hawaii. In 1974, a yard of this silk was selling for $9.50.

Application of the china paint/copaiba mixture is similar to working with water colors. For covering large areas, such as those requiring skin tones, use a *square shader* brush and paint the color onto the repaired and sealed surface, lapping it about a half-inch over the original area. Don't worry about getting it on too thick; the next step will take care of that.

Next, make the "pad"—a piece of silk wrapped around a cotton ball and held together by twisting the silk close to the cotton and holding it in that position. Put a couple of drops of copaiba on the back of the hand, and rub the pad lightly in this before using it on the already applied color. The copaiba assures even distribution. Hold the doll head (or whatever part is being colored) in the other hand and, with a light up-and-down motion, "pounce" the pad gently over the surface just painted. Do this until all the air and oil bubbles have disappeared and the color appears even. It is best to work outward from the center of the area being colored. As the pad absorbs oil and color, keep moving the cotton from the soiled part of the silk to a clean part of it. Exert a bit more pressure on the pad as you approach the outer edges of the repair. This helps to blend the new color onto the old, so that there will be no line of demarcation.

For fine-detail color work such as fingernails, toenails, and other delicate areas, use a pointed short-haired Sable brush, size 000000 (%).

In some areas—molded hair, for example—it may not be necessary to use the pad. China paint mixed *thick* with an oil medium and blended with a small square shader brush into the old color is all that is necessary.

After the paint has dried thoroughly, apply several coats of spray-on sealer. Remember—high gloss for chinas and matte for bisques. Allow ample time for each coat to dry before spraying on another.

We dollmakers and dollmenders walk a special road, one paved with aesthetic values, curiosity, patience, and determination. On the one hand, we preserve the beautiful dolls so loved by our ancestors; on the other, we create our own, which we hope will be cherished by future generations. Some day, many of you will progress from repairing dolls to making them.

Although this chapter contains much general information about techniques and methods that have been successful in my studio, no mention has been made of using liquid rubber for copying and producing missing parts, as well as copying originals you may some day sculpt. Nor have I mentioned making plaster molds for that purpose, although both methods are invaluable at times. If you develop into an expert "M.D." (Mender of Dolls), you will want to investigate the many wonderful uses of both liquid rubber and plaster molds. *The Plastercraft Handbook* by Gay Wolfe, published by United States Gypsum (101 South Wacker Drive, Chicago, Illinois 60606), is quite inexpensive, and it thoroughly covers working with plaster, making plaster, plastic, and rubber molds, and many other useful techniques. It does not deal with doll work, but the methods and procedures are easily adapted to doll restoration.

4

Setting Stationary Eyes

Stationary eyes, sometimes called "fixed" eyes, never move, in contrast to the sleep eyes that close when the doll is put in a reclining position. Stationary eyes always gaze serenely out of the doll's face in whatever position they were originally set.

For resetting stationary eyes, you will need the following:

1. Oval (flat-back) or round glass eyes
2. Plaster of Paris
3. Sticky Wax
4. A sharp-pointed blade, such as an Exacto No. 11
5. India ink (optional)
6. Size 0000 sable artist's brush
7. Old toothbrush

First, let us consider what the doll restorer needs to keep on hand, as far as eyes are concerned. A doll hospital will, of course, need a large supply of sizes, ranging from the smallest, 6mm., to the largest available. These sizes sell for a wide range of prices per pair, and so a great deal of expense is involved in keeping an adequate stock on hand. If, however, you merely want to repair your own dolls, and therefore may need glass eyes only two or three times a year, there is no need to keep a large supply. You can order what you need from a supply house or go to a nearby doll hospital— preferably the latter—since you can take your doll along and make your own selection. In this way, you will be sure to get eyes that fit perfectly. In ordering from a supply house, you cannot order one item unless its cost coincides with the minimum order they will accept; also, rarely do you receive a pair of eyes in which the pupil is exactly in the middle, where it should be, and where the pupils are identical in size. Often one pupil will be larger than the other. Irises, too, are frequently mismatched—one may be larger than the other, or one may have a darker outer ring than the other, or no outer ring at all. Supply house personnel do not have time to do a perfect matchup, and so you hope for the best and take what you get. You can almost always rely on *round* glass eyes if you're undecided between them and the oval flat-backs, for the majority of antique dolls were fitted with the round ones.

If only one of a doll's eyes is missing, you will know which type to order when you remove the remaining one. Since it is impossible to match an old eye with a new one, always put in a new pair. But keep the old eye; someday you just might find a match for it. If you are working only with the head (detached from the body), after you have removed the wig and pate place the head in a large pan and cover it with warm water. (The method of removing wig and pate is described in Chapter 2.)

Let the head soak for 15 minutes. Then, using a sharp instrument, dig carefully at the plaster. If you do not succeed in removing all of it, or if it is very hard to remove, put the head back in the water and let it soak for another 15 minutes. This soaking can be repeated as often as necessary until you have been able to gouge out most of the plaster. Don't be afraid to use a bit of pressure. Unless the head is already cracked, a little pressure will not damage it. (It is always a good precaution to examine the porcelain first with a magnifying glass, to be sure there are no cracks.) Small fragments of plaster still clinging to the porcelain can be scraped off with a fingernail; sometimes even a stiff toothbrush, wet and then dipped in scouring powder, will do it. Dry the inside of the head thoroughly.

Place the can of Sticky Wax on a stove burner turned as low as possible. While the wax is heating, select the eyes you will use (if you have not already done so). The majority of antique doll heads had the eye sockets trimmed to fit round glass eyes, but oval flat-back eyes will usually fit satisfactorily.

Test the fit of the new eyes first. When using round eyes, wet the end of your index and third fingers on the tip of your tongue, place the back-of-the-eye projection between these two fingers, insert them into the head, and hold one eye in place. (The wetness of the fingers will hold the eye in your grasp.) Test the fit of the other eye also. For testing oval flat-backs, only the tip of the index finger need be moistened. Place the eye on the end of that finger, insert it into the head, and fit the eye into place.

Often you will have to try several pairs of eyes before you find one that gives the desired expression (unless you have only one pair on hand). A serene look is obtained by setting the eyes as shown in Ill. 5. Note that the iris is centered, with an equal amount of white showing on either side; the lower curve of the iris seems to be partly under the lower lid, with part of the upper curve under the upper lid.

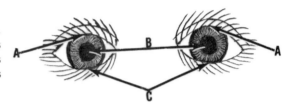

Ill. 5. Setting the eyes for a serene look. Note that the upper curve *(A)* of the iris is partly under the upper lid. The pupil *(B)* is centered. Lower curve *(C)* of the iris is partly under the lower lid.

Ill. 6. Setting the eyes for a surprised or startled look. Set the eyes looking straight ahead as in Ill. 5, but leave a tiny bit of the white showing below the upper lid and above the lower lid, as shown here.

A surprised or startled look can be obtained by setting the eyes as shown in Ill. 6. The iris is centered, with an equal amount of white appearing on both sides, but the upper curve of the iris shows below the upper lid and the lower curve shows above the lower lid. This look can be achieved only if the iris is small enough in diameter to make such positioning possible. Often the new eyes you receive will have very large irises and you will have to go with the serene look. Or, if the startled look is a must, order a pair 2mm. smaller than the corner-to-corner measurement of the eye socket. If smaller eyes are used, a tiny bit more plaster shows at each corner than if you use eyes the exact measurement, but the plaster is hardly noticeable.

Ill. 7. "Googly" or "Flirty" eyes are set looking to left or right, with half of the white showing. The full pupil is visible, as shown here.

The same principle applies if the eyes are to be set slightly off-center—that is, not looking directly at you but gazing past your ear. The only change is that more white will be showing on one side than on the other. So-called "Googly" or "Flirty" eyes have *no* white showing on one side. (See Ill. 7.) The eye is placed so that only the iris shows in one corner; the rest of the eye is white. This gives the doll an impish or flirty look.

At this point I must stress that if a doll has one eye remaining (it must be removed prior to setting new ones), the new eyes should be set exactly as the old ones were, as evidenced by that single eye. If, however, a doll is completely eyeless, try to find a picture of that doll in a reference book. From studying this you can determine in what fashion to set the eyes. A serious doll collector would be horrified to see, for instance, "googly" eyes set in a doll that should have a serene look.

Before proceeding to the permanent setting, an important precaution must be taken to protect the fragile blown-glass eye from being broken in the process. The eyes are hollow (if you're using round ones), and if you were to apply the plaster prematurely, while it is still too thin, it might accidentally get into the tiny hole in the back of the extension. To avoid having this happen, take the necessary few seconds required to plug up the hole. A tiny ball of clay, Plasticine, or play dough, even a piece of wet paper towel rolled between the fingers to the size of the hole and placed securely in or over it will prevent accidental breakage when plaster is applied later.

By now the Sticky Wax will be melted. Place a thick towel, folded over a couple of times, as close to the wax container as possible. As you apply the warm (not hot) wax, hold the head over the towel. Place a toothpick near the container of wax.

Fit one eye into position as you want it to appear permanently, and hold it there. From this point on, move slowly and carefully; any sudden movement will cause the eye you are holding to shift position. Dip the toothpick into the warm wax, hold it over the

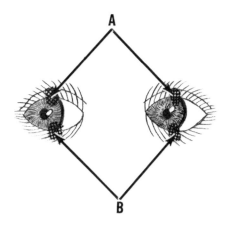

Ill. 8. The dark shaded spots, indicated by *A* and *B*, show where Sticky Wax is dropped to "tack" the eyes in place before they are set into permanent position with plaster.

center of the *lower* lid, and allow a *small* drop to fall partly on the glass eye and partly on the porcelain lid. You may have to touch the wax-coated end of the toothpick to this area if the wax is not warm enough to drip (Ill. 8). Immediately repeat this procedure on the *center* of the upper lid. (If, in the process of moving the toothpick from the container of wax to the desired location on the eye, the wax drips on any other surface of the doll's head, don't panic. It can be removed later.)

In about 30 seconds, remove the finger that is holding the eye in place. The wax hardens quickly; it will hold the eye in position until the next step can be completed. Now "tack" the other eye in place, following the same procedure.

Next, mix the plaster solution that will affix the eyes permanently. Small throwaway plastic or foam cups are useful for this mixing, as are very small plastic spoons. If these are not available, a regular teaspoon and an old cup can be used. The size of the doll eyes will determine the amount of plaster of Paris to be used. As an example, assume that the eyes to be set are 16mm. size.

Measure 3 tsp. of *cold* water into the cup. (If hot water is used, the plaster mixture sets up too fast.) Dry off the spoon before inserting it into the plaster. Put 3 *heaping* tsp. of plaster into the water. At first it will look as if this is far too much plaster for the amount of water, but as you stir the mixture, it will become like a thin pancake batter in consistency. Continue stirring and, as air bubbles form on top, stop long enough to blow on them to make them burst. (Too many air bubbles in the applied plaster will weaken it.) The stirring time is variable, depending on the condition of the plaster and atmospheric humidity and temperature.

The mixture will begin to thicken gradually as you stir it. When it begins to feel thicker, every few seconds hold a spoonful above the cup and let it drop back. When the mixture slides from the spoon in one thick "glob," it is ready to be applied to the back of the eyes. Work quickly now. If flat ovals are used, simply let the plaster fall oval flat-backs   rounds

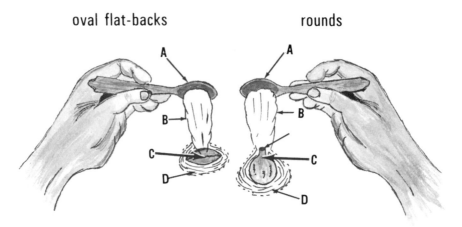

Ill. 9. Tip the spoon *(A)* so that the plaster *(B)* will slide out onto the center of the eye *(C)*. If its consistency is right, the plaster will flow over the entire eye surface and down onto the porcelain to form a plaster "puddle" *(D)*. (For clarity, the eyes are shown outside the head, although this procedure is done with the eyes inside head.)

directly on the middle back of each eye. If round glass eyes are used, be careful not to strike the eye extension with the spoon; you might break it. In either case (if you remembered to plug the tiny holes in the extension), let the plaster drop over the center of the eye and flow down onto the porcelain. After one spoonful has been added to each eye, alternate additions of the plaster until both eyes are covered generously (Ill. 9). Do not disturb the head for at least 30 minutes after you place it, face down, on the folded towel. This is ample time for the plaster to set.

If you have plaster left over, wipe out the cup with a paper towel; clean the spoon in the same way, and throw the paper into the trash can. Never wash plaster into a sink unless you want to pay a big plumbing bill.

Spread a newspaper over a work area, and arrange on it a sharp pointed tool (Exacto knife with a No. 11 blade recommended), a small container of water, a paper towel, and a small, stiff brush. These will all be useful in removing the drops of wax from each eye and any plaster that has seeped through from the backs of the eyes.

Hold the head, face up, in your left hand, placing the index finger of that hand inside, against the plaster of one eye. The pressure of your finger will prevent any pressure you exert on the *outside* from pushing the plaster loose inside the head.

Remove the wax first. Insert the pointed end of the blade *between* the eye and the wax. A twisting motion of the blade will flip the wax loose, usually in one piece. (The wax can be put back in the can and remelted for future use.) A thin film of wax will remain on both the porcelain and the glass eye. Scrape this off with the Exacto blade. If drops of wax missed their target when you were applying them, scrape them off too. Even after you think you have removed all the wax, a close examination will disclose that the formerly waxed areas are still shiny. Since it took heat to melt the wax, heat must be used to remove these spots. Heat a small amount of water to the boiling point, dip a Q-Tip into the water, and quickly rub it over the shiny areas. Keep the end of the Q-Tip hot and continue rubbing over these spots until all traces of the wax are gone.

To remove any overflow of plaster, run the sharp tip of the blade around the eye socket. Keep the area clear of plaster scraps by shaking loose your trimmings onto the newspaper. Tiny pieces will cling to the eye, particularly around the lids; keep that area brushed clear at all times so that you can see what you are doing.

After the trimming is completed, dip the end of a paper towel into water and squeeze out any excess. It is important *not* to let water seep into the plaster, for water will weaken it. Carefully wipe off all remaining plaster scraps and dust with the dampened towel.

This next step is optional: dip a small sable brush, size 0000 (4/0), into India ink and, working from the front, color all visible plaster around the eyes with it. The ink accentuates the eyes and gives them a bright, alert look. Any ink that gets onto the glass eyes and the porcelain surrounding them can be removed in the same way as the plaster scraps and dust were. If plain water does not clean off the ink, use a dampened piece of paper towel that has been rubbed over a bar of soap.

Doll eyes are purchased according to millimeter size, as mentioned earlier. To measure for them, place a small piece of white paper inside the head and, with a very sharp pencil, draw around the circumference of the eye socket. Then use the eye ruler you make from the instructions in Ill. 10 to measure from corner to corner of the outline you have drawn. Add 2mm. to that measurement. For instance, if the outline measures 10mm., order 12mm. eyes.

Ill. 10. This ruler is the exact size needed for working with doll eyes. Each mark represents 1mm, and the ruler is marked off in divisions of 5mm for easier computation.

CLEANING ANTIQUE EYES

Even if a doll's eyes are filmed over with the grime of ages, they can be successfully cleaned. A surprising number of collectors come to my studio with this problem. Sometimes they have paid a staggering amount for a doll, and are afraid of damaging its eyes by attempting to restore their sparkling beauty. Usually plain soap and water will do the trick. Dip a Q-Tip, or a toothpick with one end swirled in cotton, into warm water, squeeze out the excess, and rub the Q-Tip across a bar of soap. Gently clean the entire surface of each eye.

It is not necessary to push hard against the eyes; too much pressure can push them out. The concentration of dirt is likely to be trapped around the eye where it comes into contact with the porcelain. Here again I recommend the use of an Exacto knife. If the wig and pate are off the head, exert pressure inside, with the index finger, against the plaster of the eye you're working on. If not, be very careful in applying pressure; avoid any twisting motion of the blade. Plaster deteriorates with age, and undue pressure or twisting can dislodge the eyes.

When the surface of the eyes is clean, dip another Q-Tip or cotton-tipped toothpick into clear rinse water, squeeze out the excess, and remove the soap film from the eyes.

If soap and water do not do a thorough cleaning job, other agents may be used, such as lighter fluid, gasoline, denatured (wood) alcohol, or turpentine.

When cleaning sleep eyes with waxed lids, *never* use anything but turpentine!

5

Setting Sleep Eyes

Dolls with sleeping eyes—eyes that open and close—have been traced back to as early as 1700. In the early part of the nineteenth century, some dolls had eyes that could be manipulated from the outside. However, it was not until the latter part of the nineteenth century that *counterweight* sleep eyes gained great popularity, although they had appeared on the scene in the first half of that century. They are the type of antique eye mechanism I will discuss in this chapter. Ill. 11 shows a completed eye rocker.

Counterweight eyes consist of round, blown-glass eyes with a hollow extension on the back, a twisted wire framework attached to the eyes, and a lead weight attached to the end of the wire framework. The entire unit is referred to as a "rocker." When the doll's head is upright, the lead weight rests on a thin piece of cork glued into the chin area. Place the doll in a reclining position and she sleeps; the weight of the lead causes the unit to *rock* downward, rotating the eyes in their plaster sockets. They remain "closed" until the doll is again held upright. The cork in the chin area acts as a cushion for the lead weight, since when the doll is moved abruptly

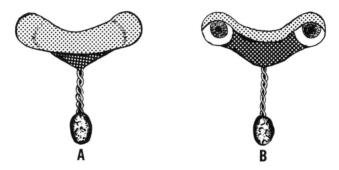

Ill. 11. Back *(A)* and front *(B)* views of a completed eye rocker.

upright, the impact of the weight against the bare porcelain of the chin area might crack or damage it.

In restoring a doll, it is often necessary to reset the sleep eyes. This is one of the most exacting procedures to learn, but quite easy once the techniques have been mastered. However, unless the old eye rocker is intact, you will have either to make or buy a replacement.

I unequivocally recommend making one. If the instructions in this chapter are followed, the rocker is *custom made* for the particular doll head you're working on. It will be strong enough to hold its shape throughout all procedures and, installed correctly, it will be there to stay.

Commercial eye rockers (referred to in catalogs as frames) can be purchased "frame only," or as a frame with the eyes attached. They are adjustable, true, but they are made of brass and very soft. You must still go through all the procedures outlined in this chapter for measuring—across (eye to eye) and down (T-arm to lead weight). And because the wire is so soft, it is extremely difficult to work with; even the slightest bump will distort it.

I tried one—and that was enough. After measuring, snipping off excess wire, building across the T-arm with proper materials, painting eyelids, waxing them, glueing on eyelashes, adjusting the lead weight, and installing the completed unit inside the head, I felt uneasy about it. And so I put the head in a cabinet. For two weeks, I "rocked" the head several times each day. At the end of that time the eyes were completely out of position. The daily rocking had bent the small bit of wire between the lead weight and the T-arm just enough to cause the eyes to fall about 1/8″ short of opening and closing properly.

As mentioned in Chapter 4, eyes are ordered by millimeter measurement. Chapter 4 contains an illustration (Ill. 10) of the

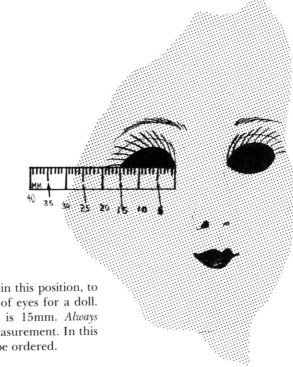

Ill. 12. Put the eye ruler in this position, to measure the correct size of eyes for a doll. Here, the measurement is 15mm. *Always* add 2mm to the ruler measurement. In this case, 17mm eyes should be ordered.

homemade eye ruler I use. It is made of heavy bond paper, 1⁹/₁₆″ long (40mm.) and a scant ¼″ wide. It is marked off 25mm. per inch, as shown. (This ruler is not only invaluable for measuring eye size, but indispensable when taking measurements for constructing the eye rocker, to be described later in this chapter.)

Place the left end of the ruler in one corner of the eye, and note where the other corner of the eye touches the ruler. Ill. 12 shows the eye ruler in proper position; the socket being measured is 15mm. from corner to corner. Eyes must be bought larger than the socket measurement: always add an extra 2mm. So this socket requires 17mm. eyes.

Before setting sleep eyes, it is necessary to remove the head from the body. Whether the body is made of cloth, leather, or jointed composition, the removal procedures are simple, and they need only be reversed for reassembly.

SOLID-DOME HEADS

This category includes any doll head that is solid, such as those of the Bye-Lo, the Dream Baby, and other similar dolls. They do not have a large opening in the crown. Their necks are flanged, and the flanges fit *inside* a neck opening in the body, which is usually made of cloth. When the body was made, a casing was stitched around the neck, and a strong cord or wire was threaded through the casing. At one point—sometimes at the side, sometimes at center back—an opening was left so that the ends of the tie thread could be pulled through to the outside and securely fastened. The loose ends were then tucked inside, out of sight.

To remove this type of head, locate where the cord or wire was tied and cut through it; but before severing the knot, be sure you are grasping the doll head firmly. Otherwise it may fall out and break when you cut the cord. (When ready to reassemble the doll, you will have to use a new cord or wire.)

After the head has been removed, you will see a piece of cardboard glued to the bottom of the flange. This was done to prevent the body stuffing from being jarred into the hollow head. Remove this cardboard (replace it with new after the eyes have been set).

If the new wire is difficult to thread through the casing, wrap one end of it with a small piece of masking tape. The wire will then slide through easily without puncturing the cloth. If a cord is used, thread it through a short bodkin (a large-eyed blunt needle available in knitting departments) and run it through the casing. Be sure, when you fasten the tie, that it is very tight against the porcelain neck; and use a square knot (what I call a "safety knot")—it's the safest one. (See Ill. 13.)

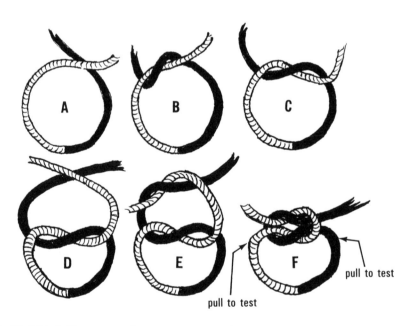

Ill. 13. This is the way to tie a security (square) knot. Start with *A* and follow the steps through *F*. There, if the knot gets tighter the harder you pull, you have tied it correctly. The security knot is the most important knot used in doll work. When it is tied correctly, it will never slip.

OPEN-CROWN HEADS

A doll with the head, neck, and shoulder plate all in one piece is called a shoulder head. One that has the head and neck in one piece and the shoulder plate separate is called a socket head or swivel neck. Its head will turn from side to side; the shoulder-head is rigid.

It is not necessary to remove a head from its shoulder plate to set sleep eyes.

These types of heads have two things in common—open crowns and wigs. Wigs and crown pates must be removed. Refer to Chapter 4 for directions on removing them.

Although it is possible to accomplish this without removing the head from the body, since the setting of sleep eyes is done through the opening in the top of the head, my personal preference is to remove it. Even when you're working with a small doll, it is very awkward to handle as you go through the techniques involved in setting sleep eyes. Too, you run the risk of chipping or breaking parts of the arms and legs (on those made of porcelain), as the body is turned hither and yon. Better be safe than sorry. Removal is simple and will actually save time in the long run.

If the shoulder plate is glued onto an inner body lining, with an outer covering of leather that fits *over* the bisque, the outer leather pieces must be partly removed from the body lining, in order to free the head. If the adhesive is old, you can probably peel the leather away from the bisque easily. Leave as much of the lower part of it glued to the body lining as is practical. To remove the shoulder plate from the inner body lining, insert a blunt tool (perhaps the end of a rounded spoon handle) under the porcelain. Gently rock the handle *downward* into the stuffed portion of the body. This will separate the porcelain from the inner body lining. Work carefully all around the edges of the shoulder plate until it can be removed.

REMOVAL OF BISQUE HEADS
FROM BALL-JOINTED BODIES

This category includes both solid-dome and open-crown heads, but more of the latter type.

If you are not familiar with the stringing of ball-jointed bodies, read Chapter 10. It will help if you know what is *inside* the body, so that you understand why the head can be removed without destroying the stringing.

You will need a rigid "holding stick" on which to loop the elastic while you work on the head. You can use a pencil, two craft sticks (one on top of the other, for strength), or a strong piece of wood 6″ long and ¼″ thick. Make a stringing hook like that shown as *G*, Ill. 80. If the head hook is *clamped* onto the elastic, you will also need a pair of needle-nose pliers. Assemble these items in your work area before beginning.

If you have a helper, let her hold onto the body. If you're working alone, sit in a comfortable chair and grip the doll body between your knees. Grasp the doll head in one hand and, with the other, hold the stringing hook. Slowly pull the head away from the neck socket. When you can see the elastic fastened to the head hook, slip the stringing hook *under* the loop (or loops), keeping tension on the elastic. Tilt the head to one side and free the head hook, but maintain tension on the elastic at all times. If it gets away from you at this point, it will snap back inside the body and you will have to restring the doll. Lay the head to one side. Pick up the holding stick and slip it between the elastic loop(s), allowing the two ends of the stick to rest on the rim or edge of the neck socket. Ease the elastic down onto the holding stick, and remove the stringing hook.

If the head hook is *clamped* onto the elastic, do not try to remove the head. Instead, pull the head upward, far enough away from the body, to slip the holding stick under the elastic. This will protect the stringing while you pry open the head hook to release the head. Sometimes a metal head hook breaks as it is being pried open. Even if it remains intact, examine it carefully for any structural weakness. If in doubt, replace it with a new one when you put the head back in place.

New hooks, referred to in the trade as S-hooks, can be purchased commercially, or one can be made from coat hanger wire. I prefer the latter because, for a large head in which a large wooden neck button was used, even the longest commercial S-hook will not reach from the top of the neck button and through the neck hole with enough clearance to hook into the elastic. Use the old hook for a pattern.

Materials needed for setting eyes:
  Eyes
  Plaster of Paris
  Sticky Wax (see list of suppliers)
  Vaseline
  Homemade rocker tool (Ill. 14)

Materials that may be needed:
  Cork or plastic wood
  Small soldering iron
  Solder

Ill. 14. To make an eye rocker tool, cut a 6″ length of wire from a thin coat hanger. Bend it into the shape shown here. Slip the hook (at left) under the "tail" of the eye rocker, just above the lead weight. Manipulating the rocker with the hook forms the eye sockets in the plaster.

Step 1   After the wig and crown pate have been removed, place the head in warm water to soften any plaster remaining on the *inside,* following the cleaning directions in Chapter 2. Scrape off all plaster, and make a detailed examination of the head. Inside, at the *outer* corner of each eye, is a white area—much whiter than the rest. This is where the old plaster was, and this is where the new plaster should go.

Step 2   Using a soft cloth and mild soap and water, give the head a good washing inside and out. Remove any grime remaining around the nose, ears, and eyes with a soft or worn toothbrush dipped in the suds. If the doll has teeth, use the toothbrush gently on them too, but do not exert much pressure; you may push them loose.

Take care to do all work over a thickly folded bath towel, and hold the part you're working on as close to the towel as possible. Suds make the parts slippery, and if you drop the head or the eye rocker, the towel will probably prevent any breakage.

Step 3   Clean the eye rocker unit in the same suds, but handle it carefully and use a suds-dampened cloth instead of the brush. Never use hot water, for there is always danger of melting waxed eyelids and damaging the lashes, if there are lashes. If waxed lids do not respond to the soap and water treatment, go over them with a Q-Tip dampened with turpentine. Turpentine is the only commercial product I have found that will not damage the wax.

Step 4   Dry the head, inside and out, with a soft lintfree cloth. It can also be safely force dried in an oven set no higher than 125° F, but never put the rocker unit in the oven. Pad *it* dry with a soft cloth until all visible moisture has been removed; then let it air dry.

Step 5   Check the chin area. Is the cork still intact? It may have come loose when you soaked the head, or it may be missing. If you have the cork and if it's thoroughly dry, reglue it into position. If the cork is deteriorating or is missing, replace it with new cork or use plastic wood.

Occasionally you will find a doll in which the lead weight not only struck the chin area on the downward swing of the rocker, but also was of such length that it struck a point on the back of the head when the doll was laid down. If this piece of cork is missing too, replace it with new cork or plastic wood. There is almost always visible evidence as to the original location of one or more such cork stops, unless soaking the head to remove the old plaster has destroyed it. Look for signs of old adhesive. If there are none, the locations can easily be gauged later on, after the rocker is placed inside the head. Put the new cushions at the points where the lead weight strikes the porcelain.

To use plastic wood cushions: roll a small amount of the plastic material into a ball and place it in the depressed area of the chin. It will take on the contour of the chin if you apply a bit of pressure. Then, while the plastic is still pliable, place the eye rocker into position inside the head. This must be done immediately, to ascertain the correct height of the cushion.

Hold the rocker unit in position inside the head, with your index finger placed at the pivot point (center) of the unit and the weight resting against the plastic wood. Keep the head upright, but turn it to face you, so that you can see whether the eyes are positioned correctly.

If they are "looking" too far upward, the plastic wood cushion needs to be raised higher. Remove the rocker unit. With your fingertips, squeeze the plastic wood a bit higher at the point where the lead weight strikes it. Check the eyes again. If they now "look" down too much, do *not* remove the rocker unit. Instead, exert slow pressure on the lead weight while you continue to watch the eyes. As you press the weight against the plastic wood, you will see them gradually move until they are gazing straight at you.

In dolls that also had a cork "stop" in the back of the head, simply press an adequate amount of plastic wood in position there as well. Here the height is not critical, as it is in the chin area. The purpose is merely to protect the back of the head from damage. The chin cork or cushion not only protects the porcelain; it also controls the position of the eyes.

If you decide to use new cork for the cushion instead of plastic wood, cut a thin slice from the small end of a medium-sized bottle cork and glue that in place. Prior to glueing, however, test out the correct position. Place the piece of cork in the chin area, put the eye rocker in place, and check the position of the eyes; repeat the procedure until the height of the cork is exact.

After glueing the cork, check the position of the eyes again. Often, just the necessary small amount of glue will raise the height sufficiently to spoil the position of the eyes.

Step 6 After the plastic wood or cork (glue) has dried completely, again place the eye rocker unit inside the head as it will be when permanently installed. Let's assume you are working with eyes without eyelashes (eyes with lashes will be covered later) and with an open-crown head. Place the head face down on a folded bath towel. Reach inside and, with the tip of a finger, press firmly against the lead weight and, at the same time, put pressure against the bridge holding the eyes together.

Slowly turn the head until it's facing you so that you can make a final check for eye position. Then remove the eye rocker. Cover the glass section of the eyes, the lids, and areas on the "T" section as indicated in Ill. 15 with a *heavy* coat of vaseline. Return the rocker to its position inside the head and carefully place the head face down, open crown toward you, on the folded towel. The head must *not* be jarred or moved at all until much later (Step 9).

Ill. 16, an inside view (right interior) of a doll's head, shows what is accomplished by following the directions in Steps 7, 8, and 9. The

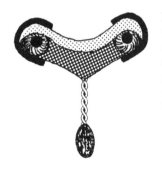

Ill. 15. This drawing shows the finished "T" section of the eye rocker. Apply a heavy coat of Vaseline over all the surfaces—front, sides, and back—on areas indicated by the heavy black curved lines. The Vaseline prevents plaster from sticking to any part of eye surface or rocker, and creates the small amount of clearance between eye and plaster socket that will permit eyes to open and close freely.

neck hole

B

C

eye rocker

A

Ill. 16. This view of the inside of a doll head shows how the spoon *(A)* is tilted so that the plaster *(B)* slides toward *(C)* (the eye) and separates, allowing a small amount of plaster to flow above and below the outer third of the eye.

eye rocker is included in this drawing so that you can see where to tilt the spoon, as well as the shape assumed by the wet plaster as it slides toward the eye, separating at the corner and one part going above the eye and one part below.

Step 7 For mixing plaster, use foam egg cartons; they make good throwaway containers. An old cup will also do. To set the eyes permanently, always mix more plaster than needed for the actual setting. Whatever is left over in the container should be checked every few seconds, for a reason I will explain later.

WARNING: Never rinse any tools or mixing containers where the rinsing water will go through drain pipes; old plaster scraps will quickly clog plumbing. Instead, saturate paper towels with soapy water and wipe off any items that need to be cleaned. Work over a newspaper or wastebasket. Soap and water cleanup can be done when all traces of plaster are gone.

Measure 3 tsp. of cold water into your container. Add 3 *heaping* tsp. of plaster* to the water. Always use a *dry* spoon to dip into the container of plaster. The slightest dampness causes crystallization to begin, and once it has started, it will ruin your supply of plaster. Wait until all plaster has gone *into* the water; then stir. The mixture will first turn "creamy"; as you continue stirring, it will become thicker. When you think it is thick enough, dip up an amount about

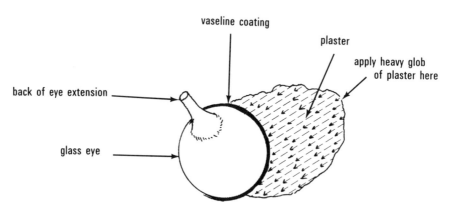

Ill. 17. Enlarged view of eye without any part of eye rocker. Here it is easy to see correct direction of the plaster flow: around the sides and slightly under and below the glass eye.

---

*If a new box of plaster of Paris has small lumps in it, it is not fresh. Crystallization is in progress and it should not be used. Return it to place of purchase and get a fresh box.

the size of your thumbnail, tip the spoon, and let it fall back into the container. If the mixture seems "runny," stir a bit longer. When it slips off the spoon with a solid "plop," it's ready to use.

Step 8 With one hand, brace the head in its position on the towel. With the other, dip the spoon in the plaster and remove an amount the size of your thumbnail. Carefully insert the spoon inside the head to *your right*, about where the ear is located. Tip the spoon toward the *outer* corner of the glass eye and allow the plaster to slide out. If the consistency is right, the mixture will ooze toward the eye; a small part, when it hits the side of the vaselined glass eye, will slide above it and a small part below it (Ill. 17).

If the mixture is too thick, give it a little help in flowing toward the eye by pushing it with your index finger. Be careful not to push too much, above and below the eye. If the mixture is too thin—i.e., if it flows rapidly around the upper and lower part of the eye and will not stay in place—clean it out and try again.

Immediately follow the same procedure for the other eye.

Step 9 Leave the head undisturbed, but keep a close watch on the leftover mixture in the container. (After you become accustomed to setting sleep eyes, this will not be necessary, but for the first few times, you had better do it.) Grease an index finger with vaseline and touch the leftover mixture every few seconds with your fingertip. If it clings to your finger, wipe it off, again grease the fingertip, wait a few seconds, and try again.

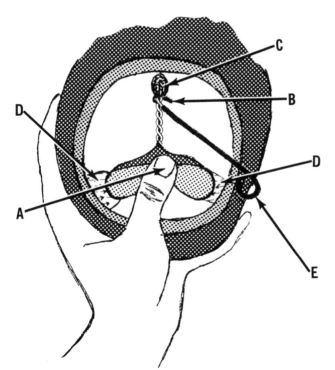

Ill. 18. Making an eye socket. Hold the thumb *(A)* in the center, at the pivot point of rocker arm. *B* is hook of the eye rocker tool. *C* is the weight, and *D*'s indicate the plaster. *E* is handle of the eye rocker tool.

When the fingertip test shows that the plaster does *not* stick to your finger, pick up the head in one hand with the face toward your palm, the open crown facing you, leaving your thumb free. Place the thumb in the *center* of the rocker arm. Insert the hook of the eye rocker tool down next to the lead weight and, keeping the thumb pressure very firm, slowly lift the weight in an arc up and toward the back of the head (Ill. 18). This forms eye sockets in the plaster. Hold it there a second, then release it. If the weight does not freely drop back to the cork in the chin area, gently ease it back with the eye rocker tool.

Wait 15 minutes more to allow the plaster to harden. Then hold the head upright to check the eyes. Are they still in position? If they were *before* you applied the plaster, and *if* you did not dislodge them, they will be. Now tilt the head to a sleeping position. If all steps have been followed to this stage, the eyes will "sleep."

It is necessary to do this test only once. You can tell if the eyes drop back and close erratically (wobble). If they do not work correctly now, they never will. And you will have to start over by removing all plaster while it is still somewhat damp and cleaning all parts just as you did in the beginning.

RESETTING EYES WITH EYELASHES

If the doll had (or is to have) eyelashes, many of the same procedures are followed. Prepare the head as directed in Steps 1 and 2. If the old eye rocker is intact, complete with lashes, clean it as described in Step 3, being especially careful not to loosen or damage the strips. If they are already loose in places, remove them and clean the eye rocker unit as described in Step 3; dry it thoroughly, and either reglue the old lashes or add new ones.

If the old ones are used, remove all the old glue adhering to them with your fingernails or tweezers. Rub the *solid edge* across a drop of fresh Duco contact cement, being careful not to get any on the lashes (Ill. 19). Quickly press the solid edge of the lashes against the glass of the eye—right up *against,* but not *on,* the painted or waxed lid (Ill. 20). Lightly coat the point of a needle with sewing machine oil and wipe off any excess. Using the oiled point, carefully work from one end of the lash strip to the other, pressing the solid edge so that it firmly abuts the lid.

If the old lashes are not usable, buy human hair eyelashes from a local store. I find these preferable to the lash strips available through doll supply houses because, from one pair, you can usually make two or three pairs of doll eyelashes. The quality is much finer,

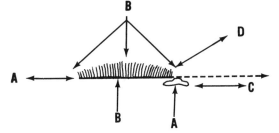

Ill. 19. Recommended method of applying glue to lashes. Starting at the drop of glue *(A)*, rub the *solid* edge of the lashes *(B)* across the glue in the direction of the arrow with the broken line.

Ill. 20. The lashes are placed against—not *on*—the lid. *A* indicates the painted and waxed lid. The dark curved line *B* is the eyelash strip. Clip a few lashes from each end *(C)* of the strip so that none will catch and drag as eyes open and close.

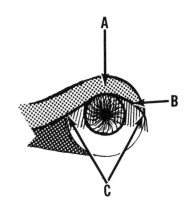

too. They are a bit more expensive, but the cost is justified by their delicate beauty.

To work smoothly on sleep eyes—not drag at the corners—the lash strips must be cut short enough so that there is a small amount of clearance at both inner and outer corners of the eyes. Trimming the lash hairs for length can be done after the sleep eyes are permanently set. The adhesive (solid) edge of the lash strip should be trimmed *very* thin, leaving just enough to hold the hair in place (Ill. 21). From this point, follow the preceding instructions for using old lashes.

Complete Steps 4 and 5 as previously outlined.

In Step 6 and later, when you place the eye rocker unit inside the head, make sure the lashes project *through* the eye socket and that none are caught inside.

Vaseline must be applied more carefully when installing eyes with lashes. It should be put on *only* those parts of the eyes that can be reached from *inside* the head. All other procedures in Step 6 are applicable. Continue with Steps 7, 8, and 9.

Finally, trim the length of the eyelash hairs, shaping them so that the longest hairs are in the center, the shorter at the sides.

Ill. 21. On the solid edge *(A)* trim off as much as possible, and as close to the lashes as can be done without making them come loose. Some of the more expensive adhesive lashes require no trimming.

6

Making an Eye Rocker

In your work area assemble the following: two 6″ lengths of firm but flexible wire (not brass; large paperclips, straightened and re-shaped, are ideal), round glass eyes, Sticky Wax, plaster of Paris, eyelashes (optional), an oblong lead fishing weight with a hole through the center, flesh-colored Flo Paque paint, pink finishing wax, wire cutters, and needle-nose pliers.

Step 1   The eyes must first be securely fastened into position. To do this, melt the Sticky Wax by placing the metal container (remove the lid!) over the lowest heat possible. While it is warming, place a toothpick near it. Put one eye in its socket and maneuver it around until it is where you want it. Hold it there. By now the wax should be partly melted around the outer rim but still fairly solid in the middle. Dip one end of the toothpick into the partly melted wax, and put one generous drop of wax in the center of the upper eyelid, allowing part of it to flow onto the glass. Put another drop on the lower eyelid, also in the center, and allow part of it to touch the glass (Ill. 22). Continue to hold the eye in place with your finger until the wax cools, a matter of about 5 seconds. Repeat for the other eye.

This is called "tacking" the eyes in position. Only two drops are used on each eye in this initial step, to allow for comparison. Are the pupils aligned? Is the same amount of white showing to the right and left of each iris?

If so, continue dipping your toothpick into the wax and letting drops of wax fall onto the surface of both eyes, until they are entirely covered. Make sure the wax not only covers the glass surface but also extends at least ⅛" *onto* the porcelain all the way around each eye (Ill. 23). Unless this covering is thick and strong enough to prevent the eyes from slipping, you may accidentally jar one or both of them loose as you proceed. Place the head in your

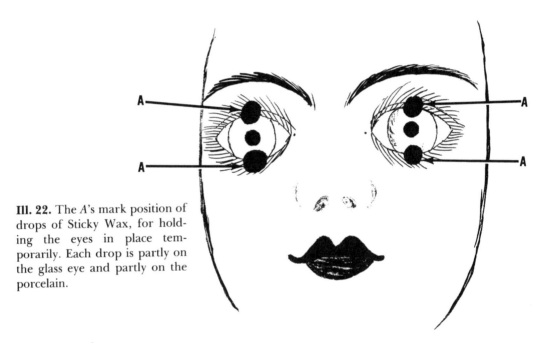

Ill. 22. The *A*'s mark position of drops of Sticky Wax, for holding the eyes in place temporarily. Each drop is partly on the glass eye and partly on the porcelain.

Ill. 23. To apply wax to the eyes, use as many drops of Sticky Wax as necessary to cover the entire glass area and extend ⅛" onto the porcelain.

refrigerator for 30 minutes. The cold temperature makes the wax get harder and stronger.

Step 2   When the 30 minutes is up, remove the head. Place the eye ruler inside it, with one end in the *center* of one of the back-of-eye extensions, the other end across to the same position on the other eye (Ill. 24). Make a note of the measurement and add an extra ¼″ to both ends; i.e., if the measurement is 1¼″, add another ½″ to that to allow for the turnunder. The total needed is then 1¾″. Divide that width in half: ⅞″.

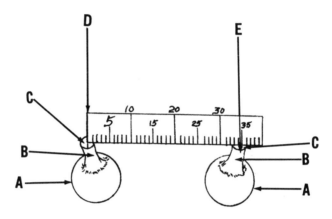

Ill. 24. Measuring width of "T" arm of rocker. (This is a simplified drawing. Visualize the situation with the eyes fastened inside the head.) Hold end of ruler *(D)* at center *(C)* of hole in back of eye extension *(B)*. Note the measurement indicated at *E* (center of hole in other eye extension). To this measurement, *always* add another ½″ (13mm) for a ¼″ bend (6½-mm bend) at each end.

Now you're ready to begin work on the two wires. From one end of a wire, measure in ⅞″ and bend it as shown in Ill. 25. Repeat for the other wire. Hook the two wires together at the point where they were bent (Ill. 26) and, using your thumb to hold them tightly together there, start twisting the wires. The motion can be compared to that of closing a bread wrapper with the little piece of wire provided for that purpose. In that, too, you twist the two *ends* of wire together. Ill. 26 shows how the wires should look when you have finished twisting them.

Finally, grasp one end of the *straight* portion, which looks like the horizontal part of a capital *T*, in the jaw tip of the needle-nose pliers (Ill. 27). Hold the thumb firmly over the center point where the wires are *hooked* together and bend one end of the wire down (away from you) ¼″. Repeat at the other side. Recheck your measurements. From side to side, not counting the turnunder, the overall width should be 1½″.

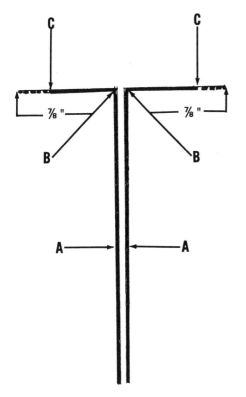

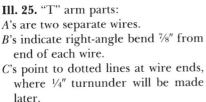

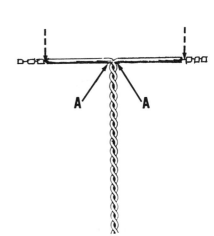

Ill. 26. To put the "T" arm together, hook the two wires together at point A, and twist them together all the way to the lower ends, to form the "tail" of the rocker unit. (Broken lines at top indicate where ¼″ turnunder will be made.)

Ill. 25. "T" arm parts:
A's are two separate wires.
B's indicate right-angle bend ⅞″ from end of each wire.
C's point to dotted lines at wire ends, where ¼″ turnunder will be made later.

Step 3   Now measure the length of the twisted wires: hold the doll head, face down, and insert the ¼″ prongs you have just bent, into the holes of the extensions on the backs of the eyes. Let the twisted wire drop to the chin area. If it's too long, snip off a little with wire cutters. Measure, with your eye ruler, from the center of the rocker arm down to the chin area where you have placed a "cushioning material" (Ill. 28).

Ill. 27. Skeletal structure of eye rocker, and the next step in construction: at B, the thumb and fingers brace the unit. The needle-nose pliers (A) grip the outer ¼″ of wire (dotted line C), and bend it into final position, represented by the solid line C.

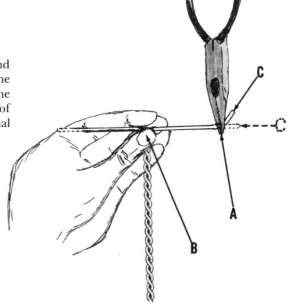

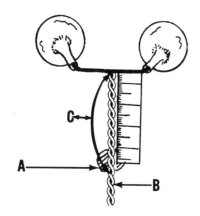

Ill. 28. Measuring the length of the twisted wire tail, with the unit inside the head (not shown). With the bent wire ends inserted into the eye extensions, let the "tail" fall to touch the chin-area cushion pad *(A)*. Snip off the wire (at *B*) if it is too long. Measure length *(C)* to the cushion pad and add ¼″ for a bent "stop." *C* marks the length the "tail" should be before the addition.

For purposes of illustration, let's say the measurement is 1⅞″. Make a note of it. You'll need to refer back to it soon. Remove the wire frame.

Step 4 For the weight, use an oblong lead sinker, such as fishermen use. Be sure it's the type that has a hole through the center. Slip the end of the twisted wires through the hole and slide the sinker up toward the rocker arm, out of the way. Remember that the *exact* measurement you noted was 1⅞″. Measure down that far from the rocker arm. At that precise point, bend the twisted wire in an **L**-shape, and cut off all but ¼″ (Ill. 29). The direction in which you make the bend does not matter, for its only purpose is as a stop for the weight.

Slide the weight back down, against the stop, and place the rocker inside the head. Check to see that the weight rests on the cork or

Ill. 29. Adding the lead sinker.

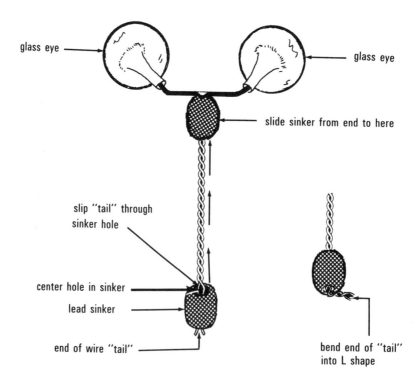

plastic wood in the chin area, and that it does not make contact anywhere with the porcelain.

If it fits, remove it. With the lead weight down tightly against the stop (bent end), lay the rocker flat on concrete and give the lead weight a solid whack with a hammer. This will flatten the lead securely against the wire so that it will stay in place.

If minor adjustments are needed, however, make them before flattening the lead weight.

Step 5   Place the eye rocker unit back inside the head, inserting the ¼″ turnunder (on each end of the arm) into the back-of-the-eye extensions and letting the weight rest on its cushion in the chin area. This is the exact position the unit must hold for permanent sleep eyes. Put the head aside, face down.

Mix together about ¾ tsp. plaster of Paris with enough Elmer's Glue to make a *very thick* paste. Make the first application of the paste to the holes in the back of the eyes, where the ¼″ wire extensions go. The mixture must be extremely thick because we do *not* want it to run down into the hollow eyes. Use a toothpick to lift small amounts at a time to apply to this critical area. (See Ill. 30.)

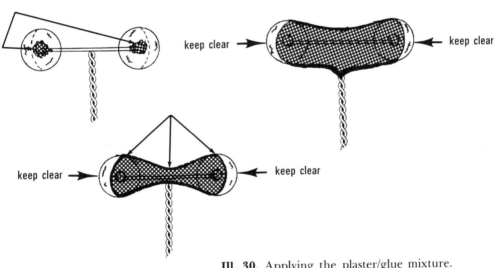

Ill. 30. Applying the plaster/glue mixture. First, apply paste mixture to the holes in the back-of-the-eye extensions, as indicated by the two arrows at top left. Always keep outer third of eye clear (see arrow at top right).

The three arrows in the center drawing indicate the area to be covered with thick paste.

At bottom is the eye rocker, as it will look when Step 5 (see text) has been completed. Use a dampened finger or wet brush to smooth the surface as you work.

Next, start applying the mixture *down* the glass eye extension and onto the round part of the eye, then across the straight section, and on to the other eye. Do *not* let any of the mixture run down the *outer* third of the eye, for this area will later form sockets for the sleep eyes. Continue applying thick paste, working back and forth across the arm of the eye rocker, around the glass eye extensions, and over the holes.

Some of the mixture will slide off the wire and drop to the porcelain underneath. Scoop it up and dab it back on the wire. Keep the porcelain underneath the unit as clean as possible.

The main purpose of this first application and succeeding ones is to secure the eyes to the wire arm so tightly that they will *not* slip out of position when you remove the Sticky Wax from the front of the eyes, after construction has been completed.

When the mixture has set and dried, which takes several hours, you will have a good base on which to build the next layer of material, Sticky Wax.

Step 6   With the unit still *inside* the head, warm the Sticky Wax only until it's melted enough that a "glob" of it will adhere to a toothpick. A "dip and dab" motion gives the best results, and facilitates the needed buildup. Study Ill. 31 to determine the approximate *shape* the eye rocker should have when completed. Be especially careful to avoid a buildup of material on the *outer* round

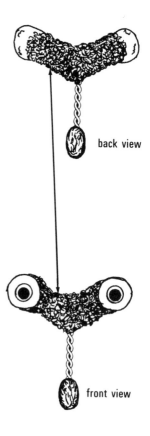

Ill. 31. Front and back views, showing the application of Sticky Wax. The two arrows at top point to the outer third of the glass eye, the area that is to be kept clear. The long arrow indicates the rough uneven surface left by the "dip and dab" method of applying wax. Follow text instructions in Step 7 for smoothing out the surface.

back view

front view

area of the glass eyes. The buildup must slant inward, leaving the outer third of the glass eye exposed. It is this area that later forms eye sockets in the plaster, as described in Step 9 of the overall directions for setting sleep eyes.

Step 7   When the buildup is completed and dried, remove the Sticky Wax from the *front* of the glass eyes by bracing the rocker unit from *inside* with one hand. Slip the sharp end of an Exacto blade under the edges of the wax, and with a quick twisting motion flick off all the wax holding the eyes in place. Remove the rocker unit. If it needs still more buildup across the arm, add more.

Scrape off all wax scraps adhering to the porcelain head and any clinging to the exposed glass section of the eyes.

The wax you have "dipped and dabbed" on while building up the rocker arm will be very rough and unsightly. To smooth it, heat a rounded piece of metal (handle of a kitchen knife, large nail, or other suitable object) until it is just warm enough to melt the wax slightly as you run it back and forth and around over the surface. If, when you touch the metal to the wax, the wax immediately starts to run, the metal is too hot. Let it cool down a bit and try it again.

Save all Sticky Wax and put it back into the container. It can be used over and over again.

Finally, let the unit dry overnight.

Step 8   For applying eyelids, first locate where they should be by placing the rocker unit back in position inside the head. Brace it with one hand. With the other, take a finely sharpened soft lead pencil (a film-marker is ideal) and put the point of the pencil, slanted a trifle upward, into the corner of one eye. Letting the contour of the upper lid serve as a guide, draw an arched line across to the other corner. Examine the line to make sure it's easy to see. Sometimes wetting the pencil point will make the line darker. Repeat for the other eye.

Remove the eye rocker unit. Using flesh-colored Flo Paque paint (see list of suppliers) and a small artist's brush, apply the lid, keeping on the lines you have just drawn. Ill. 32 indicates all other areas to be painted (and later waxed). Let dry several hours.

Pink wax, specially made for this purpose (see list of suppliers), is used for waxing the lids. It comes in thin sheets. Tear several sheets into small pieces, put them in a metal container, and melt over low heat until the wax becomes transparent. Flow it onto the painted area by loading an old, but clean, artist's brush and just letting the tip touch the area to be coated. It's best to run a line of pink wax across the arc of the eyelid first because this is the area most tedious to do. The rest of the eyelid and painted areas can be quickly covered.

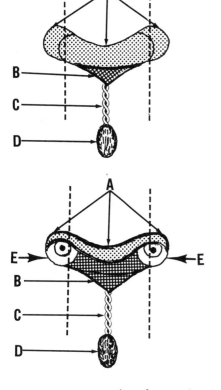

Ill. 32. Areas to be painted and waxed, front and back views. WARNING: Do not paint or wax until the shaping is smooth and round *outside* the area indicated here by vertical broken lines. Areas indicated by *A* are to be painted first with flesh Flo Paque, permitted to dry, then coated with pink wax. *B* indicates Sticky Wax, *C* is the wire "tail," *D* is the lead weight, and *E* the glass eyes.

An alternative method is dipping. This must be done fast, for if the eye rocker is held too long in the hot wax, the heat affects the Sticky Wax used in building up the rocker arm. It is also impossible to get the wax precisely where you want it with dipping, yet some people do it. Its only advantage is the smoothness of the wax application. Wax adhering to areas other than those you have painted should be scraped off. In addition, if you plan to add eyelashes, all traces of the wax must be removed with turpentine, followed by a soap and water washing. The adhesive used for applying lashes will not hold unless the surface is absolutely clean and dry.

Step 9 When the wax has cooled enough to allow handling of the eye rocker, the lashes may be applied following the procedures shown in Ills. 19, 20, and 21, and explained under Resetting Eyes with Eyelashes. Then follow the overall directions for permanently setting the eyes for sleep.

If eyes move easily in their sockets but seem sluggish in opening and closing, the cause will usually be lack of enough weight on the end of the eye rocker. To add more weight, plug in your soldering iron. (For doll work, the only kind suitable is the pencil type, made especially for intricate work.) While it's heating, fold a tissue to use as a pad and slip it *under* the weight, to prevent hot solder from dropping onto the porcelain.

Hold the soldering iron in one hand and a coil of solder in the other. Extend the *end* of the solder directly *over* an area of the lead weight, and touching it. Insert the soldering iron in the head, carefully slanting it to avoid touching the porcelain. If the iron is hot enough, even a quick touch of its tip against the tip of the solder will melt off a small portion onto the lead weight, where it will adhere. Repeat, until a layer of "drops" covers the surface of the lead. The solder should add enough weight. If not, more can be added.

The surface of the solder will be rough. Let the iron cool down just enough so that, if you touch it to the solder, it will smooth out the surface but not make it melt and run.

Remove the folded tissue. If enough weight has been added, the eyes will open and close smoothly.

Finally, clean all traces of vaseline from the front of the eyes. Use Q-Tips moistened in turpentine over the largest portion of the glass. For areas a Q-Tip will not reach, wet the end of a toothpick, swirl cotton around it, dip it in turpentine, and clean the remaining surfaces.

The techniques described in this chapter will work on all antique sleep-eye dolls. Naturally the measurements used will vary according to the size of the doll.

You learn by doing. Though it has taken quite a few pages to present the detailed directions, setting sleep eyes can be accomplished in as little as 45 minutes, exclusive of the waiting periods, once you are familiar with the routine and the techniques. And not only will you save yourself considerable expense by learning to set sleep eyes; you can earn good pay doing the job for other collectors.

Recently I received a letter from a customer who lives in a small California town. A doll shipped to her by parcel post had arrived with the eyes jarred out. When she removed the wig and pate, she discovered the eye rocker unit intact, but both plaster eye sockets were broken. Although this customer is a do-it-yourselfer who has repaired her own dolls, she had never learned to set either fixed or sleep eyes. So she took the doll to the nearest doll hospital, only to be told that they didn't set sleep eyes; they would put them in as fixed eyes, though. In all, she went to six places before she found one that would set sleep eyes—and they wanted $50.00 for the job.

When she wrote to me about the problem, I immediately forwarded a copy of this chapter to her. About two weeks later came her reply: "I did it four times before I got it right, but now Hilda is my most prized possession . . . I'm so proud of myself. I've always wanted to learn to set sleep eyes, but could never find specific instructions before."

7

Wigs-Making
New Ones

Little definitive information has appeared in print about making doll wigs, and so this chapter will attempt to repair that omission by describing various methods of making such wigs from human hair. Of course synthetic hair wigs can be bought ready made, but many serious collectors consider synthetic wigs incompatible on an antique doll.

Dynel wigs do have some specific merits in the restoration of dolls, however. For one thing, they are more lustrous (sometimes too lustrous), more easily styled, and much cheaper in the long run if one takes into consideration the time required in making a wig. The high sheen of a Dynel wig can be toned down by a generous dusting with ordinary talcum powder or spraying with a canned talcum, followed by a thorough combing and brushing. (This high sheen is caused by the chemicals used to make it fireproof.)

The final choice of material is up to the customer—or to you, if you're working on your own dolls. Dynel or human hair—one or the other; they are the only two materials I use consistently in my studio.

Where can you find wig materials? Auctions, garage sales, and similar events are good sources for all types and all colors of hairpieces. Sometimes a friend will give you one or more hairpieces. Beauticians are sometimes willing to save long hair for you. Whatever the source, be sure the piece is shampooed, rinsed, and dried thoroughly before you take it apart (if you're working with a manufactured hairpiece). Hair obtained from a beauty shop is usually shampooed before it's cut, thus eliminating one step.

All supplies needed for making wigs can be purchased commercially, too, if you want to pay the prices (see list of suppliers).

Although the methods described here will refer only to the use of human hair, you can use the same methods if your source of hair is a synthetic wig or fall—with a few exceptions. For example, you cannot put a permanent wave in a synthetic wig, nor can you dye it another color. Also, synthetic hair has usually been precurled, so it is more difficult to handle than straight hair.

To remove the curls from a synthetic wig or fall, soak it 15 minutes in Woolite to remove any spray or dirt, then rinse it thoroughly. The hair may be blotted to take out some of the water, but be sure it is quite wet when you place it on a wig block. (See Ill. 33 for directions on how to make a doll wig block.) Comb it out

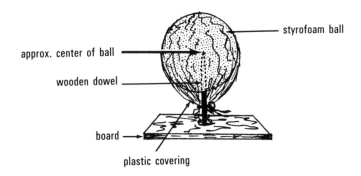

Ill. 33. To make a doll-wig block, start with styrofoam ball of appropriate size and a piece of board no less than 6″ square. You will also need plastic to cover the ball and a short piece of dowel rod to connect the ball to the wood base.

Sand and varnish the board. In the center drill a hole for No. 5 wood screw. Then drill a hole to countersink metal washer. (The washer gives the block greater stability.) In the bottom of the ball, punch a hole somewhat smaller than the dowel, extending to the center of the ball. Fill the hole with Elmer's Glue, invert ball, and let excess glue run out; then force ball down on sharpened end of dowel. Let dry. Cover ball with plastic, and fasten plastic covering by tying it to the dowel.

(WARNING: Never allow more than 2″ of dowel rod between the upper surface of the board and the opening in the styrofoam ball. If the ball sits too high above its base, it may be top heavy when a wig is put on it.)

straight. Then cover it with a large white cloth, drawn tightly down to the base of the block and secured with a heavy rubber band or string. When it is dry, handle it as you would human hair. The only precaution that need be taken is in the type of glue used, where glue is necessary. Some glues are not compatible with synthetics, so if you are using a glue other than what is recommended, test it first. Instructions for curling and styling synthetic hair will be given later in this section.

If you use a human hair wig or fall, clean it as described above. Towel-dry it, comb it, place it on a wig block, comb it again, and let it air dry. It is not necessary to cover human hair with a white cloth.

PREPARATION OF HAIR

Assuming the hair has been conditioned—all foreign matter washed out and the hairpiece combed and dried—are you satisfied with the color? If not, perhaps you can do something about it. A blonde hairpiece can be "stripped" and redyed, following directions on the commercial product you buy. (Directions are not given here because the manufacturer of such products includes specific instructions.)

A large, shallow cardboard box like those used by department stores for packing bulky garments is a good container in which to lay the strands as you prepare for wig making, regardless of which type of wig you plan. Pad the bottom of the box with an old bath towel. Work always in a place where there is no breeze—not even a breath of air stirring—to displace the strands.

To remove the wefts from the base of a secondhand hairpiece, use a single-edged razor blade—but handle it carefully. Locate the spot, usually in the back, where the wefts were overlapped and stitched. This is your starting point. As you remove each weft, put it in the box. Continue until all of them are removed. Some wefts will have shorter hair than others. Place the short ones together, as well as all other lengths, but in separate layers—do not pile them up. And don't cut the hair from the weft until directed to do so. When you have a thin layer stretching from one end of the towel to the other, wrap the unused part of the hairpiece, wefts intact, in plastic and store it for later use.

Read through this chapter, study the various types of wigs, and decide which one you want to make. Then prepare your work area accordingly. The line drawings are as visually comprehensive as possible, the techniques and procedures broken down into step-by-step illustrations. The various methods are presented in the order of their difficulty, from the easiest to the most demanding. And I strongly recommend the use of Duco waterproof cement any time glue is needed in wig work. The words *glue* and *cement* are used interchangeably here.

It is advisable for beginners to start with the simplest wig construction and proceed to the next, and the next, until finally they are ready for the most difficult, wig weaving.

Refresh your memory on how to tie a "security knot," as illustrated in Chapter 5, Illustration 13. This is the only knot I use in making wigs. It has many practical uses in all phases of doll work when you need a knot that will not slip.

TOPKNOT WIG

Of all the types of wig construction, this is the easiest. Unfortunately the use of a topknot wig is limited to small dolls, baby dolls, and little-boy dolls. The open-top crown suitable for this type of wig must be so shaped that a topknot wig can be used without spoiling the "roundness" of the head. Study Ill. 34. It shows three types of heads.

1. *Solid Dome.* The 4″ to 5″ Bye-Lo, designed by Grace Storey Putnam (1925), is an excellent example of a solid-dome head. Most Bye-Lo's had painted hair, but the rare ones had a small hole in the top of the solid dome, into which a topknot wig was inserted (Ill. 34, line *A*).

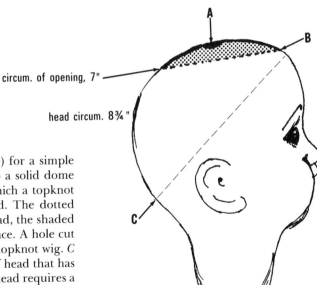

circum. of opening, 7″

head circum. 8¾″

Ill. 34. Heads suitable (and unsuitable) for a simple topknot wig. The arrow at *A* points to a solid dome with a hole (the only opening) into which a topknot wig of hair can be inserted and glued. The dotted line at *B* represents an open-crown head, the shaded area being a skull crown glued into place. A hole cut in the center of this will also receive a topknot wig. *C* indicates the upper edge of the type of head that has most of its dome cut out. This type of head requires a full wig.

2. *High open-crown.* A good example of this type of head is the K*R Simon & Halbig 117. Although there are countless others, this is the one I chose to represent in Illustration 34, line *B*. Notice that only the very top of the head was removed (in the greenware state), leaving the curved contour in the back of the head. Topknot wigs are, if not ideal, at least practical on dolls of this type as long as the crown opening is not more than 7″.

3. *Low open-crown.* French (or other) dolls may have an open crown slanting from the top of a high forehead to a low point in line with the ears (either the top or the lobe). Note line *C* in Illustration 34. Dolls with such a low open-crown should never be fitted with a topknot wig.

Procedure

First, measure the diameter of the crown opening. In Ill. 34 the crown opening is 7″ and the head circumference is 8¾ ″. (If you were ordering a wig, you would have to order a size 9, since wigs are not available in fractional measurements.)

Regardless of the type of wig you make, you will need a skull crown (pate). These are made of finely pressed buckram, and are inexpensive. It is a good idea to order a one-dozen assortment. They come only in even sizes, but can always be cut down to fit perfectly. For the 7″ crown opening shown in Ill. 34, you need an 8″ skull crown cut down to 7″.

Other supplies needed for a topknot wig are scissors, thread to match the hair color, Duco waterproof cement, and a sharp-pointed tool, such as an awl, to bore a hole in the skull crown. Follow the step-by-step instructions in Ill. 35.

If you're making a topknot wig for a solid-dome head, simply use shorter hair strands and follow the instructions in Ill. 35, *C* through *F*. To fasten it inside the solid dome, squeeze out a small amount of Duco waterproof cement on waxed paper, dip the end of a toothpick into the glue, and apply a thin layer all around the inside edges of the hole before inserting the hair knot through the hole. The hair knot should be large enough that it comes into contact with the glue all around the opening. Test the hair knot first before you apply the glue.

Continue following instructions in Ill. 35 for final arrangement of the hair.

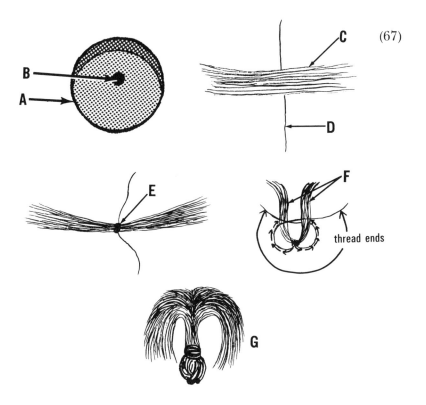

Ill. 35. Making a topknot wig. Drawing at top left shows a skull crown. Light area *(A)* is under side; dark area is part of the top, showing. *B* indicates a hole pierced through the skull crown.

At upper right, *C* indicates hair strands 10″ long. Arrange these over center of long thread (same color as hair) that is marked *D*. At *E*, the thread is tied in a security knot. *F* shows the hair doubled over, to be wound around and around with the thread ends in opposite directions. Tie thread ends in a safety knot and cut off excess thread. *G* is the topknot, ready to be pushed through hole *B*, until nothing shows outside except loose hair.

Run a solid ribbon of Duco waterproof cement around the hole and the hair, from *inside* the skull crown. Let dry. Then glue skull crown to doll's head and let dry.

Finally, distribute hair evenly over head: lift hair, one section at a time, and spread *very thin* coat of *fresh* Duco waterproof cement under each section. Allow each section of hair, in turn, to fall onto its own cement-covered surface area (only a few hairs on the under side of a section should be caught in the glue).

To make hair lie flat, wet it, comb and arrange it, then cover with a damp white cloth fastened at neckline with string or rubber bands until dry.

STRIP WIGS

This type of wig is made on strips of cloth cut on the *straight* of the fabric. Old cotton cloth, either the color of the hair or flesh color, is used. Construction can range from a single strip to multiple strips placed at strategic spots on the doll's head.

If you make a strip wig that is glued in part to a skull crown, paint the skull crown a flesh color, matching the color as closely as possible to the skin tones of the doll. Do not attempt any glueing until the paint is thoroughly dry.

One-Strip Wig

This is the simplest type of strip wig to make. Begin by measuring from the forehead, where you want the hairline, then over the center top of the head *toward* (not to) the center nape of the neck. The measurement should not go beyond an imaginary line drawn from the top of one ear across the head to the top of the other. To illustrate, if the measurement, from the front hairline to the imaginary line, is 3″, add another inch so that, later, ½ ″ of fabric can be turned and glued under at each end of the strip. Make the fabric strip no more than ½ ″ wide.

Very long hair is needed for this type of wig, for reasons that will be clear later.

Study Ill. 36, which shows the placement of hair in relation to the fabric strip. This determines whether you make a center part or a side part. Cut a square of tissue paper large enough to accommodate the length and width of the strip wig you're making. Place the fabric strip on the tissue paper and arrange the hair over it. If a center part is desired, spread the hair across the strip with the strip in the middle. If a side part is desired, place the hair atop the strip so that more hangs down on one side than on the other.

Next, make a "sandwich" by placing another piece of tissue paper *over* the hair. Then slide the tissue paper-hair-tissue paper "sandwich" under the presser foot of the sewing machine. This will prevent the feed dog of the machine from "chewing" at the fabric, which it will do if the tissue paper is not used. Without tissue paper it will also tangle the hair.

Run two lines of stitching as close as possible to each other on the strip. The length of the stitch is important. The smaller the straight stitch (never use zig-zag), the better it will hold the hair in place. Experiment with a small test strip "sandwich" before sewing the permanent strip.

After sewing, tear off the tissue paper; then cut off the fabric as

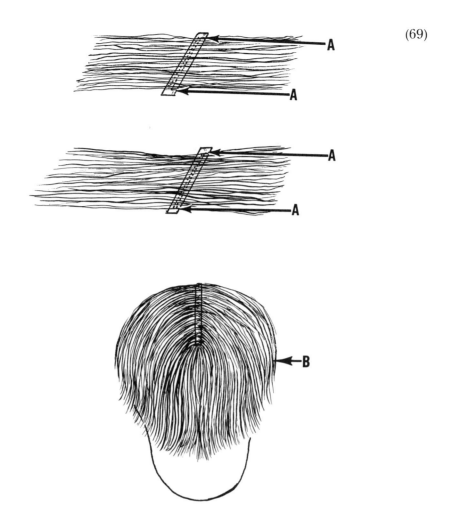

Ill. 36. Making a one-strip wig. For a center part (top drawing), equal lengths of hair must fall on either side of the strip. Glue the ends under at *A*. For a side part (second drawing), one side of the hair must hang longer than the other. Again, glue ends under at *A*. In back, the hair must be combed as shown in the lower drawing *B*. The under layer is held in place with a very thin coat of Duco waterproof cement.

close to the stitching lines as possible. Glue the half-inch extensions of fabric under, Ill. 36, onto the wrong side of the fabric. Use glue sparingly here.

The one-strip wig can now be permanently attached to the head. Apply glue the entire length of the fabric strip (underneath), being careful not to use so much it will ooze into the hair when pressure is applied. Place the strip (which is actually the part in the hair) into position and hold it there for a few minutes. If you're using Duco glue it will bond quickly.

When you're sure the glue is dry, lift the hair on one side of the head and spread a very thin coat of Duco waterproof cement on that side. Ease the hair into place and press gently with your hand. Repeat on the other side. To cover the back of the head with a thin layer of hair, apply the thin coat of cement and comb the hair, working from both sides of the strip, around and down. If the combing is done correctly, the back of the hair will look as shown in Ill. 36 *B*.

Dampen a piece of white cloth, preferably cotton, and bind it tightly over the wig. It can be held in place by securing it with a rubber band around the neck of the doll. Let it dry at least 24 hours.

Long hair strands must be used in one-strip wigs because you are depending on their length to provide hair for both sides and the back of the head. When you're ready to style the wig, you will have to do some trimming to even up the hair length.

Although it is possible to "set" the hair by using tiny rollers or bobby pins for pin curls, simply letting the hair fall straight is most attractive, particularly on dolls representing children. Or, for a slight curl on the ends, an electric curling iron can be used.

Ill. 37. The two-strip wig. *A* is the bangs strip, glued in place. *B* is a long strip constructed the same as a one-strip wig. *C* shows how the front and back ends of the long strip are turned under and glued, before the long strip is glued onto the head. When glueing down the turned-under ends, it's a good idea also to turn under a few of the end hairs. Be sure to place the long strip so that it covers the edge of the bang strip.

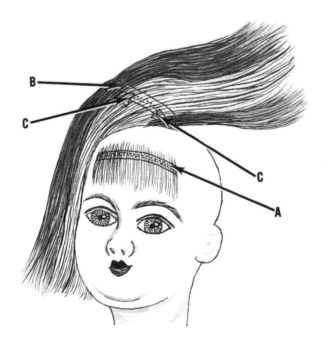

Two, three, four, or more hair strips can be constructed according to the foregoing instructions; only the measurements will be different. However, it is extremely important to plan the hairdo before making the strips. If you want a demure hairdo with center part and bangs, for instance, first measure a small strip of cloth the width of the bangs. Prepare it as you did the single strip, and glue it in place first. The longer strip that constitutes the rest of the wig is then glued far enough over the bang strip to cover it. Ill. 37 shows a two-strip wig.

Three-strip Wig

A lovely hair-style can be made with three strips: a short one for bangs; one that fits from one side of the bangs, around the desired hair line, to the other side of the bangs; and another long strip that is glued directly over (on top of) the second strip. Be sure you have enough long hair to finish this one. It takes quite a bit.

Make and apply the bang strip first. Then measure, as indicated by *B* in Ill. 38, from one end of the bang strip around the head to the other end of the bang strip. Cut the fabric strip this length plus 1″, to allow for turning ½″ under at each end of the strip.

Ill. 38. Strip wig hairstyle using three strips. Measure for the bang strip as indicated by the *A*'s. Make it of short hairs; glue it in place and let dry. Measure the head from one end of bang strip *(A)* around *B* to the other side of bang strip *(A)*. Use long hair for this strip (#2). Glue it in place and let dry; trim off irregular ends projecting above both strips. (See Ill. 39 for next step.)

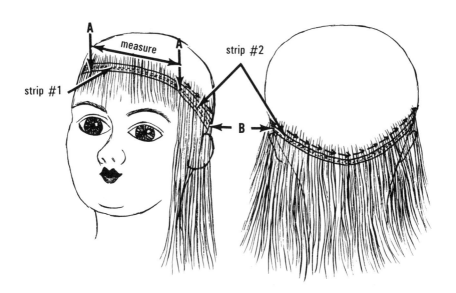

In making bang strips, as well as the other two needed for this wig (see Ills. 37 and 38), note that irregular ends of hair project above the strips. These must be trimmed off as close to the stitching line as possible; then a minute threading of Duco cement run over it and worked into the hair and fabric. Without the glue, some of the hair would come out when you comb it. As each strip dries, apply it in position on the head.

The third and final strip is glued directly on top of the second one, so when you measure for it, be sure its length is the total length of long strip 2 plus that of the bang strip. Ill. 39 shows, in shaded

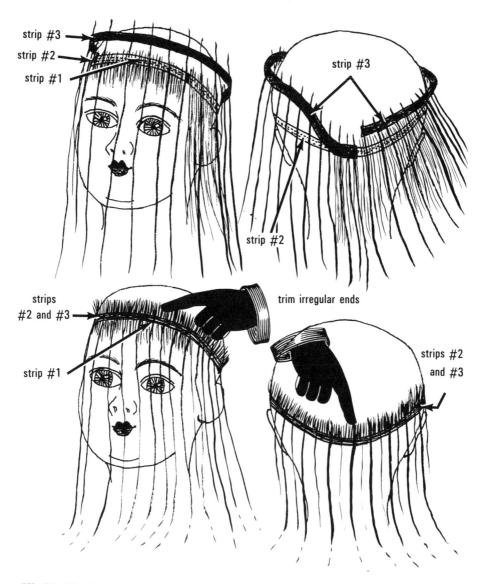

Ill. 39. The four drawings here indicate the procedure for adding the third wig strip to the two that were glued on in Ill. 38.

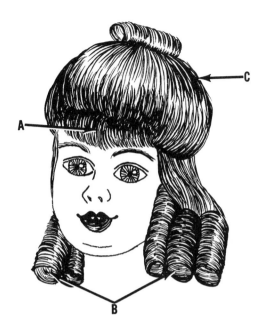

Ill. 40. Styling the three-strip wig. *A* indicates the bangs (strip #1) now combed down and shaped. *B* points to the fat curls made in the hair of strip #2. Strip #3 *(C)*, combed upward and puffed, ends in a curl on top of the head.

black, the positioning of strip 3. Start glueing one end at center back; take it around the head and end at center back. For the purpose of clarity, only a few long strands of hair are shown on strip 3 (Ill. 39)—but keep in mind that it should be as full as strip 2. Later, when you style it, the hair on strip 3 will be drawn upward, ending in a bun or a single large curl; the hair on strip 2 will hang down and may be left plain, or curled. See Ill. 40 for a suggested hairstyle.

GLUEING HAIR DIRECTLY ONTO A SOLID DOME

In my research into the various methods used in wigmaking, one name kept cropping up. I was told that this particular woman had, many years ago, gained quite a reputation for her "Heirloom Dolls." No one remembered what the dolls were made of—they remembered the gorgeous wigs made by this talented lady; and so I called her. Because she is now in her late eighties and wants no publicity, her name will not be given.

"My eyesight is gone," the woman explained over the phone, "but I'll be glad to show you my dolls, and teach you how I made the wigs. Don't bring any hair—I have lots of it. Just bring a solid-dome doll and some Duco cement." Later, she welcomed me into her home, and taught me the following method.

Lay various lengths of hair on a bath towel, with all shorter lengths together, and medium and long strands likewise separated and placed together. As you prepare the hair according to length, comb it thoroughly before placing it on the towel. Cover your work area with an opened brown paper bag like those groceries come in. You'll need a pan of clear water, an old washcloth, a piece of white cotton cloth large enough to cover the doll's head and reach to the neck, some rubber bands, and a pencil sharpened to a fine point. Sketch the desired hairline onto the bisque very lightly with the pencil.

Thin strands of hair are first glued around the marked hairline. Squeeze out one drop of Duco, take up a hair strand with no more than a dozen hairs in it, dip the blunt end of the strand into the glue, then quickly place it against the pencil mark at the nape of the neck. Press your thumb against the hair ends to distribute the hair thinly. This step must be done fast. It's a quick push-distribute-remove movement, and if it is not done this way, the strand will stick to your finger instead of to the doll's head.

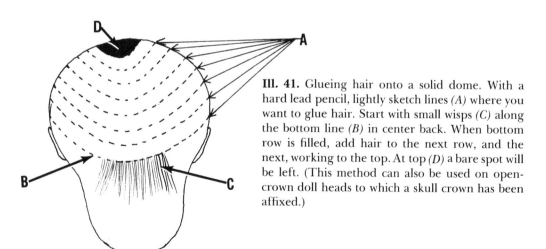

Ill. 41. Glueing hair onto a solid dome. With a hard lead pencil, lightly sketch lines *(A)* where you want to glue hair. Start with small wisps *(C)* along the bottom line *(B)* in center back. When bottom row is filled, add hair to the next row, and the next, working to the top. At top *(D)* a bare spot will be left. (This method can also be used on open-crown doll heads to which a skull crown has been affixed.)

After each strand is put in place, wipe as much glue as possible off the fingers, using the wet washcloth. Since Duco is waterproof, a thin layer of it will stick to your fingers no matter what you do. Continue this procedure until the first row of hair is in place. Ill. 41 shows how this first row is positioned and how the location of the succeeding rows should be marked. No specific measurement between the rows can be given because the location of the rows depends on the size of the doll head. Fill in each row until you have just a small bare spot left on top of the head (*D* in Ill. 41). This can be covered by following the directions given in Ill. 43.

Saturate the white cloth, squeeze out the excess water, and place the center of the cloth at the center top of the hair. Pull the cloth down tightly over the head and secure it firmly at the neck with rubber bands. Allow the hair to dry at least 24 hours; then it can be cut and styled. You can even give it a permanent wave. Duco glue is impervious to permanent waving solutions.

When it has been applied skillfully, the hair seems to be actually growing from the doll's head. Of course, hair applied in this manner must have a hairstyle that utilizes the "comb down, then back" look, particularly around the front of the face. The Gibson Girl hairdo is a prime example of this style. Ill. 42 shows how to make a "widow's peak."

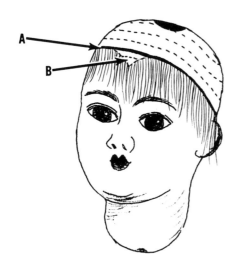

Ill. 42. Making a widow's peak. The method described in Ill. 41 is extremely versatile. For example, the widow's peak at *B* can be made by simply marking its shape and glueing wisps of hair along the lines. This variation may be useful to doll artists who make original creations. On antique dolls, the conventional hairline *(A)* should be followed.

After the glue is dry, you can use any method of hair curling you would use on your own hair, and the style possibilities are limitless. You never have to worry that the edge of a wig cap will show, as it almost always does on commercial wigs.

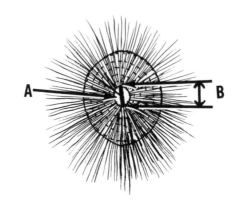

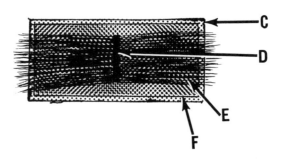

Ill. 43. Filling in the bare spot. *A* indicates bald spot to be covered. *B* shows where to measure, to determine length of the hairpiece needed. If the area measures 1½", cut a strip of flesh-colored net or fabric 1½" long and ½" wide.

Lay a rectangular piece of tissue paper *(C)* on a flat surface. Put the net or fabric strip *(D)* in the center. Place long strands of hair *(E)* over the strip, distributing them evenly. On top, lay a second sheet *(F)* of tissue paper.

Set sewing machine for smallest stitch possible. Slide the tissue paper "sandwich" under presser foot of machine and make one row of stitching down the net or fabric strip. Turn strip and stitch a second row down it, as close to first row as possible.

Tear off both layers of tissue paper. Trim strip to the lines of stitching. Glue strip in place on bald spot.

Once you work with "home-grown" hair, you will find it is much softer and more manageable than hair obtained from manufactured hairpieces. The hair used in wigs has been subjected to various chemical processes to obtain the colors we see today, whereas hair in its natural state is more lustrous and a delight to work with.

By the time you've finished applying the hair strands, your fingers will be uncomfortably coated with layers of waterproof glue even though you have been using the wet washcloth faithfully. Solvent used in thinning plastic wood does a fairly good job of removing the heaviest accumulation, but be prepared to peel off offending fragments for several days.

SEWING MACHINE WIGS

If you've ever examined a factory-made wig, you know that the top of the wig base has stitching lines that seem to go helter-skelter, in all directions, and that long machine stitches are always used. From the center top to the hairline the stitches are thickest. This is where the part of the hair is made (middle or side). Then the rows, even on a small size-7 wig, are spaced almost an inch apart. Wig bases are rarely the same color as the hair, and around the front "hairline" the base must be trimmed close to the line of stitching. I have seen white hair stitched with black thread, black stitched with white; I've worked with wigs that were thick in some places, and so thin in others it was almost impossible to restyle them.

The making of commercial doll wigs is a big business, a production-line business. As in most large operations, the aim is to turn out as many as possible in the shortest length of time. This is not to "run down" commercial wigs, for they are important to us. But I must point out that many things done in a factory can be done at home, and done better, because we are interested only in the final product, not in how fast we can make it.

Study Ills. 44 through 51, which show the steps to be followed in producing a facsimile of a factory wig. The first one you make will be the most difficult, but each one becomes easier until finally you will be able to make this size-12 wig in an hour or less.

As you work, remove any loose hairs from around the feed dog and bobbin hole of your sewing machine. Form the habit of doing this after each section of hair is sewed to the wig base; otherwise the machine may "lock up."

Begin as shown in Ill. 44.

Ill. 45 describes the manner in which each fill-in is stitched, folded, and stitched again.

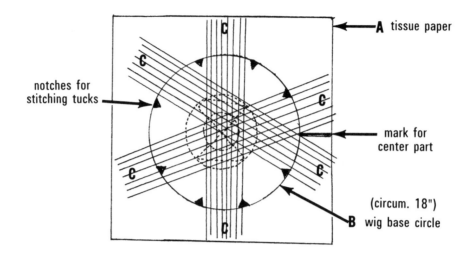

notches for stitching tucks

A tissue paper

mark for center part

(circum. 18")
B wig base circle

≡ strands of hair

·················---. stitching pattern to follow

Ill. 44. Near sewing machine presser foot lay a square of tissue paper *(A)*. Put wig base circle *(B)* in the center of the paper. Position long strands of hair *(C's)* crisscrossing wig base circle. On top, lay piece of Saran Wrap or any see-through plastic (not shown).

Set stitch length at #2 (12–13 per inch). Slide the "sandwich" assembly under presser foot and stitch inner circle as indicated. Then stitch outer circle, and leave needle in the work. Raise presser foot, rotate "sandwich" to position where you can stitch cross lines as indicated. Tear off and discard plastic. None will be needed from here on.

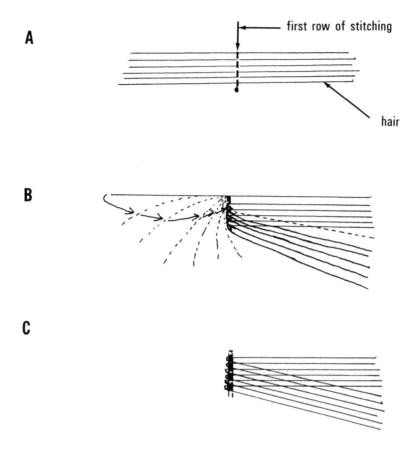

Ill. 45. Shown here are the steps in stitching hair strands to the wig base. At the end of the first row of stitching in *A*, take two extra stitches beyond the last hair, leave needle in work and rotate work.

B shows hair folded back over the first row of stitching. Comb it in the direction shown. Holding hair firmly, make a second row of stitching over the first row. Rotate wig and sew a third and final row over the first two.

C shows the folded hair at an angle to the underneath layer. All hair subsequently stitched to the wig base is handled in the same manner; only the positions will be different. These later strands will be referred to as fill-ins.

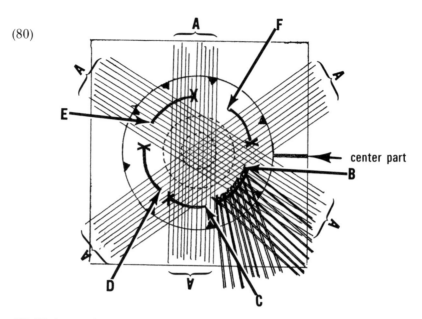

Ill. 46. Approximate locations for stitching fill-ins. The strands identified by *A*'s are the first three that were stitched to the base. Starting at *B* (near the center part), stitch over hair and keep adding fill-in strands, spreading them thin and stitching until, when the strands are folded over at an angle, the ends are even with the ends of the *A* strand underneath. (Follow the instructions in Ill. 45.) End the third row of stitching at *X*. Fill-ins *C*, *D*, *E*, and *F* are affixed in the same manner as *B*. Tear off and discard tissue paper.

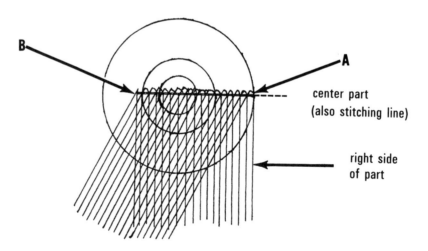

Ill. 47. Stitching right side of center part. All unnecessary lines have been omitted here and in Ill. 48 in order to make clear how the hair is handled and stitched to form a center part with no stitches showing. Begin laying the hair flat at *A* and make a few stitches; add more strands and stitch over them. Continue in this way to point *B*. Then fold all hair back over the first row of stitches (as in Ill. 45) and make a second row of stitches. Only two rows of stitches are needed here.

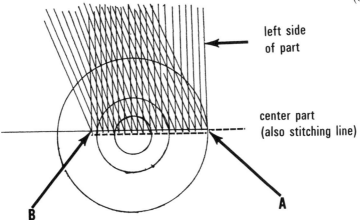

Ill. 48. Stitching and handling left side of center part. Start at *A* and end at *B* as you did for the right side; but here the stitching must be ¹/₁₆″ to the *right* of the two rows beneath, which are represented by the solid line in the drawing. (The broken line indicates the two rows you are now making.) Do not fold the hair over this time. Instead, stitch the second row back over the first one, ending at *A*. Do this stitching very carefully; otherwise the part will be crooked.

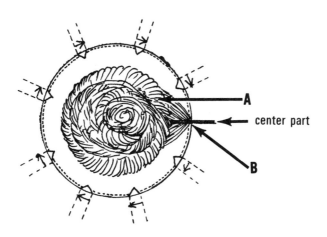

Ill. 49. Steps in shaping the wig base. Gather together all the hair stitched to the wig base and twist it *(A)* into a knot. Secure knot with hairpins to keep it out of the way. Begin at *B* to stitch as close as possible to edge of the cloth. Each time you come to a tuck, fold it in the direction indicated by the arrows and stitch over it. This gently shapes base into a cap form. To add last row of hair, turn wig base wrong side out (the knot of hair will then be on the inside). Slide wig base under presser foot and insert needle at *B*. Take a couple of stitches along the edge (Ill. 50) before starting to sew the final row of hair in place.

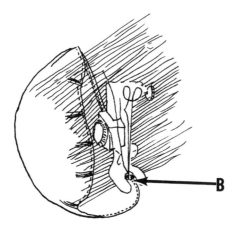

Ill. 50. Starting at *B*, push thin strands of hair under presser foot (with an equal length on each side of needle) and stitch them, a few at a time. Keep stitching as close to edge as possible. Continue all the way around the wig base until you reach point *B* again. Remove work from machine.

The hair you have just stitched to the edge must be folded over (as in Ill. 45) and stitched down. Do only a small section at a time. Comb a section over the first row of stitches, hold it firmly, stitch down; comb, hold, and stitch until again you reach point *B*.

Clip off thread ends. If any raw edges project too far, cut them off close to the stitching. Turn wig right side out.

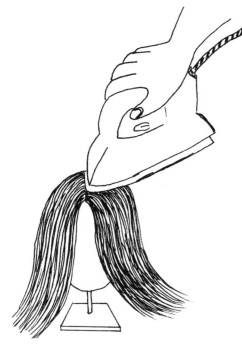

Ill. 51. Ironing the center hair part to make it lie flat. Put the wig on a *padded* styrofoam wig block and fasten it down with wig pins. Fold left side of part back over its two lines of stitching and comb the hair. Then iron it into a neat, straight center part. WARNING: Don't touch the iron to the wig until you have determined the ideal heat setting. Test various settings on loose strands of hair.

With the same heat setting, the ends of the hair can be curled. Lay wig flat on ironing board; twist ends of hair into curls (like pin curls without pins); hold iron on each curl until it is set. (Any kind of iron with a controlled heat setting can be used.)

Ill. 46 shows regularly spaced notches where tucks are to be made, and Ill. 49 gives directions on how these are to be sewed to shape the wig. These illustrations are for general instructions only. If you're making a wig for a specific doll, cut the wig base circle, dampen it, and fit it tightly over the doll's head, securing it with rubber bands. Let it dry. This will automatically place the tucks where they should be for a perfect fit. Mark the center front, as well as where and how wide each tuck should be. And for the most perfect hairline, trim off all excess material from the circle while the wig base is still on the doll.

Hand-press the wig base as flat as possible on top of a square of tissue paper. Then follow the step-by-step instructions that accompany Ills. 44 through 51.

When you have styled the wig to your satisfaction, glue it to the doll's head.

WOVEN WIGS

To weave a wig, you must have something to weave it on. That item is a weaving board, sometimes referred to as a wefting board. Hair is woven in and out, under and over, threads to produce a "weft" that, when completed and tied off, is sewed to a wig base.

Although these boards are available commercially (if somewhat expensive), you can easily construct a weaving board at home. The only tools needed are a saw, hammer, electric drill, and screwdriver. If you'd like to try making a small wig before going to the trouble of making a permanent wooden board, you can use heavy cardboard, following the instructions in Ill. 52.

Making a Weaving Board

Ills. 53, 54, and 55 show how to make a flat weaving board, and Ill. 56 shows how to construct an upright board.

For either of the wooden boards you will also need metal screw eyes, a small can of Satin Clear Varnish, and some fine sandpaper or steel wool (0000). In addition, if you make an upright board, you'll need one half-inch dowel rod to be used as the end posts.

In either case, prepare the board before beginning construction. Sand it until it is as smooth as you can get it. Any roughness will catch the hairs and make working with them more difficult. Apply four to six coats of varnish, allowing each coat to dry, then giving it a light runover with fine sandpaper or steel wool before applying the next coat. If, when you pull a strand of hair over the surface, it slides easily and doesn't catch anywhere, the board is ready to use. You can then go on to construction of the type of board you have decided to make.

The flat board is a bit harder to use, but it is more portable and can be held on the lap. A crochet hook, to pull strands of hair in and out through the threads, will facilitate the weaving process. The main difficulty with this type is the small amount of clearance between the threads and the board. The upright board presents no such problem, but while in use it should be kept in one place.

After the board has been sanded and varnished (for an upright weaving board), cut two 9″ posts from the dowel rod. To prepare their positions, use a wood screw pilot bit—one that drills not only a hole to accommodate a No. 4 or 5 wood screw, but also a wider area to countersink a metal washer for greater stabilization of the post. With this pilot bit, drill through the base at premarked positions: 2″ from each end, at the center of the board. Do not allow the countersunk area to get any deeper than the thickness of the metal washer.

Replace the pilot bit with a regular twist drill bit, which will bore a hole approximately ³⁄₁₆″ in diameter. Drill one hole 3″ down from the top of one post, completely through the dowel. Two inches below this—on what will be the *back side* of the post—screw in a metal eyelet. This post will be installed on the right side of the board. The hole 3″ from the top is for insertion of the weaving threads. The metal eyelet on the back side is for tieing the threads.

On the other post, which will be installed on the left side of the board, measure down 2″ and mark that position. From that mark, measure down another inch, and mark again. Continue until you have four pencil marks in a vertical line. Four metal screw eyes will go at these points. If the dowel rod is smooth, they can be installed immediately, as soon as you sand down any roughness left from sawing the dowel. If the rods are rough, however, give them the same finishing treatment as you did the board.

If it is necessary to sand and varnish the posts, mark the metal eye positions by using a small nail; hammer it in no more than ¹⁄₁₆″ at each pencil mark, to leave a small depression in the wood. This will preserve the locations (pencil marks would be eradicated in the finishing procedure) and also be a start for screwing in the metal eyes later.

To fasten the posts to the board, use wood screws no less than 2″ long. The metal washer should completely fill the countersunk area. To facilitate starting the screw into the post, find the center of the post. Using either a small drill bit the same size as the wood screw or a hammer and nail, make a small hole, no more than ⅛″ deep, in

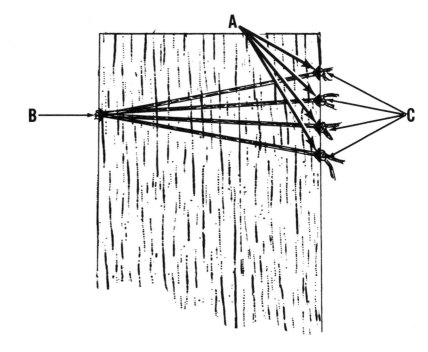

Ill. 52. An inexpensive weaving board can be made of thin wood or heavy cardboard. Cut four notches (or a sufficient number for the number of threads you plan to use) on the right-hand side. These are indicated in the drawing by the *A* arrows. Cut one notch in left side *(B)*.

Cut four pieces of strong thread the same color as the hair, each long enough to wind around the board and tie with a security knot *(C)*.

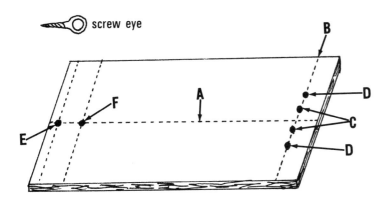

Ill. 53. Making a flat weaving board. Prepare the board according to the instructions in the text. The board should be ½″ thick, 7″ wide, and 16½″ long. With a marking pencil, draw a line through center of board *(A)*. Measure in 1″ from the right end and draw another line *(B)*. On line *B*, measure ⅜″ above line *A* and the same distance below line *A* and mark these two points. In the drawing, they are indicated by *C*. Measure ¾″ from each of the *C* dots and mark two more heavy dots *(D)*.

Measure in 1″ from *left* side of board and mark a dot *(E)* on line *A*. Measure in 2½″ from left side and mark a second dot *(F)* on line *A*.

In all, you now have six dots on the board. Insert a metal screw eye (like the one shown in the drawing) in each of the six dots.

Ill. 54. Positioning the metal eyes. When they are screwed into the board, the four metal eyes at right and the first one in from the left edge (*A*'s) should be positioned so that the holes face you. The metal eye marked *B* should be tightened down with its hole facing the ends of the board.

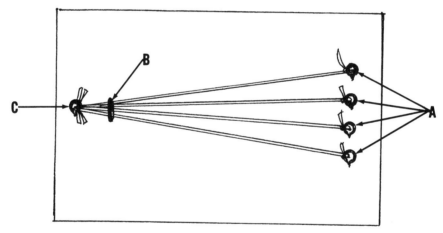

Ill. 55. Threading the flat weaving board. Cut four strands of thread, each the length of the board plus 6″. Attach each strand to a metal eyelet (*A*) at the right end of board, fastening it with a security knot. Thread the four strands through the metal eye marked *B*. Run two of these strands through one side of metal eye *C* and the other two strands through the opposite side of metal eye *C*. Tie them with a security knot, making sure all strands are as tight as possible. Do not cut off excess thread. (If it hinders your work, tape it out of the way.)

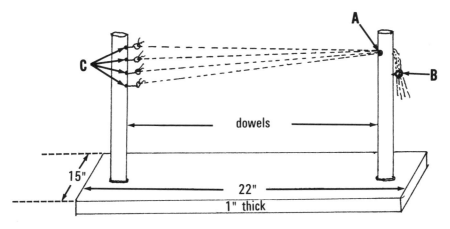

Ill. 56. Making an upright weaving board. Follow instructions in text for inserting two dowels in the wooden base. Drill a hole at *A*, 3″ down from top of right-hand dowel. Insert screw eye *(B)*, 2″ down from *A* but on the *back* side of the dowel.

Measure 2″ down from top of left-hand dowel and mark for insertion of first screw eye. Add three more screw eyes *(C)* at 1″ intervals below the first one.

Dotted lines indicate the weaving threads. Each is tied individually with a security knot to a metal eye *(C)*. All four are then inserted through hole *(A)* in the other rod. Put two of the threads through the metal eye *(B)* from one direction and two through the same eye from the opposite side. Draw the threads as tight as possible and then tie them in a security knot.

the center of the post. If you do this beforehand, the screw will go in dead center and the post, when securely fastened, will be solid.

Ill. 56 shows a completed upright weaving board.

No matter what type of weaving board you use, the method of weaving remains basically the same. You will feel awkward when you start learning. Just remember that, after a while, every wigmaker develops her own methods, and you will develop yours. The instructions here will simply help you get started.

Weaving the Wefts

When the hair has been prepared and separated into short, medium, and long lengths, place it near the weaving board. If you have ripped up a used hairpiece but left the commercial wefts intact, cut the hair from the weft. This leaves a "blunt" end, and when you place it in your work area, always lay it blunt end away from you (up). This will facilitate handling it.

In this section I will cover weaving on two and three threads, as well as instructions on how to weave a "part." Study Ills. 57, 58, 59, and 60 for the patterns.

Keep a glass of water and a comb handy, for each strand of hair used should be dampened and combed just before it is woven through the threads. Always push the *blunt* end under the lower weaving thread. The hairs at the blunt end are cut straight across; the other ends are of various lengths. Even though you lead with the blunt end, you will still lose some hair as you weave, but not nearly as much as if you had started with the uneven ends.

There are two things to be careful of: 1. Do *not* use thick strands of hair. The tendency of a beginner is to do just that. Large strands are easier to handle, and the weaving threads fill up much faster, but the end result will be hair so thick that it will be totally unmanageable. 2. Make every effort to keep the last end woven as long as the first one, where you started.

At this point, a careful study of Ills. 57 through 60 will be more helpful than a long, detailed set of instructions. Begin weaving, one step at a time, referring constantly to the illustration. After you've woven a few strands you'll be able to do it with your eyes closed— almost.

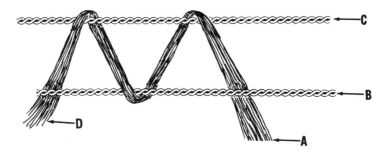

Ill. 57. Pattern for weaving on two threads. NOTE: Dampen each strand before weaving. *A* is starting point. Hair goes *under* the lower thread *B*, over thread *C*, under thread *B*, under top thread *C*, and under (bottom) thread *B*. Grasp *A* and *D* together and pull downward. This tightens threads *B* and *C*. When they are as tight as possible, slide the hair strand to the far left. Continue weaving hair strands in this manner until no more room remains on the weaving threads.

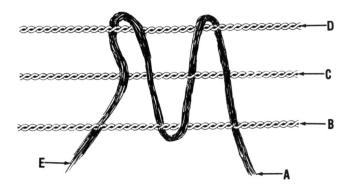

Ill. 58. Pattern for weaving on three threads. NOTE: Dampen each strand before weaving. *A* is starting point. Strand goes under *B*, over *C*, under and over *D*, back under *C*, over and under *B*, over *C*, over and under *D*, over *C*, and under *B*. Then grasp *A* and *E* together and pull downward, to tighten threads *B*, *C*, and *D*. When threads are pulled as tight as possible, slide woven strand to far left. Continue weaving hair strands in this manner until the threads are full but not crowded.

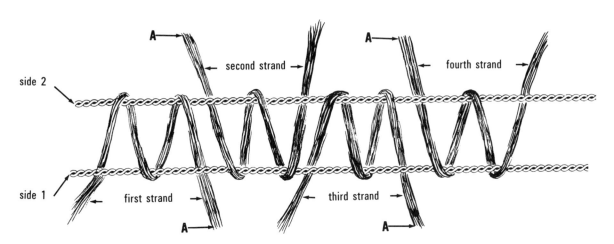

Ill. 59. Weaving a side or middle part on two threads. NOTE: Dampen each strand before weaving. A flat weaving board is recommended for this pattern. Always weave from right to left, starting at *A*. Odd-numbered strands (first, third, fifth, and so on) are all started from side 1. The even-numbered strands (second, fourth, and so on) are all started from side 2. As these alternately woven strands are tightened and slid to the left, equal portions of hair fall on either side of the weft, to form a part. It makes no difference how weaving board is held as long as this pattern is followed.

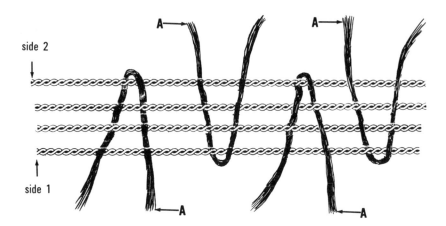

Ill. 60. Weaving a side or middle part on four threads. NOTE: Dampen each strand before weaving. Again, a flat weaving board is recommended. Weave from right to left, starting at *A*. The odd-numbered strands (first, third, fifth, and so on) are all started from side 1. Even-numbered strands (second, fourth, and so on) are started from side 2. As the alternately woven strands are tightened and slid to the left, equal portions of hair fall on either side of the weft.

If wig weaving is simply not your "ball of wax," you *can* use the already woven strips of hair from the hairpiece you dismantled. This is a shortcut, but it gives splendid results. The strips can be hand-stitched to the wig base the same way you stitch on the hand-woven wefts. However, you will have to weave the top, which contains the part, whether that is on the side or in the middle.

One weft may be enough if you're making a very small wig, but a large doll will require several. The only specific advice that can be given at this stage is to sew each weft to the wig base when it is completed, starting at the back center edge for the first one. Each successive weft, spaced ½" apart, should be sewed in place. In this way you can judge when you're nearing the end and weave a short weft accordingly.

Study Ills. 61 through 65 for directions on finishing the ends of the weft, whether it's a short one or the full length of the weaving threads.

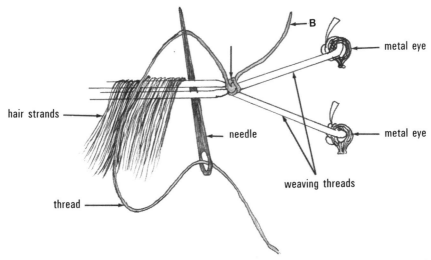

Labels on illustration: B, metal eye, metal eye, hair strands, needle, weaving threads, thread

Ill. 61. Tieing off the weft. To tie off the weft and prepare to remove it from the weaving board, use a sharp needle with a single thread. Starting at the right side, weave the needle through the threads in the same pattern as the hair strand was woven. Tie a security knot (A) and leave 10″ of the needle thread hanging (B). (This will later be tied off with the weaving threads, when weft is cut loose from the board.) Insert the needle under the weaving threads and do a buttonhole stitch as illustrated. Slide this over against the security knot.

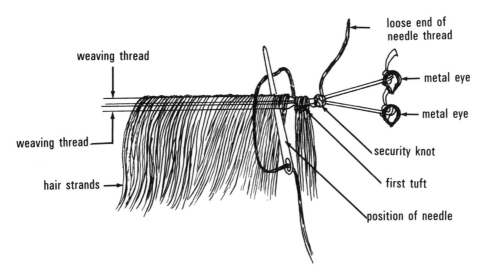

Labels on illustration: loose end of needle thread, weaving thread, metal eye, metal eye, weaving thread, security knot, hair strands, first tuft, position of needle

Ill. 62. Using buttonhole stitch to group hairs. This exaggerated-detail drawing shows how to secure small tufts of hair together with buttonhole stitches across length of the weft. Make tufts of no more than a dozen hairs, and work each tuft as far to right as possible before starting next one. Whichever type of board you use, position it so that you can work comfortably. (NOTE: Procedures for tieing off ends and tufting the hairs are same whether weaving was done on two, three, or four threads. No tufting is done on wefts woven for middle or side parts because these go on top of the head where hair must be smooth.)

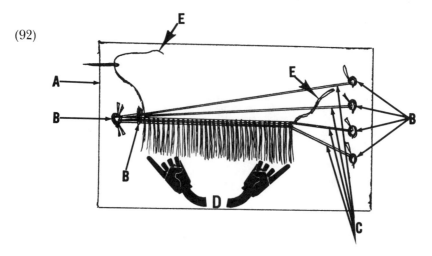

Ill. 63. View of completed tufting, with weft still on the board.

A. weaving board

B. screw eyes

C. four weaving threads (only two are used here)

D. hair strands after tufting

E. loose end of needle thread

Leave the needle attached to the thread. The final stitching must be done after security knots are tied at each end of the weft.

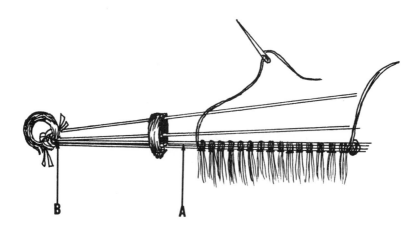

Ill. 64. Fastening off ends of the weft. Before starting, mix together one drop of Elmer's Glue and one drop of water and place mixture near the weaving board. Grasp tightly the two weaving threads at *A*. At *B*, cut them free of the metal eye. Still grasping the threads, rub glue/water mixture between thumb and index finger of your free hand, then over the two loose ends of thread you are grasping. This should moisten them slightly, not saturate them. Tie them in a security knot.

At the other end of the weft, repeat this procedure to fasten off the ends there.

When both ends of the weft have been tied off, keep the weft straight and lay it on a piece of waxed paper until the moistened threads are dry.

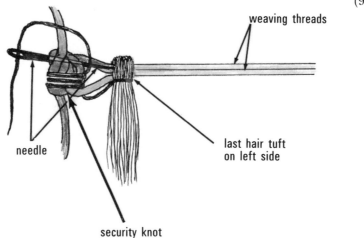

weaving threads

needle

last hair tuft
on left side

security knot

Ill. 65. Finishing the weft. Only one tuft is shown here. (Reverse these directions to finish the opposite [right] end of the weft.) The details are exaggerated in this drawing to show needle position as the final stitches are made.

The needle goes *under* the security knot and then up between the last hair tuft and the gap between the tuft and the knot. The thread is looped behind the needle to make a buttonhole stitch around the knot. Make several of these stitches, pulling each one very tight. Remove needle.

Now thread the needle onto the free end of the needle thread at the other (right) end, and repeat to finish that end. With a toothpick, apply a small amount of glue/water mixture to the stitches. Let dry; then cut off all loose thread ends.

MAKING A WIG BASE

Although there are many materials that can be used in making a wig base—crinoline, canvas, and similar fabrics—none has the versatility of stiff, coarse netting like that used in old hats. This was "sized" with a glutinous mixture, and it will work *for* you in shaping the wig base.

Where can you find such hats? Go to auctions, to house sales. Often you can buy a large boxful for little money. Besides obtaining net for wig bases, you may also get a collection of beautiful ribbons, feathers, velvets, satins, flowers, veiling—the list is endless—to use in doll costuming and hat making. Quite often, too, if you explain your needs, friends will dig into their closets and come up with many well-preserved old hats that were "just too good to throw away."

In color, the netting for a wig base should match either the hair or "skin" of the doll as closely as possible. You may not find old hat netting of the color you need, but you can treat it with fabric dye. It takes only a small amount mixed in hot water, and one quick dip of light-colored netting.

For illustrative purposes, we will make a wig base for a doll with a head circumference of 8¾". Cut a circle 4" in diameter from the net base of an old hat. Let's assume the cork (or other type of) pate is glued on. Tear off a piece of plastic wrap large enough to go over the head and down to the neck, where it can be tightly secured with a rubber band. This is to protect not only the pate, but the doll head, from getting wet. Cut out a piece of white cotton cloth the same size as the plastic and lay it aside. It will be used later.

To protect the doll body, wrap it in plastic or stick it down inside a plastic bag and secure the edges with a rubber band at the neckline.

Saturate the net circle in water, if you're using the color "as is." If you want to dye the net, dip it in the solution, and when it reaches the desired density of color, squeeze out the excess (water or dye). The net will feel a bit "gummy." That's the sizing referred to earlier. Place the center of the net circle in the crown area and smooth it over the doll's head. As you force it to conform to the shape of the head, tucks will form. These, when the net is dry, will remain. Now put the dry white cloth over the net and secure it at the neck with a tight rubber band. This will hold the dampened net in place until it dries. When the rubber band is in place, gently tug at the cloth all around the edge to tighten it on the head. Set it aside to dry. Do not be concerned if the sizing makes the net stick to the cloth—the cloth will peel away easily, leaving a beautifully shaped wig base.

Cut the wig cap (base) to conform to the desired hairline. Then sew a narrow ribbon, selected to match the color of the net, around the edge. This is called facing the edge. Study Ill. 66.

Now you can begin sewing the wefts to the wig base, starting at center back, Ill. 67. A simple whip stitch is the most practical one to use. Always insert the needle through the wig base *above* the weft and bring the tip up *through* the weft. Concentrate on keeping your stitches firm enough to hold, but loose enough not to "gather" or pull the wig base; otherwise, when you're finished, the wig will no longer fit the head you made it for.

For those who have literally been driven up the wall in their search for ready-made wigs suitable for boy dolls and baby dolls, this method works beautifully. In making a wig for a boy doll or baby doll, however, you must use the hair strands more sparingly than when weaving for other types of wigs such as those for toddlers and lady dolls.

If a wig is needed for a Negro doll, use black netting and black hair.

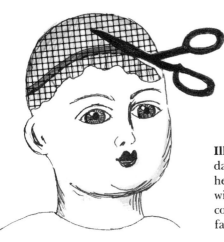

Ill. 66. Making a net wig base. Follow directions in the text for dampening the net used for the wig cap and fitting it over the head. Cut off net to the desired hairline and face the edge with very narrow ribbon matching the wig base or the hair in color. Wide dark line in the drawing indicates the ribbon facing.

Ill. 67. Sewing the wefts to the wig base. Starting at center back *(A)*, sew first weft *(B)* *under* the edge of the base. Then sew a second weft *(C)* ½″ above the first one but on the *outside* of the base. The spacing between the wefts from this point on will depend on the size wig being made. The dotted lines here merely suggest how the spacing should be. Use a needle with a single thread, and whip the wefts *loosely* into position. Every time you rethread your needle, tie the new thread to the old one with a security knot.

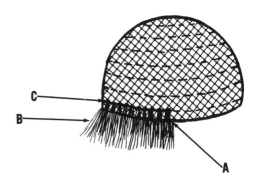

Ill. 68. Making a center or side part. These directions are for a center part, but a side part can be made by following the same basic procedure. The area indicated by *A* is to be left "bare." Sew the first and second wefts to the wig base as shown in Ill. 67. All additional wefts should be stitched to end short of the center, as indicated here by the solid black area. Ills. 59 and 60 show how wefts are woven for the parts. Carefully place one of these specially woven center-part wefts over the "bare" spot, and sew it in place with a stab stitch, i.e., needle down through wig base, back through top, down and back, the length of the weft.

Ill. 68 outlines the procedure to follow for completing the wig with either a center or side part.

STYLING THE WIG

There is little waste when using human hair. For example, even the most badly tangled balls of hair can be used—and without combing. I learned this trick several years ago while vacationing in Port of Spain, Trinidad, where I was intrigued by the towering coiffures on the ladies' heads as they paraded in and out of the hotel. After watching them for several days, I made an appointment at the hotel beauty shop—I had to learn their secret.

The first thing I noticed was enormous *wads* of tangled hair lying in front of several patrons, obviously local residents. Then I noted that these customers on whom the tangled hair was being used had extremely long hair to begin with. As an operator worked on combing out her customer's hair, she "teased" the long hair, and as each strand was pulled up preparatory to teasing, she reached over and picked up a wad of the tangled hair, which she placed near the scalp. Then she began teasing the customer's hair into it. As she worked up a long strand, the beautician kept reaching over and getting more tangled hair to tease into the strand. By the time she'd finished, the ball of hair was gone, and the customer's hair stood at least 18″ high.

Some 30 minutes later—after the application of what must have been an entire can of hair spray—the customer strutted out under one of the sleekest, most elegant, and most towering hairdos I have ever seen.

"How can she sleep like that?" I asked my operator.

Shrugging, she replied, "She comes in every morning for a comb-out."

The comb-out cost $8.00, and that was in 1964.

This story is included for one reason. Always be alert for new ideas. I have rarely met a person who didn't, sometimes unconsciously, sometimes consciously, teach me something. This Trinidad experience taught me still another way of styling hair. On dolls, it is particularly useful if the style you're trying to copy is unusually high, like some seventeenth- and eighteenth-century styles. By saving "tangled balls" of hair—all colors—and preserving them in small plastic bags, you'll always have a color to match the wig you're working on. It's much better than padding with cotton balls, as some doll-wig stylists do.

If you've been working with dolls, chances are you have already discovered some common household items that can be used in styling both synthetic and human hair wigs. For the beginner, I suggest the use of any small, round object, such as pencils, the smallest permanent wave rollers, toothpicks, bobby pins, hairpins, even paperclips. These, combined with inexpensive end papers like those used by beauticians in giving a permanent, will give good results. In rolling up the hair for a Negro doll, I always use plastic-covered wires like those used to fasten bread wrappers. Beware of any covered with bright red paper, because when they are wet the red dye comes off on the hair. This type of "curler" is easy to handle—all you need do is wet the hair with a good waving solution, wrap an end paper around the ends of the hair, roll it up, and fold under each end of the plastic-covered wire, to hold the curl in place. When the hair is dry and the curlers have been removed, you will have a tightly curled wig that needs only a good brushing and, possibly, a bit of trimming. Electric clippers do a marvelous job in evening up this type of hairstyle.

When human hair is rolled up for setting, let it air dry. For synthetic hair, use the highest heat setting on your hair dryer.

Are curling irons safe? Yes and no. You can produce beautiful curls with them. Take care not to let the iron get too hot. The safest ones I've found are those with a Teflon coating and a temperature control. Some synthetic wigs can be curled this way, some cannot. Try a lower wisp of hair in the back of the wig. If the hair turns out fuzzy, if it loses its shine, don't use a curling iron.

Familiarize yourself with the various styles worn during the period in which a doll was made. Several books on today's market include line drawings and photographs of old-fashioned hairstyles. Along with what you learn, however, use some common sense. Never do an elegant lady's hairstyle on a doll that was, or is to be, dressed in calico or gingham. Match the hairstyle to the type of doll you're working on. For instance, in today's world of hair fashions, in everyday life we want our hair to look attractive but not require much fuss; we save the more elaborate beauty shop hairdos for some special event, for a dressup occasion. And so it has always been in the women's world. If your doll is elaborately dressed, give her a hairstyle to go with it; if she's simply attired, give her a simple hairstyle.

If you have difficulty getting curls to stay in place, or if locks of hair pop out even after you've sprayed the hair and put on a tiny doll's hairnet (and this does happen), thread a needle with transparent nylon thread and sew or weave the stubborn strand(s) in place. If the thread is not pulled too tight (unless absolutely necessary to secure a curl, pompadour, or the like), no one will ever know it's there.

One of the greatest differences between synthetic and human hair is in the methods of styling. Curls are put into synthetic hair by the application of heat; human hair is rolled and styled just as you would do your own. Putting synthetic hair up on rollers and letting it air dry is a waste of time. It will fall out just as straight as it was before you rolled it up. While the synthetic hair is in rollers, it must be subjected to heat. If you have a blow-dryer, the kind held in one hand, turn it as high as the heat will go. Holding the head in one hand (this, of course, is after the wig has been glued to the doll's head), expose the rolled-up hair to the heat, keeping the dryer tip at least 2″ from the wig. Synthetics do not take long to dry. Do not remove the curlers until the hair is absolutely dry and has cooled off. Test it first for any remaining dampness you could not detect while it was cooling. Use the dryer again if you suspect any moisture is still present.

For hairstyling, certain tools and supplies are "musts." In this, as in other specialized areas, if you lack the proper equipment, you simply cannot do a first-rate job, so spend a little and get a lot. Buy a pair of thinning shears, inexpensive hair clippers, doll hairnets, tiny bobby pins, and other items you find yourself needing as your work progresses and improves. The smallest hairpins I've found are 2″ long, therefore unsuitable for all but the largest doll wigs. When I receive a supply, I immediately cut them down to about an inch in length, using wire cutters. This leaves rough ends hard to insert into a wig. So, while I'm cutting the pins down, I heat a small can of paraffin to a liquid state. A quick dip of the hairpin tips into the paraffin eliminates their roughness.

8

Wigs-
Refurbishing Old
Ones

Refurbishing an antique doll wig can be time consuming or it can be done quickly, depending on the individual. When a little girl is first taught to comb and brush her own hair, often she will smooth only the top layer in her rush to finish if she is left on her own. But mother sees the tangles underneath and patiently works with the child until, she hopes, good grooming habits will become an integral part of the child's personality. In learning good habits relative to doll work, you must be your own disciplinarian. I cannot think of one task that can be rushed and done correctly.

Look beyond the grime on a wig. Ignore the musty odor that assaults your nostrils. Disregard the unkempt appearance of the hair, its tangles, its all-around offensiveness. See the beauty that's waiting to be discovered. Preserve the wig if you can. Unless the hair has been cut right down to the wig base, you can salvage it. And even if it has, save the wig base. It too is a part of the doll's history. Make a new wig on the old base following instructions in Chapter 7.

I have read of many products alleged to be safe to use for

cleaning old wigs. I have been told of others. And, being a naturally curious person who would rather experiment than eat cake, I have tried them all—but very cautiously. My all-around favorite is still the one I started out with many years ago—cold water and Woolite. But even in using this combination, there are commonsense precautions that must be taken. For example, if you're refurbishing the wig on an operative mechanical doll and think it's too much trouble to remove the wig, I must warn you that the water-based solution *will* get into the mechanism no matter how careful you are. In trying to save time you will have destroyed the most valuable part of the doll.

If the head is on a composition body, you *will* damage the body. Invariably some of the solution will drip onto the surface and soak in. Tiny cracks will appear (these are called "crazing"). Then they will begin to separate and curl up. Finally they will flake off. Water, alone, will cause this to happen on composition.

The lesson to be learned from these examples is this: always remove a wig *before* you start refurbishing it. The less an antique doll is handled, the less chance there is of accidental breakage. And you will also find that the wig is much easier to handle.

Never reglue the wig to the pate until all other work on the doll is completed (including the costuming, if that is a part of the job). Protect the body, or the costume, by covering up everything from the neck down. If you should apply too much glue to the pate, the covering will protect the doll body or the costume from any that might drip down.

The two materials you are most likely to find in doll wigs are mohair (from the Angora goat) and human hair. Other materials—including caracul, a short curly fur often found on boy and baby dolls; Thibet, the hair of the Tibetan goat; and even wool—are rarely seen.

How can a beginner tell the difference between mohair and human hair? Try combing a very small strand on the lower back edge. If it's human hair some will come loose, but you can comb out all the tangles. If it's mohair, it cannot be combed. Instead (and particularly on an antique wig), what you're trying to comb will pull loose from the base completely. Even new mohair cannot be combed, though it is much stronger than the old. Mohair is finer than human hair, so after you have handled a few wigs of each kind, you will merely have to feel the texture to know which it is.

Assemble the items you'll need for removing, refurbishing, restoring, and replacing the wig:

1. A rat-tail comb for picking out tangles.
2. A Twinco slicker brush. This item can be found in pet stores or ordered from a veterinary supply house (see

list of suppliers). It consists of rows of short, tin-plated wire bristles set closely together in a live rubber pad and supported by a steel back. Buy the smallest size for doll work. It's about $3'' \times 1\frac{1}{2}''$.

3. A Twinco comb, sold in conjunction with the slicker brush. Buy the smallest size. The teeth have blunt ends and will never damage the hair.
4. An empty Windex spray bottle (you may not need it, but keep one handy).
5. Woolite
6. Towels
7. Elmer's water-soluble Glue
8. Hairstyling aids and hair spray (Final Net is my recommendation).

REMOVING THE WIG

Although these instructions can be found in Chapter 2, they bear repeating here. First, grasp the edge of the wig, preferably in the center back, and pull upward in an attempt to peel that portion of the wig base away from the doll head. If it comes loose, move your hand to another spot and do the same thing. Continue until the wig comes off.

It's possible that the wig was never glued to the head, but instead attached to the cork or wooden pate with metal "points" (like pins without heads). In any case, remove the wig carefully, trying not to stretch it, but don't be surprised by whatever you find under an old wig.

To digress for a moment: I once discovered a blackened coin wedged into a slightly concave hole in the top of a solid cork pate. At the time I didn't know it was a coin, so I put it aside. Beneath the coin was what appeared to be a scrap of paper, folded several times. When I tried to remove it from the concavity with tweezers, it disintegrated.

Later, I ran across the coin and decided to try to find out what it was. Metal cleaner removed the black, and there was something I'd never seen before—a copper penny measuring 29mm. across. The face side is so worn that only five stars remain clear, but the woman's profile is unmistakable, as is the word *Liberty* that goes across and down the head. The other side can be easily read: "United States of America" around the outer edge, and inside a wreath, "one cent." Even under lighted magnification, though, the date cannot be seen. Since I am not a coin collector, and am not acquainted with any, the date the coin was made and the history of this copper penny will remain a mystery. The reason it was wedged into the cork pate to conceal what must have been—to the one who placed it there—an important paper will forever remain a secret. The doll was mine, so I kept the coin out when I reglued the wig. How I wish it could talk!

You will usually find, on the underside of a wig, patches of old glue sticking to the hair. When the wig is removed from the head and soaked, the patches will usually "melt" because the glue *is* water soluble.

If you cannot peel off the wig, put some warm water in a Windex spray bottle and spray under the edge of the wig base, then pull gently on it. If the glue is water soluble but still so strong that you could not peel off the wig when it was dry, this will work. Always spray underneath, working a little at a time, until the wig comes off. Do not allow the wig base to become saturated. Some water will get on it, but protect it as much as you can from thorough saturation.

There is always a possibility that you're not working with the original wig and glue. The old one may have been replaced and a glue impervious to water used to fasten the replacement wig. If the warm water spray does not work, use a single-edged razor blade to scrape between the base and the doll head. Angle the blade so that its edge touches only the porcelain, never the wig base.

REFURBISHING HUMAN HAIR

Straighten out the tangles first. If the hair is matted, use the rat-tail comb to "pick out" the snarls. Begin at the free ends of the hair. While holding it down at its "roots" with one hand, carefully pick upward from the ends. Once the tangles are gone, comb it with your Twinco pet comb; then give it a good brushing with the slicker brush.

Shampooing can present problems if the base is made of cardboard or if it's made of a material that shrinks. If it's cardboard, remove the hair from it, for the cardboard will disintegrate or turn "gummy" when it's wet. Of course you cannot tell in advance whether a wig base made of woven fabric will shrink, but assume that it *will*. Fit the wig onto a homemade wig block (Ill. 33). (Be sure the block is as large as the wig.) Fasten it around the edges with wig pins. The pins will not only prevent the material from shrinking in size—for example, going from a size 10 to a size 8—they will also keep the base from shortening; that is, sitting much higher on top of the head when you are ready to reglue it in place.

On the other hand, if you have chanced upon a wig too large to fit any of your dolls (sometimes separate wigs are sold at flea markets, auctions, or doll sales), you can make these tendencies work for you. Remember, old wigs are always preferable to new ones.

After combing and brushing the hair, fit the wig onto a block the size you want the wig to be when it's dry. For instance, if your doll head measures 9″ in circumference and the spare wig is no more than 1½″ to 2″ too large, you can let the shrinking process work for you. After the hair is washed (try lukewarm water to promote the shrinkage), put the wig on the 9″ wig block without wig pins, and let it dry. You can style it later. Naturally, after the wig has shrunk, it will appear to have much more hair than before because, although the amount of hair is the same, the wig base has become smaller. I feel that this procedure is much more desirable than taking several large tucks in a wig to make it fit; the tucks make the hair bunch up at the points where they are made.

Shampooing is next. Mix one capful of Woolite in 40 oz. of *cold* water in a basin. (That amount of water is equivalent to about five standard water glasses or coffee cups full.) If you're shampooing a wig that is fastened to a wig block, dip it up and down and swish it back and forth in the solution, being careful at all times not to get the wig base any wetter than necessary. Continue until the water is too dirty to use further, or until you're sure the wig is clean (whichever comes first). If necessary, repeat. If you're shampooing hair removed from a wig base, ease it into the water and let it soak 3 to 5 minutes.

Rinse the wig on the block the same way you washed it—dip, dip; swish, swish—and put a few drops of vinegar in your last rinse water. This usually gives the hair an attractive shine. Hair not on a wig block can be rinsed by holding it directly under the faucet.

Always use *cold water* (unless you're shrinking a wig base).

Comb out the tangles with the doggie comb. If you plan on setting curls and need information, refer to Chapter 7, the section on "Styling the Wig," for suggestions. If you want the hair to hang straight and smooth, give it a good going over with the slicker brush, then put it in a draftfree location to air dry. This applies, of course, to any wig fastened to a wig block.

If it has been necessary to remove hair from a cardboard base and you're working with "loose" hair, it must be combed, dried, glued to the base, and *then* styled.

While the hair is drying, do whatever work is needed on the rest of the doll, such as cleaning the porcelain, repairing chips, holes, and the like.

In the old days, powders and perfumes were used freely on wigs;

today, if we want to keep an elaborate hairstyle in place, we use hair spray. Final Net—though I've tried all other kinds—is the only brand I use, though you may have your own favorite. (This is not to say that Final Net is the only one suitable.) I would rather keep the hair soft and natural, and do, on my own dolls, but some customers prefer a good holding spray. "After all," one lady remarked when I tried to discourage the use of spray, "no one knows it's there unless they touch the hair, and they have no business doing that!"

REFURBISHING MOHAIR WIGS

Mohair, so soft, so fine and silky, so beautiful, is what one might call "the devil in disguise," for it is truly devilish to work with. It was once very popular, and far cheaper to use in making doll wigs than human hair. Dollmakers were happy with it because it enabled them to make a bit more profit (human hair wigs then, as now, were very expensive), and "little mothers" didn't know the difference anyway. I have yet to see a human hair wig that holds deep, flowing waves as mohair does, regardless of its age. If the original mohair was wavy and has been reasonably preserved, I am firmly convinced such waves would last through eternity.

A case in point: Readers old enough to remember the traveling carnival shows will probably recall the copper-bright hair on the heads of the gaudy chalkware Kewpie dolls that were popular as prizes at the carnival games of chance. Many years ago, one of my first customers was a dealer in general antiques who was also a doll collector. She acquired one of these old carnival Kewpies, a badly damaged one, and brought it to me for restoration. When I saw the large hole in its back I refused the job, pointing out that even if I could fix it (and at the time I wasn't sure), the cost would be prohibitive. She insisted that I name a price. I did—placing the figure so high that I was sure she'd back off. But she didn't.

So I began by removing the filthy wig. Since it was not on a base, but was mohair glued directly to the plaster skull, it came away easily, taking paint and glue with it, of course. It took five soakings and rinsings before I saw that the wig was not the dark brown I expected, but a glorious bright copper. Often, as it dried, I pushed at the waves with both index fingers to make them deeper.

After the doll was repainted, the patched hole was invisible; the waves in the hair lay in deep ridges and valleys. The customer was ecstatic (this seems like a strong word to use, but it is the typical reaction of a customer who brings a total wreck in for restoration and carries out a doll looking as though nothing has ever happened to it); but somehow I felt sad. I think it was because the doll looked too new. At that time, though I realized that something was not right, I hadn't yet learned to match the old patina.

Mohair requires the most careful handling of all wig materials. It has a tendency to become quite matted when wet, so before you attempt to clean a mohair wig, pick out as many tangles as you can by using the metal end of the rat-tail comb. If too much hair comes out as you pick at the snarls, do what smoothing you can with a soft-bristled brush. Never use a slicker brush on mohair. Remove the wig, then the wig base if there is one. On many dolls the mohair was glued directly to the head. On others it was fastened to a cardboard base through a hole, front and center (top-knot wig). Hair was fanned out and only the bottom layer was glued to the head, leaving the upper layers free for styling.

If the mohair, free of its base, is soaked in a cold water/Woolite solution for about 10 minutes, it will usually come out of its bath sparkling clean. It should be gently eased into the solution, never rubbed (scrubbed) between the fingers. To rinse it, always slide your hand under the wig while it's in the water, so that it will lie on the palm of your hand. Turn on the cold water faucet and hold the wig under the tap until all soapy residue is washed away. If the top looks clean, transfer the wig to the palm of the other hand, thus automatically flipping it over, so that you can see the under side.

If patches of glue still adhere there, pick off as much as you can with tweezers or your fingernails; then repeat the soaking procedure as many times as necessary to rid the hair of glue.

Fold a bath towel several times; arrange the wig on it with the hair fanned out in a circle. Using another towel, press down on the wig and force out as much water as you can. Transfer the wig to a fresh towel, and put both in a warm spot to air dry.

Glue or stitch the wig back to its head or base, as the case may be, just as it was done originally. On a tiny doll, reglue the curls directly onto the doll head. Finally, smooth out the upper layers of mohair as much as you can, and arrange the hair in the desired style.

Color Plates 5 and 6 show what can be done with a mohair wig that, at first sight, appeared hopeless. The final styling is probably not like the original one, but by following the procedures outlined here the antique mohair wig was preserved, thus adding many dollars to the value of the doll.

Beware of detergents, cleaning fluids, and other products said to be safe for use on antique doll wigs. You will be handling something that, once destroyed, can never be replaced. Cultivate a warning system in your mind that says "Hold your horses! Don't go whole-hog on this thing. Try it on a small strand of hair first, to make sure it's safe!" Remember, even the water/Woolite solution can cause problems, as was pointed out at the beginning of this chapter.

If, in spite of extreme care in pinning the wig to the wig block, it still shrinks, there are several things you can do. Remove some stitches in the vicinity of tucks in the wig base (if there are any), and open a tuck or tucks. This will release a bit of fullness and may allow snug fitting of the wig.

If there are no tucks, remove the number of stitches necessary (from the stitching around the bottom weft), using the point of a seam ripper. Releasing these stiches will allow you to stretch the wig base a small amount, perhaps enough to fit the wig back on the head.

If these attempts fail, you can try an extreme measure: with a single-edged razor blade, make a slash in the center back of the wig base, extending from the bottom edge of the wig up about a half-inch, depending on the size of the wig or on how much it has shrunk. Do not cut into the hair. When the wig is fitted on the doll's head, the hair can be spread out to cover the slit if you have been careful not to damage it with the razor blade.

If the wig stretched while you were handling it, stitch in a few tiny tucks all around the edge until it again fits the head.

None of these actions will be necessary if, before shampooing the wig, you secure it to the proper size wig block with an adequate number of wig pins so that it cannot shrink in any direction.

When a doll has part of its hair remaining, but unsightly bald spots, the situation can be remedied if you can match the original hair. A beginner may find this difficult, lacking a stockpile of wig or hairpiece odds and ends to fall back on, but the advanced restorer—who is invariably a pack rat—will probably be able to find the needed hair.

After you have cleaned the hair that remains on the wig base, refer to Chapter 7, the section on Glueing Hair Directly onto a Solid Dome. Instructions given there will enable you to patch the bald spots. If a wig strip is needed, for example, where a part in the wig must be replaced, refer to Ill. 36.

The information in this chapter and Chapter 7, combined with your desire to learn, your imagination, and your common sense, will enable you to cope with almost any wig problem that ever confronts you.

9

Repairing Ball-Jointed Bodies

If women in the 1800s were capable of making composition and papier-mâché bodies at home (after serving an apprenticeship), surely you can repair them at home. Those nineteenth-century workers had their specialties—some made torsos, others legs, and some made arms ad infinitum. You, too, can develop a specialty—repairing the bodies of your own dolls and of dolls belonging to other collectors. The techniques described here are applicable to both composition and papier-mâché bodies.

It would be impossible to cover—in a single chapter—every style of jointed body ever made, even if I knew them all. I doubt that anyone has that knowledge, although a great deal is known about the various materials that were used to make both composition and papier-mâché. Every manufacturer claimed his dolls were the best, but since we cannot know what formulas were used to make the bodies, nor what finish was applied, we must follow rather general and safe procedures of restoration, always keeping in mind that we must avoid any methods that might cause more damage or further deterioration.

Water is the worst enemy of compositions and papier-mâchés. If you're ever tempted to clean soiled bodies the quickest way—with soap and water—don't do it. There's always a slight chance that it would not cause such damage as cracking or peeling, but don't take the risk.

Never pass up an opportunity to buy a damaged antique body (though its cost may shock you) because usually it can be restored. Often the torso has suffered an inward collapse. Sometimes the pieces are there, though fragmented; sometimes they're missing. Occasionally one or more of the sockets has caved in because of the tension exerted by the stretched elastic. The same procedures are used—with variations—whether the damage is in the torso, arms, legs, or ball-joints. Since the torso is the largest part and the most easily repaired, let's deal with it first.

REPAIRING A HOLE

Cut a piece of thin cardboard at least ½″ larger than the hole. The larger the doll and the more widespread the damage around the hole, the larger the piece of cardboard required to provide the strength and backing needed when filler material is applied. It is better to allow too much than too little. This cardboard is glued inside the body, extending all around the hole, to bear the weight of the filler. After you have cut the cardboard patch, assemble fast-drying glue (I highly recommend Duco cement) and a length of wire (the patch holder) cut from a heavy coat hanger (see Ill. 69). The patch holder must be long enough to reach inside the body, to hold the patch in place; therefore, before cutting it, decide which opening (neck, arm, or leg) to insert it through.

Let's assume we are repairing a 24″ German ball-jointed composition body. This body has fifteen pieces—not counting the head; they are the torso, the three parts of each leg, and the four parts of each arm (Ill. 70). If you are going to patch a hole in the torso, the legs and head must be removed. The first time you do this, it's best to have a helper. Assemble a small screwdriver, two craft sticks, and a pair of needle-nose pliers in your work area. While your aide holds the body, pull the head away from its socket until you can see where it's hooked into one or two elastic loops. Slip the two craft sticks between the loops so the elastic will not snap back into the body when the head is detached. As you ease the elastic (head still attached) down onto the two craft sticks, be sure they are positioned crosswise of the socket (shoulder to shoulder). This area is stronger and less likely to cave in.

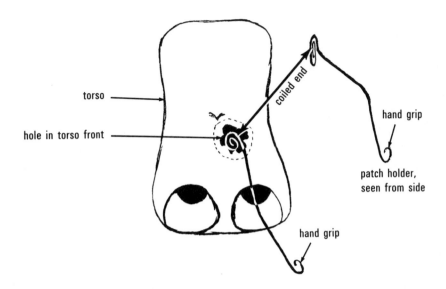

Ill. 69. Making a patch holder from a coat hanger. Each patch holder must be custom made for its particular use. Coil end that holds patch in place into a flat, springlike shape. Bend opposite end into a hand grip. Bend the wire between coil and hand grip into whatever shape will permit the coil to press flat against the patch as you exert steadying pressure from the grip.

Broken lines indicate where cardboard patch is positioned inside the torso. Patch holder can be inserted through leg hole, to hold patch in place until Duco cement "grabs."

When the elastic is secured, remove the head-hook from the elastic loop(s). If the hook is clamped onto the elastic, pry it open far enough to slip it out of the elastic. Put the head in a safe place, preferably in a box completely away from your work area. Next, slip the stringing hook under the elastic loop(s) being held by the sticks, pull the elastic away from the neck socket far enough to ease the sticks out, then allow the stringing hook and elastic to descend *slowly* to the inside of the body. As the elastic tension is released, the leg parts will loosen.

To repair the body hole, it may not be necessary to disassemble the legs. If two pieces of elastic were used, one for each leg, simply remove the legs from the torso and lay them aside. If only one piece of elastic was used for both legs, you may leave the elastic attached while you patch the hole, but it would be more convenient to disassemble one leg so that you can remove both of them. If this is done, observe the proper stringing sequence so that later you can put the leg back together as it was.

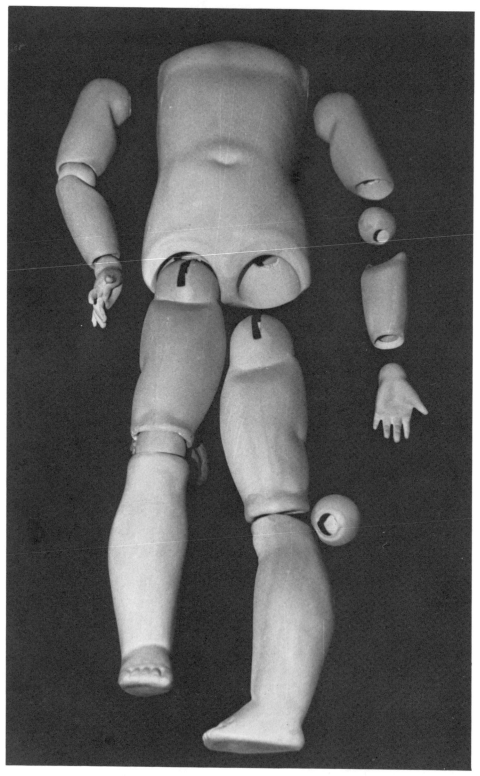

Ill. 70. German fifteen-piece ball-jointed body, unassembled.

Assume that the hole is in the center of the abdomen, just below the belly button. Since it is impossible to hold the patch in place by inserting a finger through a leg hole, make the "patch holder" mentioned earlier (Ill. 69). (A 150-watt bulb in a movable holder, placed strategically where it will shine through a body opening, will help you see inside the body and enable you to get the patch into the proper position. Try out the light before you begin work. Determine exactly where you must stand or sit to get its full benefit.)

At this point, several "dry runs" are advisable because you must work fast once the cement is applied to the edges of the patch. Practice what you're going to do before you attempt to start work. Bend the patch holder into whatever shape is best and easiest to handle by actually inserting it and going through the motions of holding a patch in place. Since the release of the patch from your fingers must be practically simultaneous with the pressure you exert with the patch holder, practice until you are sure your actions are perfectly coordinated; then go ahead with the repair.

Spread a heavy layer of Duco cement around the edges of the cardboard patch. Bend the cardboard as much as necessary to insert it through the opening you have decided to use. It takes but a few seconds for Duco to "grab." Should there be any spots not securely attached, work with each area separately, forcing cement between the patch and the body, from the outside, and pushing the patch holder against the area from the inside. Let dry.

Cut a piece of Saran Wrap the exact shape of the hole. Place it on top of the cardboard, smooth it out, and run a thin bead of glue around the edges to hold it in place. The Saran Wrap prevents the cardboard from absorbing moisture from the filler when that is applied. Although Duco is fast drying, it should be allowed to set for 24 hours before you continue. Meanwhile, if other patches are needed elsewhere on the body or any parts of the limbs, apply them in the same fashion.

After 24 hours, apply more Duco cement, using a dabbing motion, until the Saran Wrap is completely covered. Do not spread it out smooth. The uneven surface will provide a good base on which to apply the filler. Again, let dry 24 hours.

Before proceeding, do any sanding needed in the vicinity of the hole. For example, if much of the body surface has flaked off, if there is severe cracking, peeling, or curling, sand the surface smooth. The area must be repainted after the patching is completed, and so the smoother the surface, the neater will be the repair.

Many of the commercial fillers on the market require the addition of water, and I cannot recommend them. The formula I use exclusively is this: 1½ tsp. of powdered wood; ½ tsp. of dental plaster (any color you can get), and just enough Elmer's Glue to make a thick but spreadable mixture. If you live in a small town you can buy dental plaster only from a dentist, but in larger cities dental labs and supply houses carry it. As for powdered wood, I save the "dust" that clings to the sides and flaps of the box when I sift sawdust to stuff bodies. What goes through the sifter and falls to the box bottom is not fine enough to use in this formula, but that which floats and clings to the sides and flaps is ideal. Otherwise, find a carpenter who does a lot of sanding (floors, cabinets, furniture, and the like) and ask him to save the dust for you. However, if you cannot obtain enough powdered wood, use Durham's Water Putty—but *don't* mix *water* with it.

The mixture made from this formula can be applied as thickly as necessary, and if just enough glue is mixed with the other two ingredients to make it spreadable, it will stay where you put it (and not run). Always build the patched spot higher than the surrounding area and feather the edges out onto the body. When sanding, go over and over the repaired spot and onto the body until there is no line of demarcation and the contour is as perfect as you can make it. At this stage, as in so many phases of restoration, visual sighting—mental judgment—is extremely important. It is the only method by which you can judge whether you have shaped a repair so that it is aesthetically acceptable.

Since the methods of finishing are the same for all repairs done on ball-jointed bodies, those instructions will be given at the end of this chapter.

REPAIRING A FRAGMENTED HOLE

Fragmented holes are found more often than those with clean edges, and are harder to deal with. You naturally want to save as much of the body surface as possible, so first try to push the pieces back into their original position. Gentle pressure from inside the body, using a straight piece of coat hanger wire, may accomplish this. Try it on one fragment. If that piece breaks off, save it; then try the next method described.

Here the use of a hemostat of suitable length is imperative. A hemostat is a surgical instrument with long thin jaws, capable of being locked onto something—in this case, a sponge. If you are good friends with a surgeon, a surgical nurse, or anyone involved in the field of medicine, ask for their used hemostats, or order new ones from Brookstone (see list of suppliers).

You may have to enlarge the hole if you're inserting the instrument through a socket; sometimes the entire socket must be cut out. Soak the sponge in Magix Leather Preparer (see Chapter 11 for information on this product). Work in a well-ventilated area or outdoors because this is a highly flammable solvent. Squeeze the sponge slightly, clamp it into the hemostat jaws, and insert it through the hole. Gently dampen and push the fragments into their original position, or as nearly so as is possible. Work on one spot at a time. Move on to another when you have pushed the first fragments into position. While you're working, keep the sponge wet with solvent.

When all fragments are positioned, wait 24 hours before applying the cardboard patch following the preceding instructions; omit glueing Saran Wrap on top of the patch. That is not necessary here.

To glue the broken fragments into place from the outside and to glue down any others, squeeze out a pea-sized amount of Duco cement onto waxed paper. Dip the end of a toothpick into the cement and dab it onto the patch. Quickly press the fragment into place and hold it there until the cement "grabs." Continue applying adhesive and exerting pressure, but not enough to cause the inside patch to collapse or pull loose. Never use cement that is no longer fluid. Duco dries quickly and some will be wasted no matter how fast you work. Fresh Duco holds; that which is partially dried does not.

When all fragments have been glued into place, mix enough of the dental plaster/powdered wood/glue formula to cover the damaged area. Use a palette knife to apply the filler. Lay it on small areas and, pushing gently with the knife blade, force it down into the fissures, leaving it a bit higher than the original surface. Feather the edges out onto the body. When it's completely dry, sand it into smooth contours that blend with the original.

These basic methods of patching and repairing, with variations that only you can decide upon, are applicable to any part of a composition or papier-mâché body.

REINFORCING A DAMAGED SOCKET

Veteran doll collectors know what a socket is, but beginners may not be familiar with one, particularly if they have never seen a jointed body disassembled. A "socket" is a cavity into which another part fits. The mobility of the human body depends on such "mechanical wonders." An excellent example of this is the action of the femur, or thighbone, the head (or top) of which fits into a cup-shaped cavity (socket) in the hip joint. Humans suffer broken hips at this juncture. Dolls suffer damaged sockets or damage to the ball that fits into a socket.

In patching the torso, it may have been necessary to cut a larger opening in one of the body sockets in order to glue a patch to the inside. Sometimes, in so doing, you will accidentally fracture the area around the socket hole. To reinforce a damaged socket, use the same formula given earlier in this chapter, but mix in enough Elmer's Glue so that the mixture can be painted on the under side of the socket. To apply it, use an old long-handled artist's brush, not good for anything else. Keep the socket hole clear, but paint the entire surface underneath. Work through the opposite armhole or either leghole that will permit you to maneuver the brush easily. Never apply the mixture to the outside because it will interfere with correct positioning and movement of the ball in the socket.

REPLACING A MISSING SOCKET

There are several ways to replace a missing socket, but the best and, in my opinion, the easiest requires the making of a one-piece press mold. Since the sockets are perfectly round, find a round object that fits the socket and use it as a pattern. It can be a plastic ball, a marble (various sizes are available in craft shops), even the upper arm/ball unit itself can be used, but it must be protected from touching the plaster by being wrapped in a double layer of plastic. (Use of the upper arm/ball unit presents difficulties, not only in protecting it from accidental damage, but also in balancing it in position until the plaster sets. Therefore, until you have made a number of sockets using a separate round object as a pattern, I suggest you forego using the actual upper arm/ball unit.) Any round object that will fit *inside* the body hole can be used as a pattern. Ill. 71 shows—and explains—how to make a socket for an "elongated upper arm/ball unit."

When you have decided on the round object to use as a pattern, assemble the items and materials you will need for making the mold. A 16-oz. cottage cheese carton is perfect for mixing the plaster and water. The exact ratio of plaster to water is not critical for this type of mold, since it will rarely be used more than once. A large craft stick makes a good mixer.

Step 1 Coat your pattern object with vaseline, then wipe it off. Enough will cling to act as a separator. Measure 11 oz. of water into the plastic carton. Weigh out, then sift, 18 oz. of plaster (510 gm.) into another container. In mixing the two, *sprinkle* the plaster *into* the water—don't dump it in; otherwise you will have a lumpy "glop" that is hard to stir. Let the combination stand for 2 minutes, then

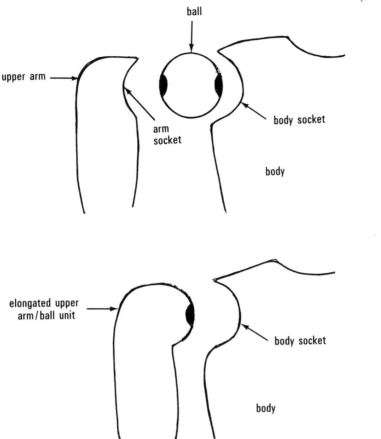

Ill. 71. Shown here are two types of upper-arm joints. At top, the joint has three parts: upper arm with socket, ball, and body socket. The bottom drawing shows an upper arm elongated into a ball unit, which fits into the body socket—in other words, it consists of two parts. (There are also other types.) Regardless of the type of arm, leg, or even waist used, when the parts are strung together for articulation, they are referred to as ball joints.

thump the container against the work table several times. This will bring some bubbles to the surface and cause those already there to burst. It will also jar the slightly mounded plaster below the surface of the water.

After 4 minutes, slowly stir the mixture with a craft stick to smooth out any lumps and achieve a creamy consistency. Keep the stirring movement of the craft stick slow and steady. If you speed up, slow down, speed up, you create bubbles in the plaster, and they are undesirable. Soon you will feel the combination begin to thicken. When the stick movement leaves swirls on the surface, remove the stick and quickly jar the carton on the table again, to burst any surface bubbles. When all bubbles are gone from the center (this is where the pattern will be inserted), put the carton aside and clean off the stick with wet paper towels. (Throw all scraps into the trash can; never rinse plaster scraps into the sink.)

Test the plaster next. Stick a fingertip into the center, press down slightly, and remove. If the finger indentation holds, quickly insert the round pattern object into the center. Push it down into the plaster until half of it is embedded and the other half sticks above the surface. As you push the object down, the displaced plaster will rise. As it does, dip an index finger into water (as often as necessary) and smooth out the raised plaster to make a level surface. If you push the round object down more than halfway (and this sometimes happens), don't panic. Let the plaster "set." After it has gone through the heating stage and cooled down, insert an old Exacto blade into a holder and carefully trim away the plaster that flowed above the center line of the round object. Until this is done, the object you used as a pattern cannot be removed from the plaster. When it is removed, it leaves its imprint in the plaster (see Ill. 72).

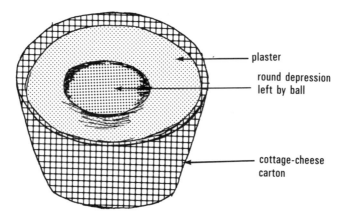

Ill. 72. When the ball is removed, a round depression is left in the plaster of the press mold.

Step 2   Items needed for use in this step are scissors, a compass, a sturdy paper bag—such as the brown bags from grocery stores—and a piece of Saran Wrap. Using the compass, draw a circle on the bag. Its diameter should be roughly that of the cottage cheese carton. Cut out the circle of paper; then cut a hole in its center. Slash the circle *almost* to the center hole. Continue the slashes all the way around, as shown in Ill. 73.

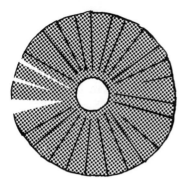

Ill. 73. Slash around the paper circle, extending the slashes almost to the center hole. When the slashed circle is pushed down into the mold, the cut sections automatically fold together and overlap one another to fit the mold contour. This action is reminiscent of the folding fans milady once used.

Step 3 Tear off a piece of Saran Wrap large enough to cover the top of the mold. Center the slashed circle over the mold and on top of the Saran Wrap. As you push the slashed circle down inside the mold, the slashes will overlap one another and allow the paper to fit snugly. Using a black felt-tipped marker—keep holding the paper down tightly inside the mold with the fingers of one hand—mark all the way around the top edge of the depression (Ill. 74). Remove the paper circle and cut away all parts of the paper outside the black mark.

Step 4 Prepare the *mold* for the next step by rolling a piece of nondrying clay (such as Plasticine, floral clay, or the like) into a

Ill. 74. Fitting the slashed circle into the mold. The clay core is put in place while the slashed circle is out of the mold. Unlike the slashed circle in Ill. 73, the circle here has been left unshaded so that its "seating" in the mold can be seen more clearly. (See step-by-step directions in the text.)

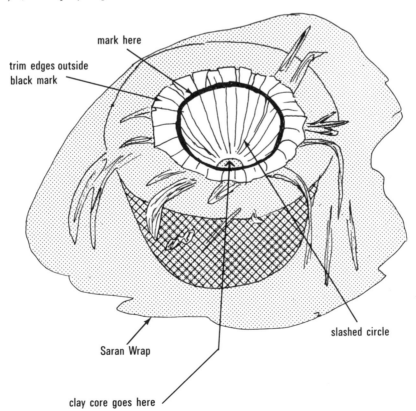

mark here

trim edges outside
black mark

Saran Wrap

slashed circle

clay core goes here

"core." It should be the same circumference as the hole cut in the center of the paper circle before you slashed it. With the Saran Wrap in place (it remains in the mold throughout this procedure), and the slashed paper circle still out of the mold, center the clay core in the bottom of the mold (see Ill. 74). Its end should project above the rim of the depression in the mold.

Step 5   Mix together 1½ tsp. of powdered wood, ½ tsp. of dental plaster, and enough Elmer's Glue to thin the mixture into the consistency of heavy syrup. Fill the mold half full. Be careful not to dislodge the clay core you placed there in Step 4.

Step 6   Ease the hole in the center of the slashed paper circle down over the clay core. Using both hands, gently push the circle to the bottom of the mold. As it goes down, the mixture already in the mold will seep through the slits in the paper as the segments overlap and adjust themselves to the contour of the round mold. When the mixture begins seeping through, start smearing it round and round on the slashed circle. If you accidentally knock the clay core out of position, replace it quickly, for the core forms the hole through which, later, the elastic will go through the socket. Be sure all surfaces of the paper circle are impregnated with the wood/ plaster/glue mixture, and that all the paper lies flat against the mold walls. You need only enough of the mixture to make the slashed circle hold its shape after it dries in the mold. It will be strengthened later.

Step 7   When the new "socket" has dried and is removed from the mold, its outer edges will be uneven. Use an old pair of scissors or a sharp knife to trim the edge off evenly.

Step 8   Prepare the same mixture used in Step 5. With your finger or an old brush, apply it to the under side of the new socket. This will turn the fragile socket into one strong enough to withstand the pressure of stringing. Apply the mixture most heavily around the center hole, leaving the lightest application for the edges, which will be strengthened when the socket is glued into its place in the body. Let dry thoroughly.

Step 9   Slip the socket into the body hole it was prepared for. If you have kept the edges rather thin, it will fit without difficulty. Run a thin line of Duco cement around the socket so that part of the cement will be on the socket and part on the body. Press down. This "tacks" the socket in place for the moment. Let the Duco dry; then, for the inside glueing, bend a long piece of coat hanger wire in such shape that you can reach the entire circumference of the circle *from the inside.* Apply Duco cement as heavily as possible. You do this by dipping the wire into glue you have squeezed onto waxed paper; or, if you have a brush you're going to throw away, glue it to the end of the wire (with Duco), and apply the cement with it. Let dry.

Step 10 When all inside glue has dried thoroughly, mix a rather thin batch of the glue formula and apply two to three coats to the outside of the socket, running each coat over the edges and feathering it out onto the body, all the way around the armhole. Light sanding will prepare it for the final body finishing.

If you want to use the actual ball (whether it's separate or a part of the upper arm), follow the same procedures with the following exceptions: at least two layers of plastic must cover any part of the composition joint that will come in contact with the plaster, and the plastic must fit as tightly as possible. It can be secured by scotch tape, masking tape, or rubber bands, but whatever you use must be kept away from the rounded portion of the upper arm/ball unit being used as a pattern. Be *sure* there are no breaks or tears in the plastic. Fit the rounded end of the upper arm into the hole where the socket will be installed, and mark how deeply the rounded part must be inserted into the plaster. And finally, be prepared to *hold* the part steady after it's inserted into the plaster—an almost impossible feat if you're the least bit nervous—until the plaster has hardened enough to hold the impression. Never leave a composition object in the plaster through the maximum heating period. The heat that develops and the expansion of the plaster as it sets could damage—even crush—the model; the heat also might damage the plastic protective covering and allow moisture to reach the composition model. It is inadvisable to try this method until you are as familiar with working in plaster as you are with making cake batter.

It is possible to make a separate ball for any that are missing by using a variety of materials; however, many supply houses now list them in different sizes—pairs only—in their catalogs. If you can buy the correct size, professionally made, it will save you a great deal of time. If you cannot, try to locate a craftsman who specializes in lathe work. Starting with a simple block of wood, he can cut and shape them and drill holes of any required size.

If you decide to make your own, try using plastic wood. It makes the strongest and most wear-resistant parts, other than wooden ones. If you're good at "sighting," you can probably make the size needed with very little effort. Prepare a "core" from nondrying clay, such as Plasticene, floral clay, or a similar substance. The core is necessary to make an opening through the round mass. It must be nondrying so that when the ball has dried, the clay core can still be pushed out and will leave a hole through which the elastic is to go. The warmth of your hands will make the clay more pliable as you work it to form the core. When you have rolled it to the core diameter you want, cut it to the length you need and freeze it.

Once the core is frozen solid, quickly add plastic wood all around it. Roll it in the palms of your hands, keeping the ends of the core free of plastic wood. (Your palms will become quite messy, but plastic-wood solvent will remove adhering particles.) When you think the ball is the right size, hold it near the socket and "sight it." You can also try it *in* the socket *if* you first protect the socket with thin plastic.

Before putting the ball aside to dry, make a last check to see that both ends of the core are free and visible. When the plastic wood is dry, punch out the clay core, sand the ball, and paint it when you paint the rest of the body.

Doll body molds are now available through many companies (see list of suppliers). The sizes range from a tiny 6½″ to 24″ (measurement taken before the head is added). If you wish to do some experimenting on your own, obtain catalogs that carry full descriptions of the available body molds. Study these before placing an order for an entire body. It will come to you in three or four molds. Be aware, though, that you can make only the size ball, hand, torso, or part that goes with the particular body mold you ordered.

If you're a ceramist, chances are you've already done some experimenting in making all, or parts, of a doll body or bodies. But if you're a beginner, visit a neaby ceramics studio. Many of these studios now carry doll-body molds in stock, and you may be able to buy one on the spot. And most studio owners are also instructors. In many parts of the country, the studio you buy supplies from will provide free instruction. Making balls from ceramic clay (freehand, without the use of a mold) is like working in plastic wood, in that you roll a clay ball the right size to fit a socket. Omit the core. A hole for the elastic can be drilled (with a ceramic drill) after the clay has dried. Your studio owner will fire it at little cost. These are breakable, however, and though they are smoother in appearance than those made of plastic wood, they are less desirable.

Still another material adaptable to ballmaking is papier-mâché. Follow the same steps as those described in working with plastic wood.

REPAIRING
COMPOSITION HANDS AND FEET

Finding an antique composition body without the fingers broken or feet damaged is a rare occurrence. Repairing broken composition fingers and toes is much easier than making the same type of repair in porcelain. Review Chapter 2 on rebuilding fingers and toes. The procedures described in that section are also applicable to composition dolls.

However, you do not need to use a hand grinder to cut anchor grooves or drill holes in composition. A sharp knife is the only tool needed to prepare the damaged area for accepting the repair material; if an entire finger or toe is missing, the point of the knife can be used to "drill" a hole in which to put the wire armature.

REPAINTING THE BODY

It may be necessary to do a bit more work on the body before repainting it. Examine it closely. Aside from the repairs you have made, is the surface severely damaged? For instance, are there places where the "skin" is badly crazed, cracked, or ready to flake off? Ninety percent of the time such damage can be "melted" back into place, and you will have preserved just that much more of the old, original finish. The product I accidentally discovered—and have since used exclusively in coping with this problem—is Formby's Fine Old Furniture Refinisher. If you cannot locate a dealer in your area, the company address is listed in the back of this book.

Many years ago, I used this product to refinish an antique oak wall telephone. Nearby, on a shelf, was what I considered a useless composition Bye-Lo head, 12" in circumference. There was not so much as an inch of good surface left, from the top of the head to the bottom of the flanged neck. What was not merely badly crazed was sticking up; much of the surface, in short, was gone. I knew the head was a "throwaway," but being a pack rat, I had failed to dispose of it. Using a wad of extrafine steel wool thoroughly saturated with Formby's, and light, circular motions, I began working on an area on the back of the head.

To my delight, Formby's began "reconstituting" the finish. It is quite thin—almost like water—but its action is somewhat like that of thin paint remover. The difference is that paint remover is used to strip off an old finish and prepare the surface for refinishing, whereas Formby's literally "melts" the skin surface of the doll, reconstitutes it, and (with the use of steel wool) smears the old surface over into any cracks, light crazing, or other damaged places. Of course it melds all the colors together—skin, lips, cheeks, hair, eyelashes, and brows—necessitating a new paint job. But after a doll head has been "scrubbed" thoroughly with steel wool and Formby's, after it has dried—even if it was badly damaged by crazing before—the defects will barely be noticeable after it has been repainted. And as for the skin-tone repainting, I use Eze-Ply spray enamel in Baby Pink (see list of suppliers).

The use of Formby's on damaged areas of the body will prepare them to receive the finishing coat of enamel. When you're ready to spray on the enamel, refer to Chapter 10, Ill. 76, which shows drying hooks made of wire coat hangers. Each piece of the doll body should be placed on a separate hanger, and the hangers hooked over nails or clotheslines, preferably outside on a windless day. If the spraying must be done inside, wear a protective mask and work in an area where there is no danger that heat or flame will ignite the fumes or spray.

There are probably other brands of good enamel, and possibly other products (besides Formby's), that will literally "melt" and reconstitute the damaged old surface of a composition body, but those mentioned are my two standbys.

Ill. 75 pictures a painted, fully strung fifteen-piece ball-jointed body.

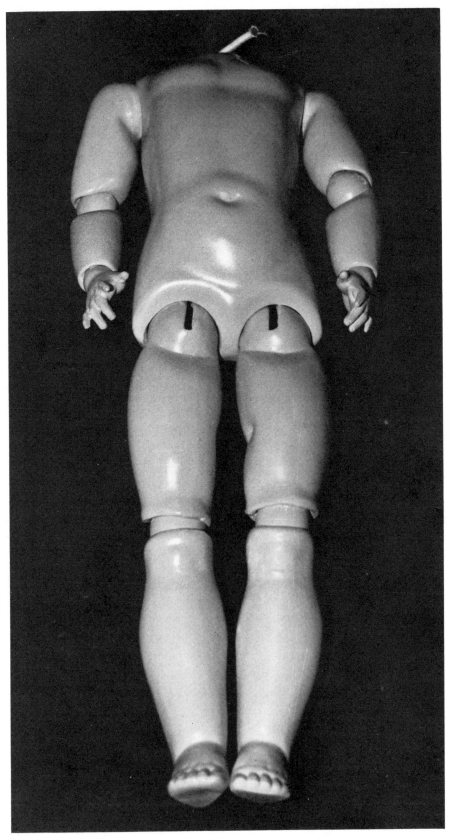

Ill. 75. German fifteen-piece ball-jointed body, painted and strung.

10

Restringing

Once you learn the basics of restringing the more complicated antique dolls, restringing others will seem simple. This chapter covers the most difficult, the ball-jointed bodies with bisque heads and the jointed compositions or papier-mâchés.

Cleaning, repairing, and painting should be done before the restringing. These things are easier to do while the doll is apart (unassembled). If painting is necessary, drying hooks can be made of wire coat hangers, and each doll part can be hung separately. (Ill. 76). Be sure all glue and paint are thoroughly dry before you start restringing.

Spread a thick turkish towel on the worktable. Whether the "patient" is barely held together by wornout elastic (which must be removed) or lying loose in a box or sack, the texture of the towel will keep the doll parts from rolling off the table when you are assembling them.

Keeping the arms and legs in exact position in relation to the torso is very important. When assembling the parts prior to stringing, be sure the right hand, the left hand, the right foot, and the left one are correctly positioned. If the tops of the legs, which fit into holes in the torso, have slots, make sure the slots are turned to the front.

Study Ills. 77, 78, and 79 for the correct laying-out of the parts of three different types of bodies. Once you learn the correct way to string these, any variations in body structure you may later encounter will present no difficulties.

The size of round doll elastic to use will depend on the size of the doll. Suggested sizes for restringing are:

Doll under 6″	Size 0
Doll 7″ to 12″	Size 1
Doll 13″ to 20″	Size 2
Doll 21″ to 28″	Size 3
Doll 29″ and taller	Size 4

Ill. 76. Drying hooks made from coat hangers. After cutting hooks of the desired lengths, bend the wire at each end as shown.

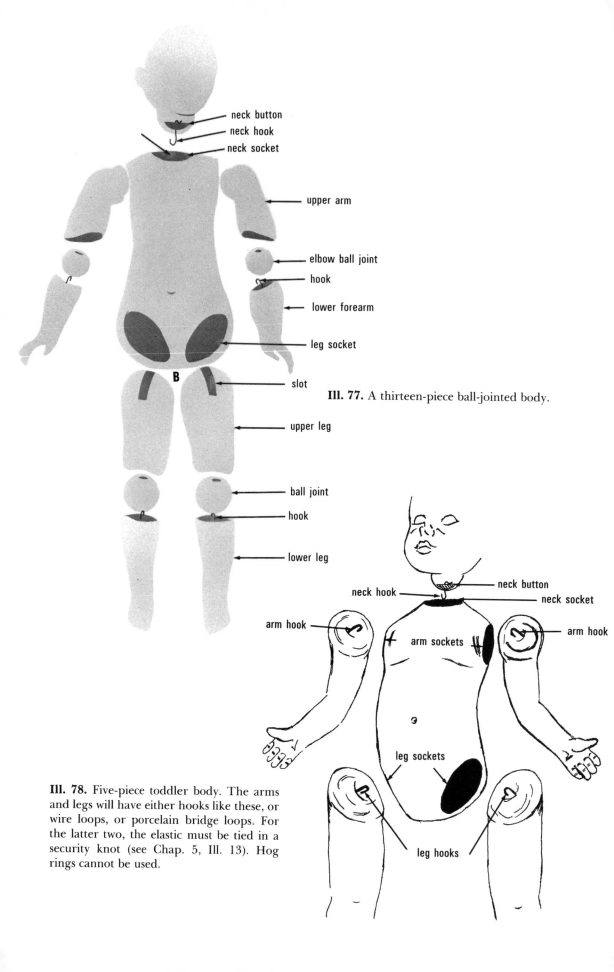

neck button

neck hook

neck socket

upper arm

elbow ball joint

hook

lower forearm

leg socket

B

slot

upper leg

ball joint

hook

lower leg

arm hook

Ill. 77. A thirteen-piece ball-jointed body.

neck hook

neck button

neck socket

arm hook

arm sockets

arm hook

leg sockets

leg hooks

Ill. 78. Five-piece toddler body. The arms and legs will have either hooks like these, or wire loops, or porcelain bridge loops. For the latter two, the elastic must be tied in a security knot (see Chap. 5, Ill. 13). Hog rings cannot be used.

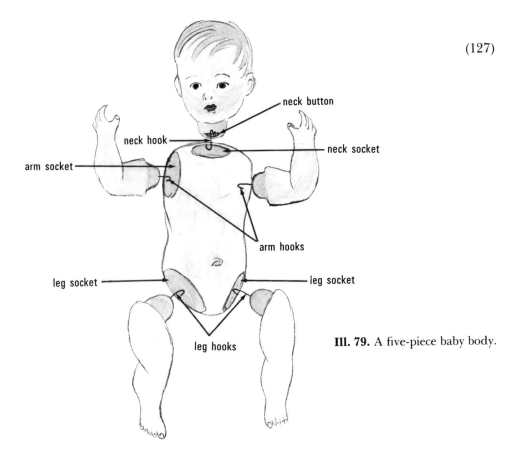

Ill. 79. A five-piece baby body.

Other items needed for restringing are shown in Ill. 80 (see list of suppliers). You can make your own stringing hooks in any size needed by straightening out wire coat hangers and cutting them to the desired length.

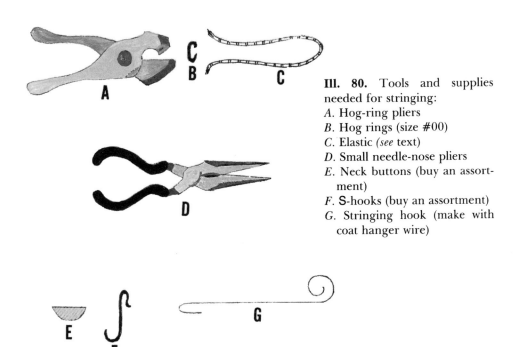

Ill. 80. Tools and supplies needed for stringing:
A. Hog-ring pliers
B. Hog rings (size #00)
C. Elastic (*see* text)
D. Small needle-nose pliers
E. Neck buttons (buy an assortment)
F. S-hooks (buy an assortment)
G. Stringing hook (make with coat hanger wire)

Once you have the correct size elastic and are ready to begin the job of restringing, here are the steps to follow:

Following Ill. 77, locate points *A* and *B*. Pick up the cut end of elastic and, without stretching it, hold the cut end at point *A*, which is the neck opening. Lay the elastic smoothly down the center of the body to point *B*, the crotch area. This will be the first half of the body loop needed for one leg. Now, continuing to hold the elastic at *B*, lay it back up to point *A* and cut it off there, even with the starting end. The piece you have cut is the correct length of elastic for firm stringing.

Cut another piece of elastic the same length for use in stringing the other leg.

Be very careful in following the next step, which is fastening the loose ends of elastic together with a tightly clamped hog ring. If the fastening is not done correctly, the elastic will not stand the tension necessary for holding the leg parts together.

From your assortment of hog rings, select the one that fits most tightly around the two loose ends of the elastic loop. Slip the hog ring over the ends (Ill. 81), place the hog ring into the jaw slots of the hog ring pliers, and squeeze the handles together as hard as you can (Ill. 82). This will tighten the hog ring. To make it even more secure, however, grasp the hog ring with the jaws of the needle-nose pliers and squeeze the pliers as tightly as possible. This will flatten the hog ring *into* the elastic.

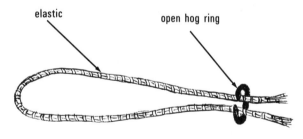

elastic   open hog ring

Ill. 81. Placement of hog ring to fasten loose ends of elastic. Leave at least ¾″ of the elastic ends extending beyond the hog ring.

Ill. 82. Fastening the hog ring. Seat the hog ring in the jaw slots, and squeeze the handles together as tightly as possible. This forces the sharp points of the hog ring into the elastic.

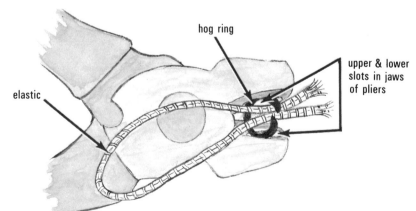

hog ring

upper & lower slots in jaws of pliers

elastic

Test the loop by stretching and pulling on it very hard. If the loop pulls apart, do it over, as it is not safe to use unless it passes this strenuous test.

Prepare and test the other leg loop in the same manner.

Before going any further, plan the position of the hog ring joinings in relation to the arms and legs. If the joinings are placed in the wrong area inside the body, they will interfere with free movement of the limbs. Keep in mind, too, that most of the illustrations in this chapter depict the elastic as though it were *outside* the body, when—in reality—very little elastic shows at any time. The drawings were made in this fashion to show the positioning more clearly.

Next, place the loop so that the hog ring joining will be inside the torso and to one side, where it cannot interfere with the movement of any part when the restringing is completed. Ill. 83 shows the elastic in place as it will appear inside the torso, with the joining in the correct position.

Hook the elastic on the lower leg hook (Ill. 84) and, using needle-nose pliers, squeeze the hook tightly over the elastic (Ill. 85).

Ill. 83. Keep the joined ends positioned as illustrated, above the waistline but below the arm opening.

Ill 84. Hook the elastic loops to the leg hooks.

Ill. 85. Use needle-nose pliers to squeeze the hooks tightly over the elastic.

With the stringing hook, pull the elastic through the ball at the knee; then, holding the elastic in your hand, detach the stringing hook and run the hook down through the next piece (top to bottom), which is the upper leg. Catch the hook into the elastic you are holding and pull it through the upper leg (Ill. 86). Push all three parts downward until they fit together snugly (Ill. 87).

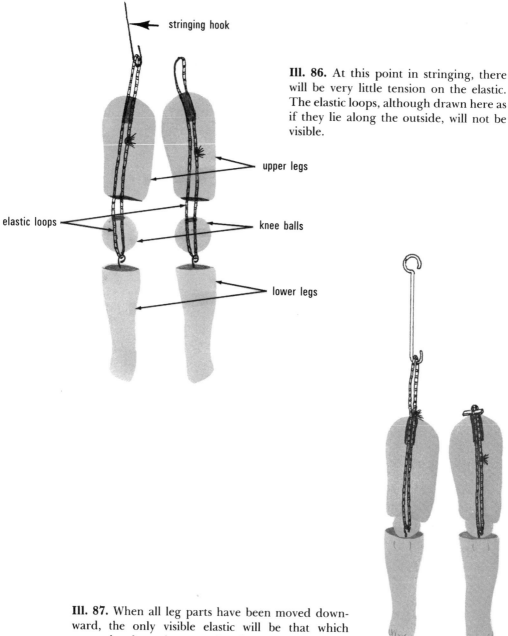

Ill. 86. At this point in stringing, there will be very little tension on the elastic. The elastic loops, although drawn here as if they lie along the outside, will not be visible.

Ill. 87. When all leg parts have been moved downward, the only visible elastic will be that which protrudes above the upper-leg slots.

stringing hook

neck opening

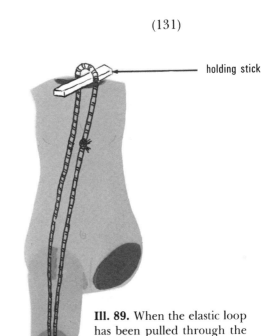

holding stick

torso

leg openings

Ill. 88. Run the stringing hook down through the neck opening and the torso, and out of a leg opening. Hook into the elastic loop, then pull loop through the torso and out the neck opening. Secure it as shown in Ill. 89.

Ill. 89. When the elastic loop has been pulled through the neck opening, there is a great deal of tension. This will be doubled when you attach the other leg. Tongue depressors or pieces of yardsticks make ideal holding sticks.

Hang on to the elastic you have just pulled through all parts of the leg, and again detach the stringing hook. Run the hook down through the neck opening into the torso and out the leg opening (Ill. 88). Catch the hook into the elastic you are holding and pull it all the way through the torso and out the neck opening.

The elastic must now be secured at the neck, to keep it from snapping back inside. For this purpose, use as wide a stick as is practical, considering the size of the doll (Ill. 89). A pencil or small craft stick will do, even a tongue depressor. Do NOT use anything too fragile or weak, as there will be considerable tension in the stretched elastic.

Repeat the same procedure for the other leg.

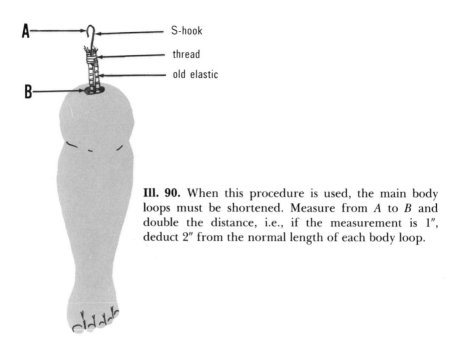

Ill. 90. When this procedure is used, the main body loops must be shortened. Measure from *A* to *B* and double the distance, i.e., if the measurement is 1″, deduct 2″ from the normal length of each body loop.

Occasionally a doll does not have a hook at the top of the lower leg; instead, what appears to be a bit of old string sticks out of the wooden ball glued into the top of the lower leg. This is actually old elastic that has lost its stretch. When cutting this type of joint apart, be sure to leave enough of the old elastic protruding to form a loop that will take an **S**-hook, as shown in Ill. 90. (Use this method only if the old elastic is strong enough to take the necessary strain when the doll is restrung.)

To fasten these two cut ends together, rub a small quantity of Elmer's Glue near the ends; then wrap heavy #8 thread round and round the ends, about ten times. Tie a security knot (see Chapter 5, Ill. 13) in the thread before inserting an **S**-hook into the loop, and squeezing the hook tight. Let the glue dry thoroughly before proceeding.

If the old elastic is too rotten to use, dig it out so that new elastic can be inserted in its place. Before you can insert new elastic, however, it will be necessary to drill a hole straight through the middle of the wooden ball (Ill. 91). For this, use a small drill bit no larger than a finishing nail.

Then double a piece of stringing elastic and push the loop end of it into the hole (where you dug out the old elastic), so that a finishing nail inserted into the drilled passageway will pass through the loop and hold it in place (Ill. 92). But before inserting the finishing nail in the drilled hole, rub Elmer's Glue on the nail or dip the entire nail in the glue and wipe off the excess. After inserting the nail in the drilled passageway, cut off the sharp point with wire cutters. You will probably also need to file the nail down even with

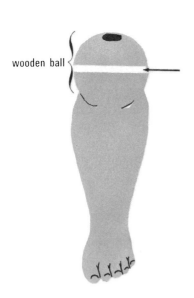

wooden ball

doubled elastic

hole

finishing nail

Ill. 92. Start the finishing nail into the drilled hole, but stop short of center. Push the elastic loop into the hole and down far enough so that the nail, when pushed all the way through, will pass through the loop and hold it in place. Cut off any protruding nail point and file it down even with the surface. Repaint, or touch up.

Ill. 91. Drill a hole straight through the center of the wooden ball, using a small drill bit no larger than a finishing nail (about 5/64″ in size).

Ill. 93. When the procedures in Ills. 90, 91, and 92 have been completed, the finished repair will look like this.

the surface of the wooden ball. Touch up this area with flesh-colored paint. The lower leg should then look as it does in Ill. 93.

You now have two elastic ends sticking out at the top of the ball, as in Ill. 93. Fasten them together, as described earlier, with Elmer's Glue near the ends and #8 thread wound around the ends. A word of caution here: when following these directions, be careful in measuring the length of the leg loops. Instead of measuring elastic from A to B and back to A (Ill. 77), the elastic will have to be shorter because of the extra length of elastic and the S-hook attached to the top of each lower leg. Otherwise, there would not be enough tension on the loop when the restringing was finished.

To figure the approximate amount to shorten the main body loops, measure from the S-hook to the top of the wooden ball, and double that measurement. For example, if the distance measured is 1″, deduct a total of 2″ from the normal measurement of the body loops. (Refer to Ill. 92.)

Proceed with stringing the legs as directed, using the two shortened body loops. When you are finished, a flat stick will be holding both loops in a fixed position outside the neck opening (Ill. 94).

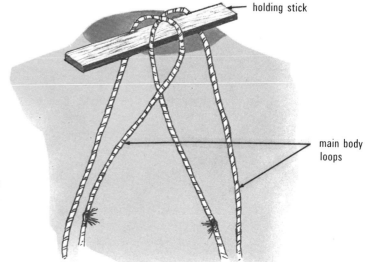

Ill. 94. Both main body loops are held in place in this manner.

Only one loop is needed for stringing the arms. Follow the instructions given in Ills. 95 through 98 for measuring the elastic and stringing the arms.

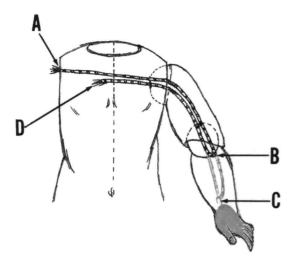

Ill. 95. Measuring elastic for stringing ball-joint arms. Assemble all the arm parts as shown, before starting to measure the elastic. *Do not stretch the elastic while measuring.*

Hold free end of elastic at *A*. Lay it straight across the chest and down to *B* (if the hook is in the upper forearm) or to *C* (if the hook is in the ball of the hand). At *B* or *C*, hold the elastic while you loop it back to *D*. Cut the elastic here. Join the two ends with a small hog ring.

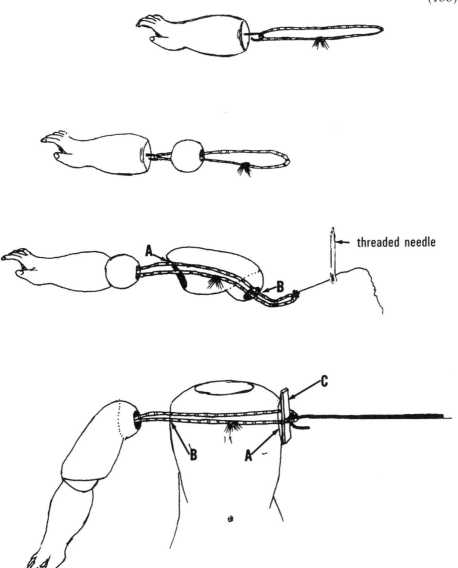

threaded needle

Ill. 96. Stringing a ball-joint arm. Arrange loop so joining is as shown at top. Slip end of loop under the hook and clamp hook closed.

Second drawing: Here elastic has been inserted through ball. If hole is too small to push elastic through, thread a bodkin with button/carpet thread, tie it onto free end of loop, and run bodkin through.

When upper arm is curved, as in third drawing, insert threaded needle at point *A*, run it through arm, and out at point *B*. Pull the elastic through and slide upper arm down.

Bottom drawing: Keeping the joining of the elastic as near the center as possible, insert stringing hook through the armhole *A*, through body, and out at *B*. Hook into the loop, pull elastic through body, out at *A*, and slip a holding stock *(C)* between body and elastic. Disengage the stringing hook.

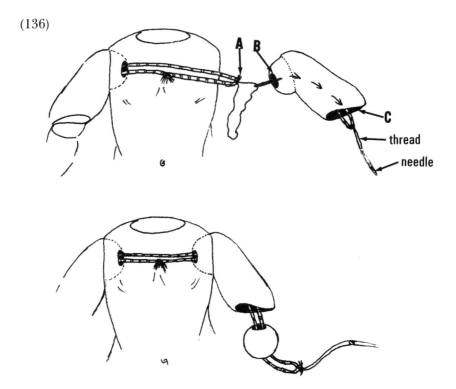

thread

needle

Ill. 97. Stringing a ball-joint arm (cont.). *At top:* Again tie the loose ends of thread to the loop at *A*. Slip the threaded needle into hole *B*. Arrows indicate the needle passing through the arm and exiting at *C*. Pull the elastic through and push the upper arm into its socket.

   Bottom drawing: Insert elastic through ball. Remove needle and thread after catching the loop with hook of the stringing tool. Now there is a great deal of tension in the elastic; unless you hold it firmly with the stringing hook, it will snap back through arm parts and body.

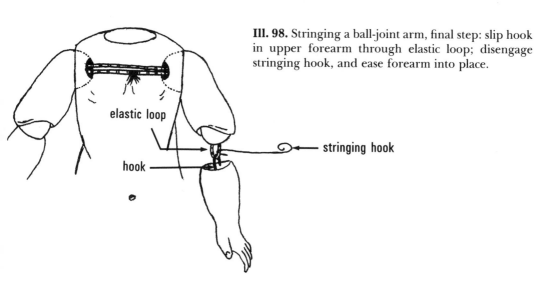

Ill. 98. Stringing a ball-joint arm, final step: slip hook in upper forearm through elastic loop; disengage stringing hook, and ease forearm into place.

elastic loop

hook

stringing hook

Sometimes the holes in a doll's limbs are too small to get the stringing hook through, and quite often the upper arms and/or legs are curved in such a way that the stringing hook cannot be used. In such cases there are alternatives, one of them being the use of a darning needle. Thread it with heavy cord and drop it through the problem limb. Then tie the cord onto the elastic, and pull the cord (and elastic) through the difficult hole; *or* make a needlelike tool of flexible steel wire. This can be used similarly to the darning needle, threaded with strong cord.

The head goes on next, and this—the final step in restringing a doll—is the one where an extra pair of hands is most welcome. If you have no one to help, a "head aid" is very simple to use. This is merely a strong metal hook screwed into solid wood so securely that there is no danger of its ever pulling loose. Study Ill. 99, which shows how to use the "head aid."

Almost all antique doll heads attached to composition or papier-mâché bodies require the use of an **S**-hook and a neck button (sometimes called a plug). The lower contour of the button fits the curve of the neck (inside). An **S**-hook goes through the center hole of the button, the upper part of the hook is bent in such a way that

Ill. 99. Use of head aid. Screw heavy metal hook into end of work table or any handy solid wood surface. Insert curved end of stringing hook into both main body loops; place round end over hook in table. Pull body away from table far enough to allow room for inserting neck hook through both body loops (the holding stick falls out when loops are pulled away from body). Disengage stringing hook and ease head into neck socket.

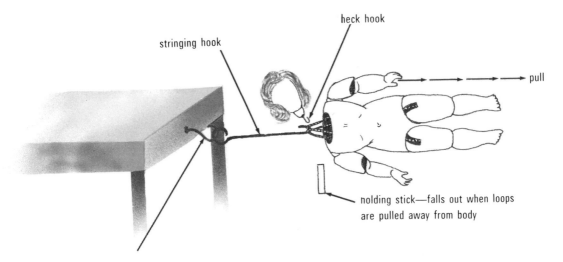

stringing hook

heck hook

pull

nolding stick—falls out when loops
are pulled away from body

it cannot slip back through the hole, and the lower part is bent into a hook, which is slipped under—and clamped onto—the elastic loop(s). This is what holds the head to the body (See Ill. 80, *E* and *F*.)

If wig and pate are intact, the old button is still inside the head. Hold the head, neck down, and coax the bottom of the S-hook through the neck opening. Clamp it onto the elastic loop(s).

If wig and pate are loose, the button unit is probably gone. You can order wooden buttons from a supply company (or substitute a thick plastic faucet washer) and use an S-hook made from a heavy wire coat hanger.

Straighten one end of an S-hook; run that through the hole in the bottom of the wooden plug and, with needle-nose pliers, twist the hook back into its original curve (on top of the plug). Then, as a safety precaution, bend the S-hook down as flat against the wood as possible. Unless this is done, the projection of the S-hook above the wooden plug may interfere with the counterweight of the eye rocker on a doll having sleep eyes.

To hook the head into place (if you have a helper), one person should hold the head firmly with both hands while the other person grasps the hook extending out of the neck hole and slips it through the elastic loop(s) being held in place by the holding stick. Remove the holding stick and gently ease the head into its neck socket.

If no helper is available, resort to the use of the "head aid" and follow the directions given in Ill. 99.

There are two methods of stringing five-piece bodies that are jointed only at the shoulders and hips (Ills. 100 through 104). The two-loop method is preferable. Study Ills. 100 through 103 for step-by-step directions.

For one-loop stringing, make the single body loop slightly longer than that used in double-loop stringing. (See Ill. 102 for method of measuring.) Two hog rings are also used here, the procedure being the same as shown in Ill. 103 as far as placement is concerned. The big difference, as can be seen in Ill. 104, is that the head, arms, and legs are all fastened to one loop.

The basic principles and procedures described here will serve you well in most restringing jobs that you encounter.

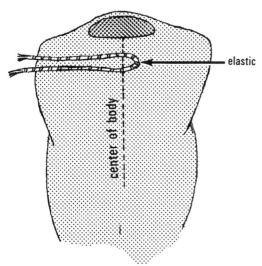

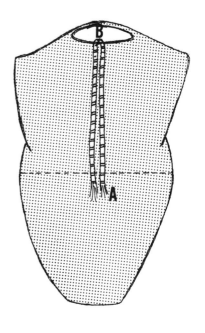

Ill. 100. Measuring elastic for arm loop (five-piece baby or toddler body). NOTE: Do not stretch elastic while measuring. (1) Visually locate center of body. (2) Lay elastic straight across from one arm socket to just past body center. (3) Loop it back and cut it. (4) Fasten hog ring about 1″ in from cut ends. Test for strength. (5) Attach arms. If loop seems too loose, remove and attach another hog ring.

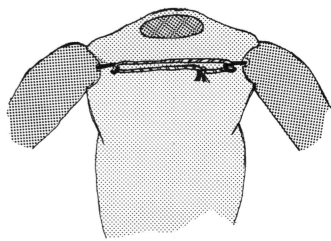

Ill. 101. Attaching arms. (1) Slip one end of elastic loop under a hook, and clamp hook so that elastic can't slip. (2) Run stringing tool into opposite armhole, through torso, then out other armhole, and hook into elastic loop. Pull it back through torso and out, and attach other arm, as above.

Note position of joining of the elastic ends. Keep it away from center of body; otherwise it will interfere with the body loop.

Ill. 102. Measuring elastic for body loop. Place cut end of the elastic at *A*. Without stretching it, loop elastic up to *B*, and back to *A*. Cut the end. Fasten cut ends together with a hog ring and test the loop for strength. Then fasten middle of the loop together with another hog ring (Ill. 103).

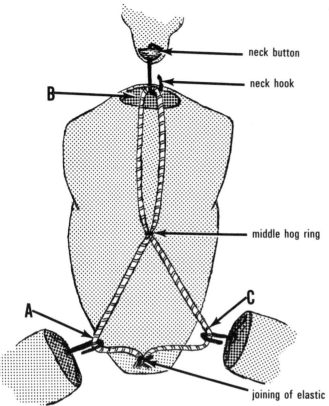

neck button

neck hook

B

middle hog ring

A

C

joining of elastic

Ill. 103. Begin stringing doll at *A* by clamping *leg* hook onto the elastic. Insert the *stringing* hook down the neck opening and torso and out the leg opening, and hook it into the attached elastic. Pull elastic out the neck opening *B* and attach the head (neck hook).

Next, insert the *stringing* hook up through leg opening at *C*, hook it into the elastic loop, pull loop out of leg opening *C*, and fasten the second leg by means of its leg hook. (At this point, there is a great deal of tension and you may need someone to aid you.)

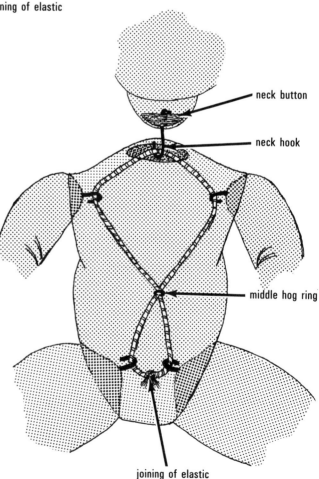

neck button

neck hook

middle hog ring

Ill. 104. One-loop stringing.

joining of elastic

11

Cleaning and Repairing Kid Bodies

Kid bodies, if at all repairable, should never be discarded. Cleaning and mending are easily done, using largely items you already have in your home or products bought in local stores. The only material that must be ordered from a supply company is the leather—unless you have a collection of white kid gloves. They make the neatest and least noticeable patches.

Items you may or may not need, depending on the type of repair, are listed below. Read the section applicable to your particular problem and assemble the necessary items in your work area.

Plain paper (not newsprint—the ink will rub off on the leather and make cleanup more time consuming)
3/16″ wooden dowel (these come in 36″ lengths)
Extrafine needle and mercerized thread
Scissors
Electric iron with heat controls
Small padded board (Ill. 107 gives instructions for making one)

Elmer's Glue
Glove leather or kidskins
Sawdust sifter (see Ill. 106 for construction)
Whisk broom
2 sponges, small and medium size
Dishwashing detergent
Soft, absorbent cotton cloth
Saddle soap
Mop and Glo
Stitch Witchery, available in rolls ⅝" wide or by the yard in
18" width
Thin iron-on interfacing
Magix Leather Preparer and White Magix Shoe Color
Spray (if not available at your shoe repair shop, write the
company for nearest dealer)

Spread plain paper, such as a brown grocery bag cut open, over the work table before beginning any repairs. It will catch the overflow of sawdust.

Make three body stuffers from the 36" wooden dowel, one 8" long, one 11", and another 17". Ill. 105 shows the simple method of preparing these. You can get by with one; however, for doing doll work, it is desirable to have many body stuffers in various lengths, not only for use as described in this chapter, but in stuffing complete doll bodies, as described in Chapter 13.

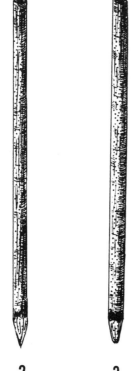

Ill. 105. Preparing a "body stuffer." Use a dowel rod ³⁄₁₆" in diameter. Drawing at left is the untouched dowel. Drawing #2 shows one end sharpened to a point. In 3 the sharp point has been rounded off with sandpaper so that, if your hand slips, point will not puncture some part of the kid body. (Dowel rods come 36" in length, so two or three stuffers can be made from a single rod.)

1   2   3

Regardless of what type of leather body you are working on—Bru, French Fashion, gusseted or nongusseted, Ne Plus Ultra hip joints, or some other—these methods will work. The object here is not to make an invisible repair—that cannot be done; rather, it is to preserve the original body as neatly as possible.

Let's take a specific problem as an example—a small tear in a leg. Keep in mind that the same method used to repair it will be applicable to a larger but similar area of damage.

Using a body stuffer, carefully work back into the leg any of the old sawdust that has leaked out. Pack this as tightly as possible without putting undue strain on the leather. You may have to add some new sawdust as well, to restore the original shape entirely. (Sawdust can be obtained free at lumberyards or cabinet shops. It should be sifted through the screen that you made according to the directions in Ill. 106. The sawdust will be very fine once the coarse shavings and wood chips are sifted out.) Continue adding sawdust and packing it tight until the leg is once again firm and shapely.

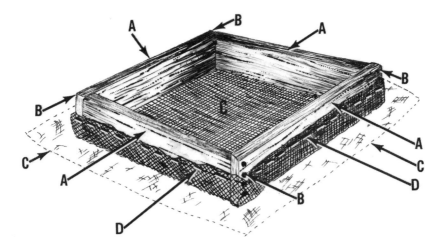

Ill. 106. Making a sawdust sifter. Completed sifter looks as shown here. The sifter should be placed over a cardboard box (as near the size of the sifter as possible). When sawdust is put inside the sifter and swept back and forth with a whisk broom, the finest dust goes through the screen and falls into the container underneath. Coarse shavings that remain are to be discarded.

Measurements can be varied, but these are the ones I have found most practical. The four boards marked *A* are each 10″ long, 5″ wide, and ¾″ thick. Nail them together in a square. (If desired, apply wood glue to the ends *(B)* butted against each other, before nailing.) *C* identifies the 16″ square of ordinary wire screen. Set the square wood frame in center of the screen. Bring sides of screen up over sides of frame, and fasten screen to frame with staples *(D)* or large-headed tacks.

Sometimes a damaged area may require a round leather patch, sometimes an oval one, sometimes a bit of both, but the procedure is the same. No matter whether the patch is made from an old white kid glove or new leather, it is very important to cut it correctly. Hold the scissors at an angle, rather than vertically, so that the edges of the leather will be automatically beveled (thinned) as you cut. To bevel the edges even more, turn the patch wrong side up on a hard surface and carefully scrape the edges with a razor blade, taking care not to cut or distort the leather. The thinner and more beveled the edges, the better the patch will hold and the neater it will look. There will be no unsightly thick edge sticking up from the body to catch on things, and the likelihood of the patch's coming loose will be negligible.

GLUEING THE PATCH

Even something as simple as glueing one thing to another can present problems—problems in the placement of the two things in relation to each other, and problems in cleanup. The most important rule is this: be generous in applying the glue to a surface; then wipe off most of it. For glueing a leather patch to a body, apply a thick "string" of Elmer's completely around the edge of the patch (on the wrong side, of course). Use your index finger to smear the glue out evenly and work it down into the back of the patch (the unfinished side of the leather). Then examine the edges to see whether any glue remains "sitting" in spots. If so, smear this out and work it down into the leather before wiping off the excess. If the glue has been properly "worked," the edges of the leather will merely look wet. (Keep a damp cloth handy for wiping the glue from your fingers.)

Place the patch over the hole; then, with the smooth, round body of a crochet hook or similar object, roll the edges of the leather tightly against the doll body or limb. Wipe off any glue that seeps out from the edges of the patch. (If there is damage on the cloth lining of a kid body, first glue fabric over the lining hole in the same manner, allowing a ½″ lapover all around. Of course, you do not bevel lining fabric.)

A long rip or tear may have jagged edges. Thin iron-on interfacing—applied, cooled, and trimmed before sawdust is packed in—makes a good reinforcement. Cut a strip of interfacing long enough and of sufficient width to fit *under* the jagged edges. Insert the strip *inside*—between the sawdust and the leather—with the *shiny* side facing you. (The shiny side has the adhesive on it.) Set the steam iron dial on "Wool." Insert the padded board (Ill. 107) under the interfacing, put a piece of tissue paper *over* the leather, and hold the iron in position on the tissue for about 10 seconds. This heats the adhesive on the interfacing and causes it to stick to the wrong side of the leather. *Do not slide the iron back and forth.*

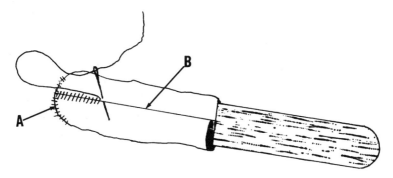

Ill. 107. Making a mini-pressing-board. Pad tongue depressor, craft stick, or one of each for two different sizes of mini-boards. Apply Elmer's Glue to half the stick, on both sides. Then wrap a strip of cotton cloth around the glued end four to six times. Tuck cloth ends in at *A* and whip stitch them together as tightly as possible. Turn under edges at *B* and stitch as illustrated.

Allow each area touched with the iron to cool for a few seconds before moving to the next spot. Repeat until the interfacing strip is fused to the leather along the entire length of the tear. The next step is trimming off the exposed interfacing with very sharp scissors, following the uneven lines of the torn leather. This trimming is necessary so that, later, the reinforced edges can be butted together before handstitching them in place.

I have suggested using iron-on interfacing because it can be found in every fabric shop. However, I prefer to use Stitch Witchery, not as well known but much easier to manipulate around uneven edges. Most large fabric shops carry it both in ⅝″-wide rolls and by the yard in 18″ width. I have never understood why this fabulous aid to seamstresses has not caught on. It has been on the market many, many years and is indispensable in my doll work. Unlike iron-on interfacing (that with adhesive on only one side), Stitch Witchery *is* an adhesive. Put a layer of it between two pieces of fabric, hold an iron on the fabric a few seconds, and the two pieces of cloth are fused together. To put a hem in any garment, curtain, or drapery, press the hem in place as you would ordinarily do prior to hand-stitching it. Then, following directions on the package, insert Stitch Witchery between the wrong side of the material and the edge of the hem. Hold the iron on it for 10 seconds, move on to the next spot, and the next, repeating until the entire hem has been treated in this fashion. Unless the article is washed in *hot* water, the hem will remain in place, without stitching.

In using Stitch Witchery to reinforce the jagged edges of a tear in leather, cut a piece of muslin to go *under* the Stitch Witchery. Put it and the adhesive under the damaged area and hold it in place with the padded board. Lay tissue paper *over* the area and, using the preheated iron, fuse the muslin to the leather. Stitch Witchery, "cobwebby" in appearance, is easily maneuvered under the contours of the damaged leather because it *is* thin, and because it can be twisted, pushed under, pleated, or shaped as needed, and so will not leave any evidence that it is there, once it's fused. Do any necessary trimming before proceeding.

Next, hold the leather together until the edges of the tear just butt against each other. (Never overlap them.) Using a fine needle and mercerized thread, sew the tear back and forth with overcasting stitches, keeping the stitches about ½" *away from* the jagged edges. This is the reason why reinforcing the damaged area is so important. Without reinforcement, the leather might well split every time you tried to take a stitch. Even with it, the stitches cannot be pulled together tightly, nor need they be. Simply make sure they are firm enough to draw the torn edges together and hold them while the next step is being completed.

Continue hand-stitching the tear until only a small hole remains, one into which a miniature funnel will fit. Glue a *beveled* patch over the damaged part but leave the opening accessible (Ill. 108). Let the glue dry completely before continuing.

If more sawdust needs to be packed in, now is the time to do it. However, be careful not to put undue strain on the stitching. Finally, stitch together the small opening and glue down the loose end of the patch.

Often kid bodies are split right up to the gusset, and sometimes even the gusset is ripped at points of strain. This problem is handled in much the same way as already described. An oval or round patch may not suit the purpose, so shape the patch to fit the damaged area and follow the same cutting and beveling procedures. Place the patch on top of the rip, overlapping the gusset whatever distance is necessary (Ill. 109).

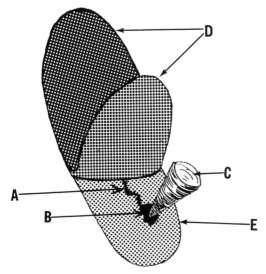

Ill. 108. Here a damaged area is stitched and a patch glued in place. Arrow at *A* points to jagged edges that have been whip stitched together as far as *B*, along the length of the tear. The opening at *B* permits addition of more stuffing, to firm up the area. A miniature funnel (*C*) can be made of heavy paper. *D* identifies the beveled patch that has been glued over part of the tear, with one end left free for access to the stuffing hole. Let glue dry before additional sawdust is added. Then stitch together the opening at *B*, and glue down rest of patch at *E*.

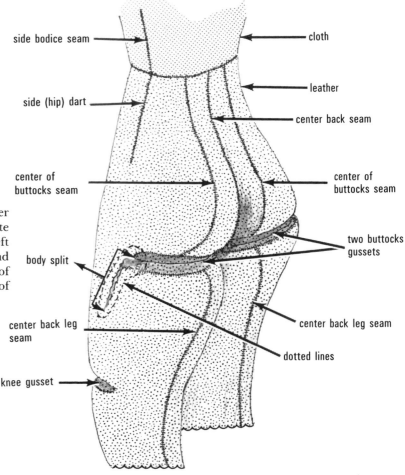

side bodice seam

cloth

side (hip) dart

leather

center back seam

center of buttocks seam

center of buttocks seam

two buttocks gussets

body split

center back leg seam

center back leg seam

dotted lines

knee gusset

Ill. 109. This is a three-quarter view of a typical Bru body. Note the body split at the end of the left hip gusset. The dotted line around the split indicates the ideal shape of the patch to use for this type of repair.

MAKING COVERS FOR DAMAGED LEGS

Many old kid bodies have muslin feet and legs that are either split or on the verge of splitting. If the sawdust is still well packed—that is, if the part still retains its original shape—make a covering for the leg. Unbleached muslin, sometimes difficult to find, is the ideal fabric to use because its color closely resembles that of old material. If you cannot locate the unbleached, buy bleached and color it. You can dye it or soak it in strong tea. Just be sure it's 100 percent cotton.

Draft a pattern from the leg you want to cover (see Ills. 110 and 111 for directions).

Ill. 110. Drafting pattern for a leg cover. Take the measurements indicated by numbers 1, 2, 3, and 4, starting at back seam, going around leg, and ending at back seam again. These will never be exactly as on the original old body, but so near that only minor adjustments are needed. Allow an extra ¼″ for seam, except for a leather cover, which needs no seam allowance.

Using these measurements, draw the pattern on paper. Fit it to the leg and make any needed adjustments. Then use it to cut a fabric leg cover.

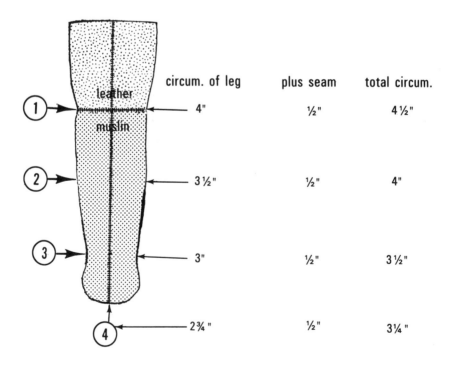

	circum. of leg	plus seam	total circum.
①	4″	½″	4½″
②	3½″	½″	4″
③	3″	½″	3½″
④	2¾″	½″	3¼″

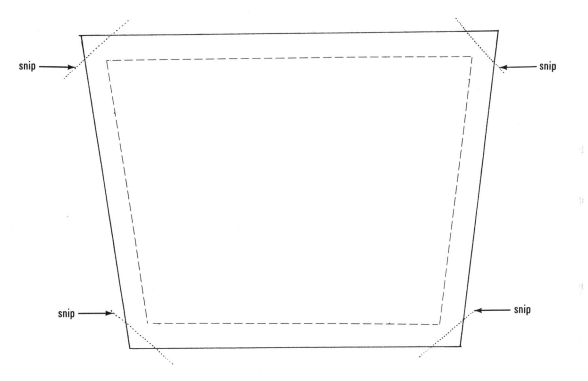

Ill. 111. A drawing of leg cover pattern made with the measurements taken in Ill. 110. The broken lines indicate the seam turnunder. Snip off corners as shown before pressing the allowance under.

The back seam of the leg covering cannot be sewed on the machine because the covering would then not slip over the foot. Iron the seam allowance under on all four sides of the muslin piece and fit the fabric around the leg. Make any final adjustments at this time. When an exact fit is achieved, run a very thin line of Elmer's Glue across the ¼″ turnunder at the top and also at the bottom. Using a fingertip, smudge the glue to the edges and wipe off any excess. Finger press the top firmly in place along the seam line where the leather and muslin are joined (Ill. 110, point 1). Then, holding the top in place with one hand, smooth the fabric down to its lower edge with the other. Finger press that in place, making certain that the turned-under back seam lines up with the original one perfectly. Let dry several hours before proceeding.

To complete the repair, use tiny whipstitches to close the back seam.

If the top circumference is not glued as neatly as you would like it, cut a small scalloped strip of leather wide enough to cover the joining and long enough to circle the leg. Glue this over the joining, half on the leather section, half on the fabric.

The same pattern-making steps can be used if the lower leg section is leather instead of fabric, but omit the seam allowances. They are used on fabric to keep the edges from fraying. Leather presents no such problems.

CLEANING A LEATHER BODY

Several cleaning methods can be used successfully if the leather body is in good condition even if badly soiled. For example, the leather can be cleaned to a certain extent by "dry sponging." Cut a small sponge into approximately a 2″ square. Dip this into a gentle detergent solution that has been whipped until a high foam stands on top. *Do not soak the cleaning sponge*; merely dip it into the sudsy foam. Clean a small area at a time.

Saturate a larger sponge in lukewarm rinse water and squeeze it out as dry as possible. Immediately after a spot is cleaned, wipe it off with the damp sponge; then dry with a soft, absorbent cotton cloth. Work over the body as fast as possible so that the leather will not become water soaked. Guard against this at all times. When you have finished, if any dampness is evident let the body dry out before going on to the next step.

After the leather is dry, any good brand of liquid white shoe polish can be used to cover the entire body. Let the polish dry about three hours; then apply Mop and Glo sparingly (available at food stores) with a soft cloth. Buff it thoroughly. Mop and Glo takes away the shoe-polish look and leaves a very white, sparkling-clean kid body.

If this suggestion gives you the "willies," rest assured that it will in no way damage the old doll body if used correctly. I have used it occasionally since it first came on the market, and the materials on which it was used (and that are still in my possession) show no signs of damage or deterioration. Any commercial product may prove unsatisfactory if it is not used precisely according to directions. That warning, of course, applies to Mop and Glo.

For bodies not badly soiled, saddle soap is an excellent cleaner. It leaves the leather soft and pliable, as it should be. Directions for its use are on the container.

Stanley E-Z clean is also good to use on bodies not badly soiled. It is gently rubbed on and buffed off with a soft cloth.

Because leathers were all dyed, depending on the purposes for which they were to be used, two products that are invaluable for working on kid bodies are Magix Leather Preparer and Magix Shoe Color Spray. Not available everywhere, they are most likely to be found in shoe repair shops or leather stores. Manufactured by Magi-Dyes Company, division of Magic Corp., Central Islip, N.Y. 11722, the "preparer" will clean badly soiled kid bodies without damaging them. It also removes the original dye and its finish (what's left of it), and that must be replaced. This is done by using Magix Shoe Color Spray in white.

With a soft cotton cloth dipped in the leather preparer, go over the entire body, a small area at a time. Keep changing to clean spots on the cloth as you work.

If the head and shoulder plate (or shoulder head), arms, and legs have been removed and you are working with only the kid body, replacing the original color is simply and quickly done. Since Magix Shoe Color Spray, which also contains a built-in finish, is in an aerosol can, paper should be spread on the work area. Brown paper bags split open are ideal. If working indoors, choose a well-ventilated spot. Lay the body on the paper and lightly spray the front and the sides first. Let dry. Turn the body over and do the back. Again, let dry. Continue turning the body, each time giving the leather a light spraying and allowing each coat to dry a few minutes before turning the body over.

When the desired color is reached, allow 24 hours' air-drying time. During this period the body should be suspended so that air can circulate freely around it. This can be done by threading a large-eyed needle with heavy carpet thread (J. & P. Coats Dual Duty Plus extra strong button & carpet thread, available in fabric shops), and stitching through the muslin top several times, forming large loops. Bend a coat-hanger hook as shown in Ill. 112. Insert the hook end through the loops and hang the other end over a large nail placed in a dustfree area. When completely dry, this spray-on color will not rub off.

A faster method of spraying the color is to suspend the body—as just described—in an area where you can walk completely around it,

Ill. 112. Making a body-drying hook. Bend a wire coat hanger as shown here. Hang, at *A*, over a nail placed in an area where air can circulate around the body. Catch the thread loops over the hook at *B*.

spraying as you go. Again, it takes several light coats to achieve a good, solid color. A deep color density, in some cases, makes the body look almost new. If you prefer an older look, examine each coat after it's dry; when you have achieved the desired "old but clean" look, apply no further color.

If the porcelain parts are still on the leather body, take precautions to avoid getting color on them. Even though the spray can be cleaned off, the cleaning wastes time that could be put to better use. Apply narrow masking tape to cover all porcelain parts. It's also a good idea to slip a plastic bag over the doll's head and as far down on the shoulders as possible. The edges of the bag can be sealed to the porcelain shoulders with masking tape.

No matter how carefully you apply the tape, however, some color will get on the porcelain, particularly in areas where the leather is glued onto the porcelain parts. After the dye has dried on the leather, remove any color from the porcelain with Magix Leather Preparer. For large areas, dip a cloth into the preparer (which is actually a solvent) and rub it over the porcelain. For small areas—if a Q-Tip is too large—swirl a small quantity of cotton over the moistened end of a toothpick, dip it into the solvent, and use it to clean off tiny specks of color. Do not let the saturated cotton touch any part of the dyed leather; it will strip off the color. If this should happen, spray a bit of color into a bottle cap, dip the end of a soft pointed brush into it, and retouch the area as needed.

REPLACING MISSING OR DAMAGED LIMBS

If a doll has an arm or leg missing, or one damaged beyond repair, reproduction parts can be obtained from supply houses or individual doll artists. When ordering from a supply house, be sure to send measurements—that is, the length of the arm or leg. (Sources having such parts available are given in the list of suppliers.) Limbs are sold in pairs only, so you must remove the old ones. The color of the porcelain will never match that of the old, but when the doll is costumed the difference will be hardly noticeable. Just be sure you use the correct terminology on your order. If you have any doubt as to whether your doll is bisque, china, or parian (the three types available), reread Chapter 1. It clearly defines the difference. As I have said, I am constantly amazed by the number of collectors who, after many years of handling dolls, refer to chinas as bisques, bisques as chinas, and parians by many names, such as sugar bisque, salt bisque, and even occasionally china.

If you want an exact color match for doll limbs, locate a doll artist in your area, show her or him the old part, and ask if the color can be matched. If the answer is affirmative, you will have to leave the old part with the artist. If you are dealing with an artist worthy of the name, the replica pair will be identical in color to the old. Custom-made parts cost double, sometimes triple, what supply companies charge, but they are well worth it.

As a collector you cannot be expected to know anything about the materials and methods used by a doll artist; however, before coming to an agreement for custom work, you should ask several questions. Knowing the correct answers and understanding why these answers are important can protect you from the artist who is not all he or she claims to be.

Hypothetical Conversation Between Customer and Artist

CUSTOMER: I have an antique doll I need reproduction arms for. Can you match this color for me? [Hand her the old arm. Never, *never* take along the whole doll.]

ARTIST: Yes, I can match the color, but I don't have a mold for arms exactly like this one.

(COMMENT: This will usually be true. A doll artist may have hundreds of molds but none exactly like the arms or legs on your antique doll. The artist will probably have one quite similar.)

CUSTOMER: You *do* make them of porcelain?

ARTIST: Of course.

(COMMENT: For the time being you will believe her. Unless you can look around the studio and immediately recognize works of porcelain on display, you have to assume she is telling the truth.)

CUSTOMER: What color porcelain do you use for reproduction parts?

ARTIST: White, of course.

CUSTOMER: Then how can you make white match this color?

ARTIST: I mix my colors, china paint them onto the white porcelain, and fire them in a kiln.

(COMMENT: Unless you get the right answers here, there is no use in continuing the conversation. Make your excuses as gracefully as possible and leave. You probably won't get these answers in the order given here, but you can elicit this basic information from the doll artist.)

A professional doll artist who takes pride in her work values the end result more than she does money. There are still many of these around. Such an artist will work conscientiously from the first step, which is selecting an appropriate mold to use, through the last, firing china paints onto the porcelain. The thought of using *ceramic* slip or nonfiring stains makes her shudder; yet there are many who peddle this cheaper product every day to the unwary, passing it off as porcelain.

The word *ceramic* is an all-encompassing one. Look it up in a dictionary or encyclopedia and you'll find that, no matter how long the definition or explanation may be, it can be condensed into thirteen words; if it started as clay and is fired in a kiln, it's ceramic. That's like comparing a red brick to a beautiful china dinner plate; or like comparing a Ford to a Rolls Royce. In the latter, they're both cars, but what a vast difference there is. Because the general public does not understand this difference, some very talented professionals who value money above their ability will take every shortcut possible to flim-flam their customers. Their attitude is that a collector "won't know the difference," and most of them do not. One of the biggest ripoffs facing doll collectors today is the artist's use of ceramic nonfiring stain to color a reproduced part. Another is the use of ceramic clay (slip) instead of porcelain clay (slip), which is five to six times more expensive.

Ceramic nonfiring stains are applied to the surface of the limb, usually by airbrush, for even coloration. If the restorer seals the color in by using a "matt spray," you may not immediately be able to tell the difference between fired-on china paints and the stains. Later, when you get home, you can check out both the material (to make sure it's porcelain) and the colors.

Since "stain" colors are *not* fired onto the porcelain, they will wear off in a short time or wash off immediately (if the color has not been sealed). If a sealer was sprayed over the color, a cloth dipped in the Magix Leather Preparer (remember, it's a solvent) and rubbed over the sealer will remove all or part of the color. It will not affect fired-on china paints.

To make sure the replacement limbs are made of porcelain and not ceramic, wet the tip of a finger, touch the *inside* of the limb with the water, and note what happens. If the water sits there until it evaporates, the material is definitely porcelain. If it is absorbed within seconds, the new limbs are made of ceramic. Ceramic is porous, porcelain is not. Do not make this test on a sealed surface, for a good matt sealer will keep the water from being absorbed by the ceramic.

If the parts do not pass these tests, do *not* be timid about taking them back. Chances are you were charged as much for these very cheap imitation parts as truly fine ones would cost.

1. Standing is a repaired antique doll, 18″ tall. The back of the head is incised "4/0 a, CUNO & OTTO DRESSEL GERMANY." The doll has blue sleep eyes, and an old fifteen-piece composition body. The costume is new but made of old materials.

2. Parian head with shoulder broken.

3. Same head, after repair.

4. Back of repaired parian shoulder head.

5. This old mohair wig, glue encrusted, was so dirty that the color was barely discernible.

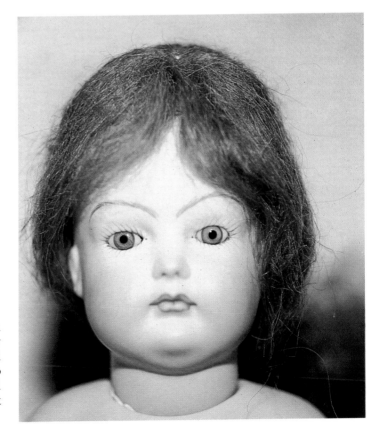

6. The wig was soaked in cold water and Woolite. Only the top layers were smoothed before the wig was glued to this bisque head (marked "XI" under the crown rim at the back).

7. S.F.B.J. 252 Paris head is here lighted from the inside to show the location of nonfired repairs. The opaque area at the rim and the long crack extending from the rim in an arc, almost to the eye, are repairs; dark spots at the outside corners of the eyes are blobs of the plaster that held the eyes in place. A triangular piece was missing at the rim. The long crack, though not separated, was repaired from both the inside and the outside to prevent separation later.

8. The same doll, seen from the outside. Even under magnification no evidence indicates that this head was ever damaged. From the inside, the white mending materials, feathered out onto the old surface, are visible only if one knows where to look for them; otherwise they would not be noticed.

9. "29 Princess 1 Germany" head lighted from the inside. The kiln-fired repairs on this head are almost as transparent as the original porcelain from which the head was made. A piece broken out of the back of the head measured 76mm. around the crown area (where only the faintest shadow is visible in the photograph), and 47mm. at the longest point—down toward the neck. All nicks and chips were filled in after the single piece was fitted into place. Four firings were required to achieve this, the ultimate in restoration. The dark spot in the neck socket and just above are *not* repaired areas, but thick droplets of porcelain formed when the head was poured and drained.

10. The same head as seen from the outside.

11. Both dolls have "Bru Jne 9" incised on the back of the head. The one at left, 22½″ tall, is a replica made by the author. At right is an old Bru Jne 9 measuring 18″ in height.

12. *Below left:*
This replica Bru Jne was poured in a mold having the same incised back-of-the-neck letters as the antique Bru Jne in Plate 13. However, its eyes were cut larger and its features water carved—while the greenware was quite damp—to make it look somewhat different. In this case, the replica doll is shorter than the antique doll.

13. *Below right:*
Antique doll incised "Bru Jne" but without a number. It is 16″ in height.

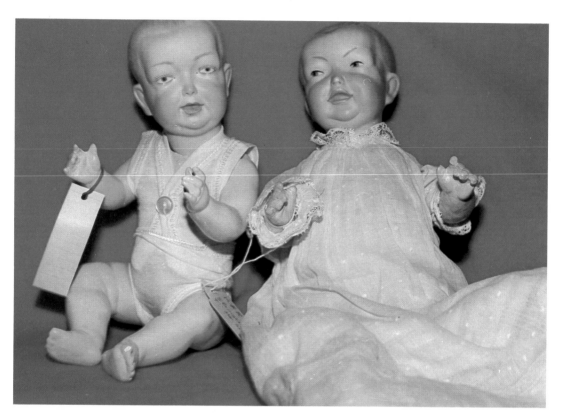

14. Signed "K*R 100." The replica at left measures 10″ around the head. The painted brown eyes look directly forward. The brush-marked hair is reddish brown. Composition body is new. The antique doll at right has a 9″ head circumference and its painted brown eyes look to the right. Reddish brown hair is brush marked. Body is composition.

15. A replica and a genuine antique A 14 T. The antique doll at left is 24″ tall. It has brown stationary glass eyes, pierced ears, and an open mouth showing two rows of *unglazed* porcelain teeth. The wig is original and of dark brown human hair. The fifteen-piece jointed body is of wood and composition. The blue costume is old, but may not be original. The replica doll at right has the same incised mark as the antique one. It is 26″ tall, has brown stationary glass eyes, pierced ears, open mouth, two rows of *glazed* white porcelain teeth, and blonde dynel wig. The fifteen-piece composition jointed body is new. Doll is costumed in pink.

16. The heads of both these dolls are incised "F.G." in a scroll on the back. Here again the replica at left is taller (24½″) than the antique doll at right (22″). Note the differences in the visible parts of the composition—the older is darker than the new composition.

17. The Bye-Lo on the right with the tuft of hair is the original, although the replica at left has an original label on its stomach. With the owner's permission, this label was transferred to the replica doll to serve as an example of how easy it can be to fool a customer.

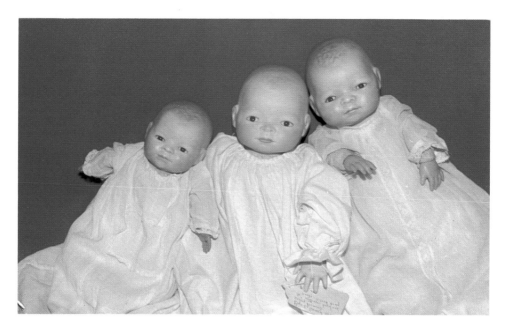

18. Note the hands of these three Bye-Lo's. All the dolls are signed "Grace Storey Putnam." Two are antique, one is a replica. Doll at left has a 10″-circumference head, brown sleep eyes, painted hair, *celluloid hands,* and cloth body. It is believed to be all original. The center doll has a 12″ head, brown stationary glass eyes, painted hair, *porcelain hands,* cloth body, and antique clothes. It is a replica. The largest doll, at right, has a 13″ head, brown sleep eyes, painted hair, *celluloid hands,* and a cloth body. It too is believed to be all original.

AFFIXING NEW LIMBS TO THE BODY

When you're satisfied with the custom-made parts—i.e., that they are made of porcelain, the colors are fired on, the length is right, the shape is as much like the old as it's possible to get, and the circumference around the top of the arm or leg is right (or perhaps only a fraction larger or smaller than the original)—insert one limb into the opening. If it fits precisely, remove it; visually locate the center back, if it's a leg, and make a pencil mark extending about a half-inch down from its top edge. (If arms are being replaced, visually locate the center of the underside of the arm and mark it with a pencil.) Apply glue inside the leather socket, smear it around with a fingertip, wipe off the excess, and insert the limb. Line up the pencil marks with the seam and push the limb into place. Hold it there a few seconds until the glue "catches."

If the limb is a shade smaller than the opening, follow the same procedure but carefully ease the leather against the porcelain. Work at it until the easement is barely noticeable and you feel the glue beginning to hold.

If the limb is a trifle larger than the opening, first dampen the inside of the socket. Try not to get water on the packed sawdust. Dampen the socket edges, scrape at the old glue with a fingernail, and gently pull around the edges of the leather. Try the part again. The combination of water and gentle pulling will usually stretch the leather enough so that you can insert the new limb unless it is very much larger. While the leather is still damp, apply Elmer's Glue and insert the limb as directed in the preceding paragraph.

After the glue has dried and it's safe to handle the doll, clean off the pencil marks.

It is always a good idea to do the repair work within a few days of picking up any new parts. If you stick the parts away somewhere and find, six months later, that they don't fit or that something is wrong with them, you cannot expect to get either your money back or a replacement.

I will not include a list of the doll artists I know who are talented, honest craftsmen for fear of doing an injustice to the ones I may not know. However, in the list of suppliers, I have included mail-order houses although I do not buy reproduction parts from them myself and therefore cannot vouch for their quality. Being damned with a perfectionist complex, I have always made any necessary replacement parts myself on the theory that if I don't make them, they won't please me: a ridiculous assumption but one I have learned to live with.

12

Taking a Pattern from an Old Body

Kid-leather doll bodies—popular since the first half of the nineteenth century—are still being made by home crafts-people. However, from the doll-related ads that appear in national publications, it is clear that today few people specialize in making these bodies. And, as of this writing, I know of only one company that sells leather bodies, though of course there may be others.

I feel there are two major reasons for this situation. First, very few patterns are available. Men or women who have painstakingly drafted really fine patterns guard them jealously, refusing to share with others the fruits of their talent. The patterns that have been made available to the public—at least in my experience—are very poor. Many years ago I ordered a book allegedly containing twenty *different* body patterns. It was quite costly, but at the time I was desperately searching for good patterns, and the advertisement convinced me that this book was *the* answer to a dollmaker's prayers. When the book arrived, I immediately noted that there were just ten *different* patterns; each one was repeated and given a different identification number, to achieve the promised total. And although the lines seemed—to the eyes of an artist—out of proportion, what did I know? I was a beginner.

The first body I made using one of the patterns in the book was grotesque. What was supposed to be a nicely rounded, shapely derrière looked like two huge knobs attached to spindly legs. I tried another one, and still another. Each one I tried—a French Fashion, a Bru, and a toddler—was grotesque. After tossing the pattern book in the trash, where it belonged, I made a couple of porcelain doll heads, painted them to look like clowns, and attached them to two of the bodies. I put the finished creations in a showcase—strictly for laughs, I thought. To my surprise, they sold within a month. The buyer was still laughing when she carried them out. The third body still hangs by its cloth loops in my basement studio. The special customers I allow into the studio invariably laugh hysterically when they see the grotesque body, no matter how many times they've seen it before. Several have tried to buy it, and one remarked: "If I had that thing hanging in my house, I'd go look at it every time I got the blues." So the book of worthless patterns—worthless, that is, to anyone who wanted lovely doll bodies—paid for itself in the dolls sold, and has proved worth several times its price because of the laughs it has brought me and my customers.

In this chapter, and in Chapter 14, you will learn of the good and bad features of the type of leather available today. Though it does not equal the thin, beautiful skins used in the old days, we must make do with it. The kind most consistently available from suppliers is Cabretta. It is sold only by the skin, not in smaller amounts, and it is quite expensive. One of its worst features—and I believe that is the second major reason why most home seamstresses stay away from this phase of doll restoration—is its "stretchiness": Cabretta stretches to an unbelievable degree *after* it has been cut out unless you take care to stretch it as much as possible *before* you cut into it. (Directions for prestretching are in Chapter 14.) Even if Cabretta has been prestretched, attempting to sew it on a machine not adjusted for leather can cause so many problems that most home seamstresses give up. (This dilemma, and how to cope with it, will also be fully explored in that chapter.)

WARNING: Before you begin the actual work, read the section "Useful Tips" at the end of this chapter.

It is very important that you see—and study—a well-proportioned leather-body pattern and familiarize yourself with the names of the many parts that go into its construction. Ills. 115, 116, 118, 119 and 121 illustrate a pantograph-reduced Bru Jne 9 pattern.

Any reader who bought this replica doll from Dollspart Supply Company's catalog #745, during 1975/76, has a doll I made, one with a body fashioned from the same pattern given here. It is the only one I used on the Bru Jne 9 during its two years of production.

To copy a leather body you will need, in addition to the antique body:

    Scissors (very sharp; otherwise they "chew" and distort the cloth)
    Straight pins—the thinnest, sharpest you can buy
    Soft lead pencil (#2)
    Firmly woven fabric, preferably broadcloth
    Tape measure
    12″ ruler
    Graph paper (size of the squares not important)
    Leather
    Muslin (for the lining)

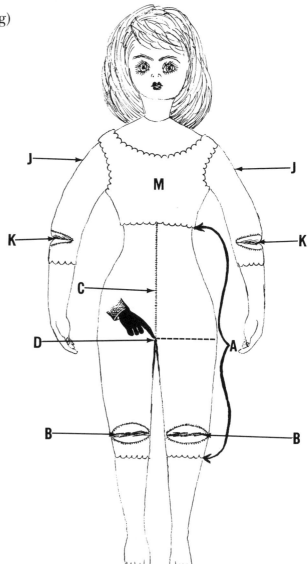

Ills. 113 & 114. Front and rear views of a Bru Jne 9 leather doll body with porcelain hands and feet. (The same identifying letters will be used throughout.) Note that side fronts overlap side backs, and front shoulder bands overlap back ones.

A. Leather torso
B. Leather knee gussets
C. Center-front seam
D. Crotch seam
E. Center-back seam
F. Side-back seam (above hip gusset) and center-back leg seam (below hip gusset)

G. Leather hip gusset
H. Side dart (Ill. 109)
I. Muslin lining
J. Leather sleeve tube
K. Leather elbow gusset
L. Sleeve seam
M. Leather lining-cover

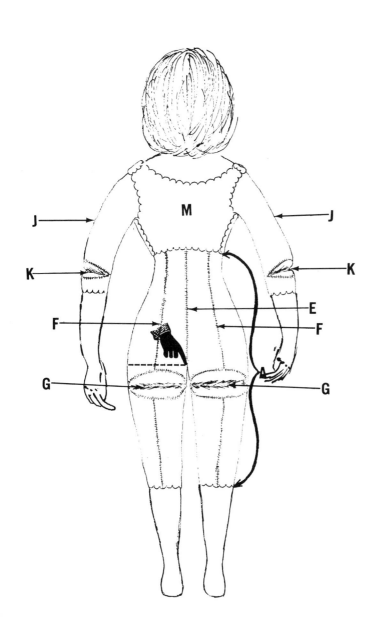

The broadcloth is used to make the original pattern (later this will be traced onto lightweight posterboard or heavyweight paper). Since it is awkward to handle a large piece of fabric—and may be wasteful as well—first cut a square or rectangular piece of the fabric a little larger than the length and width of the doll's torso.

Find the length of the torso* by holding the end of the tape measure at the waistline seam. Measure down to the scallops on that leg (Ill. 113, the area encompassed by the bracket marked A). Add 2″. Then measure the circumference of the hips, from the lowest point of C (the pointing finger and dotted line, Ill. 113), around to the lowest point of E (the pointing finger and dotted line, Ill. 114). Add 2″. The additions are made to ensure your having ample material for the pattern. Cut out the cloth using these dimensions. Follow directions in Ills. 122A, B, and C for the first twelve steps in copying a torso. Ills. 123A, 123B, and 124 show how to "true up" the torso pattern.

The torso is the only piece of a leather body on which the basic lines must not be altered. The *only* adjustment ever made is adapting the lower leg opening to the size of the porcelain leg that goes into it. Remember, only one side of the torso need be copied. In transferring the torso pattern to leather, first one side is marked; then the pattern is turned over (reversed) and marked again. This produces two identical sides—a right and a left.

Taking a pattern off the knee, hip, and elbow gussets (you need only one of each) is simple. Cut a piece of cloth larger than the gusset. Fold it in the center; then push it as far into the gusset crease as it will go. To make sure it stays there while you pin it, shove a piece of stiff cardboard into the crease. Slight pressure exerted against the cardboard will hold the cloth in place while you insert pins all around the gusset seams.

Some gussets are almost square, with gently rounded corners; some are round; some, like those in most of the bodies I make, are oval. Regardless of their shape, however, you can copy them exactly if you pin the pattern fabric as described in the preceding paragraph and then draw lines between the pins with a soft lead pencil. When you remove the pins, the guidelines you have drawn show you precisely where to cut to have an accurate pattern.

After the gussets have been copied, mark their locations on the body pattern. For the knee gusset, measure from the scalloped edge up to the *corner* of the gusset. That is where the slash will be made

*The torso is that part of the body that extends from the waistline—whether high, low, pointed, or normal—to the lower leg, whether that lower leg is porcelain and glued in, or all leather, or all fabric.

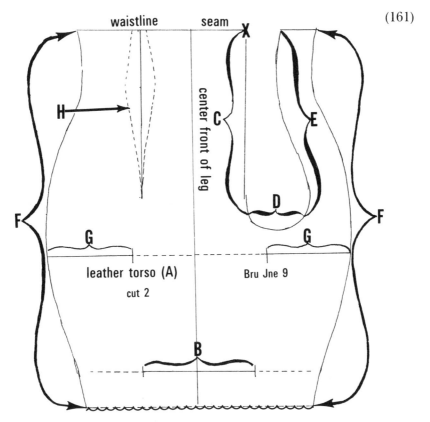

Ill. 115. The right-hand side of a leather Bru Jne 9 torso (shown wrong side up so that you can see the markings). To make the left-hand side, reverse the pattern (Ill. 124). In copying an antique body, you need copy only one side—right or left, whichever comes more naturally to you.

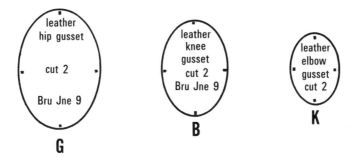

Ill. 116. The three gussets used in this Bru Jne 9 body; *G*, the hip gusset; *B*, the knee gusset; *K*, the elbow gusset. They are always cut in pairs. Before stitching in any gusset, mark it with positioning dots. To locate these, fold gusset in half lengthwise, right sides together. Press extra hard to form a visible crease. Put a dot at each end of crease. Fold gusset the opposite way, crease, and again mark a dot at either end. The four dots mark the top, bottom, and side positions of the gusset.

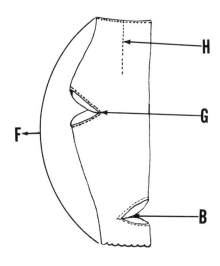

Ill. 117. Side view of assembled torso (⅛″ allowed for seams).

Step 1 Sew knee gussets *B* into torso slits *B* (Ill. 115).

Step 2 Put right sides of torso together. Beginning at *X* (Ill. 115), stitch down *C* (center-front seam), around *D* (crotch), and up *E* (center-back seam) to waistline.

Step 3 Sew both leg seams *(F)* together, *always* beginning at lower scalloped edge (never at waist). This stitching forms center-back leg seams (below gusset) and center-back side seams (above gusset).

Step 4 Sew hip gussets *G* into torso slits *G* (Ill. 115).

Step 5 Stitch side darts. Turn body right side out.

later. For the hip gusset, measure from the scalloped edge up to the *corner* of a hip gusset. Transfer that measurement to the pattern.

Copy the rest of the doll body, "trueing up" each piece on graph paper as you go. Actually, all other parts of a doll body are more or less custom made. Leather arm tubes are made shorter or longer according to the length of the porcelain arms used; their width is enlarged or reduced as necessitated by the circumference of the arms. The muslin lining (Ill. 118) and the leather lining-cover (Ill. 121) must also be custom fitted—after starting, of course, with the basic shapes.

When all parts of the *cloth* pattern have been "trued up" on graph paper, make permanent pattern pieces by tracing each one on lightweight posterboard pieces. These should be stored in an envelope with the pertinent information noted on the outside. For example, here are the envelope notations for my Bru Jne 9 pattern from which the illustrations in this chapter were reduced: "Bru Jne 9. Makes an 18- to 20-inch doll. Pattern drafted 12/5/73." If you are a beginner making your first pattern, you may think such care is unnecessary. However, you won't remain a beginner for long. Soon you'll be copying all the leather doll bodies you own, maybe even borrowing others from friends to copy. Unless you file and label each pattern, you will find it difficult to keep all the parts straight in your mind. A wise precaution that carries the labeling a step further is to ink in, on *each* pattern piece, what it is, how many to cut, of what material, and to which doll it belongs (see Ills. 115, 116, 118, 119, and 121).

After you have copied the pattern on posterboard and stored its envelope in your files, make up a body with the fabric pattern pieces. In fact, it is a good idea to make several bodies; good fabric

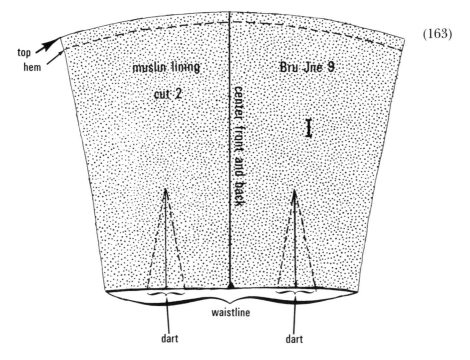

Ill. 118. Basic shape of muslin lining, *I*, for Bru Jne 9. Do not stitch side seams until torso has been completely assembled and turned right side out. Then match center-front waistline notch of lining to center-front torso seam. Measure and mark locations of lining side seams and of darts to right and left of center notch. (Front lining darts should always be deeper than those in back lining.) Follow same procedure in fitting back of lining.

Stitch in darts first. Recheck location of side seams; then stitch them. Next, stitch lining to torso, matching center fronts and center backs, and making sure side seams of lining match up with side dart seams in torso.

Glue porcelain legs into leg openings. When glue has dried, body can be stuffed and the top closed with hand stitching.

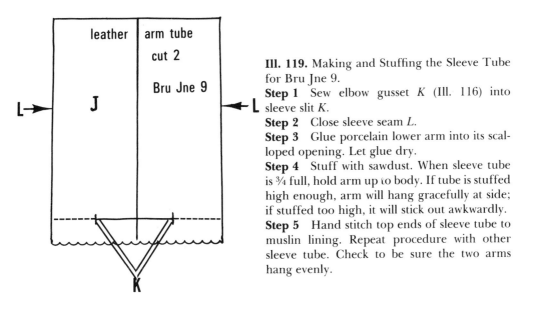

Ill. 119. Making and Stuffing the Sleeve Tube for Bru Jne 9.

Step 1 Sew elbow gusset *K* (Ill. 116) into sleeve slit *K*.

Step 2 Close sleeve seam *L*.

Step 3 Glue porcelain lower arm into its scalloped opening. Let glue dry.

Step 4 Stuff with sawdust. When sleeve tube is ¾ full, hold arm up to body. If tube is stuffed high enough, arm will hang gracefully at side; if stuffed too high, it will stick out awkwardly.

Step 5 Hand stitch top ends of sleeve tube to muslin lining. Repeat procedure with other sleeve tube. Check to be sure the two arms hang evenly.

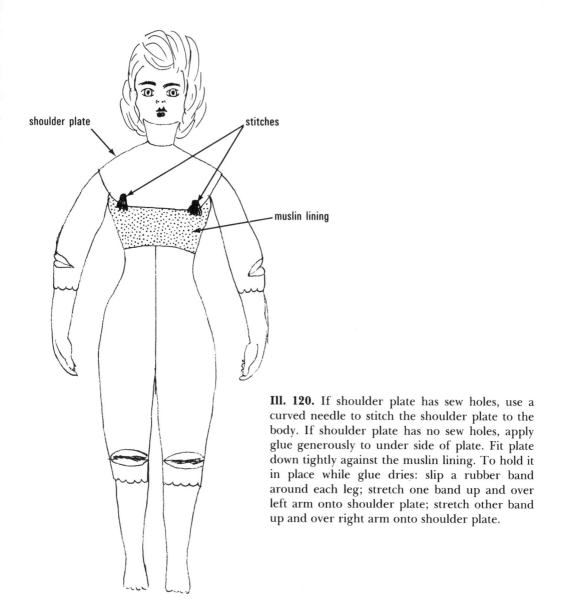

shoulder plate

stitches

muslin lining

Ill. 120. If shoulder plate has sew holes, use a curved needle to stitch the shoulder plate to the body. If shoulder plate has no sew holes, apply glue generously to under side of plate. Fit plate down tightly against the muslin lining. To hold it in place while glue dries: slip a rubber band around each leg; stretch one band up and over left arm onto shoulder plate; stretch other band up and over right arm onto shoulder plate.

Ill. 121. The leather cover for the Bru Jne 9, like the muslin lining, must be custom fitted. Back of cover is glued on first. Arrange it over the lining and fit as shown in Ill. 114. Trim broken lines into scallops. Run glue around edges and smear it into back of leather. Be sure glue extends fully to edges. Press leather smoothly into position on lining, wiping off any glue that seeps out. Let dry. Repeat procedure for front (Ill. 113).

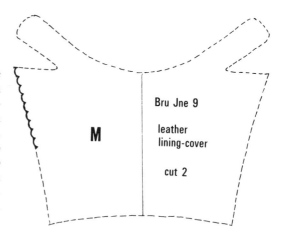

M

Bru Jne 9

leather lining-cover

cut 2

ones can always be used. It is also a good idea to practice with fabric before you cut into the expensive leather.

When the pieces are stitched together, every inward curve, every outward curve, every line must match precisely. If, in stitching, you do not hold an exact seam allowance as specified by the pattern, many things will be wrong with the body, things not evident until it's stuffed. Sometimes these can be corrected by dumping out the sawdust, turning the body wrong side out again, and straightening out the seam and its "partner," if there is a matching seam. Sometimes if you fail to "true up" the edges before you stitch them together, a back seam on the stuffed body may twist around to the side. There is no way to correct this. Or the doll's feet will turn inward or outward, depending on where and how you "goofed up." This cannot be corrected.

I mention these problems to stress how important it is to follow all steps as carefully as possible, particularly in copying a torso. All other parts of the body can be custom made (or fitted), but if you ruin the torso, you've ruined the body.

USEFUL TIPS

Whenever you are instructed to "trim" the cloth, always cut as close to the line of pins as possible. Do not allow extra for seams because the body you are copying stretched when it was made and stuffed, and the replica you are making will also stretch when it is stuffed (unless you use interfacing). In cases where the body size is critical—that is, if you want to make a new body that is exactly the size of the old one—here is a good rule of thumb to follow: after the cloth pattern has been "trued up," reduce all pieces by 1/4".

Always take your time in pushing the pins through the seams. Never stick them *into* the leather. As you work, smooth the cloth in all directions to keep it free of wrinkles. Cut and snip the cloth as much as necessary to make it lie flat. There will be times when the cloth must be held taut (but not stretched) with one hand while you pin with the other. This is strictly a one-person job, so never accept any well-meant offers of help.

I have been asked many times why Dollspart Supply lists my dolls in no specific size, but as "17–19 inches," or "19–20 inches," or "23–24 inches." This is true not only of my leather-bodied dolls, but also of the creations of other doll artists as well. The reason is that we never know what the exact height will be because some bodies stretch more than others as they are stuffed. To be honest with the customers, we list the possible size range. If a body pattern measures, for instance, 19″, we know the doll will be *at least* that tall, but we add 1″ or 2″ more to be on the safe side. It's a rare doll that doesn't end up being taller than the first number listed. Sometimes it may be even taller than the last number!

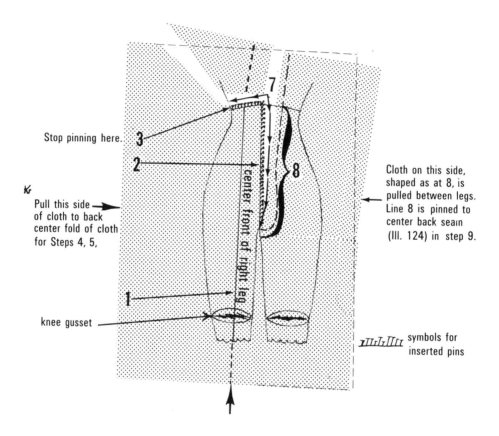

Stop pinning here.

Pull this side of cloth to back center fold of cloth for Steps 4, 5,

center front of right leg

Cloth on this side, shaped as at 8, is pulled between legs. Line 8 is pinned to center back seam (Ill. 124) in step 9.

knee gusset

symbols for inserted pins

Ills. 122 A, B, & C. These three drawings are numbered to illustrate the first twelve steps.

Step 1 Crease cloth in center lengthwise, mark center crease with pencil, then lay pencil-marked line over center front of leg. The squared-off broken lines represent position of cloth before you pin or trim it.

Step 2 Insert pins through center-front seam, beginning at crotch and ending at waist.

Step 3 Starting at center front of waist, insert pins through waistline seam, working toward side dart and stopping *in* its seam line.

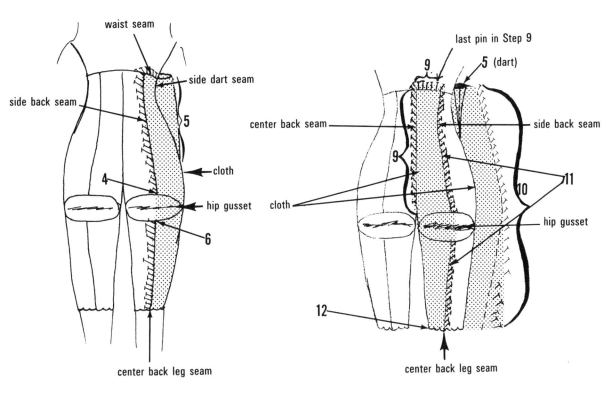

Step 4   Draw fabric taut (but not stretched) around to side-back seam above hip gusset. Starting at 4, pin fabric up side-back seam to waist, then from waist over to side-dart seam. This leaves fold of excess fabric (5) directly over dart seam.

Step 5   Pinch loose fold of fabric together from waistline to widest part of hip to create side dart. Mark its position with pencil, or baste dart. Draw lines between pins or along stitches.

Step 6   Again holding fabric taut (but not stretched), start pinning just below hip gusset on center-back leg seam, and pin through seam down toward scalloped lower edge. (Porcelain leg glued inside prevents pinning all the way.)

Step 7   Before pulling cloth between legs and to back, trim away excess cloth from crotch to waist seam, then above the waistline (Ill. 122A). Trim close to pins.

Step 8   Trim crotch curve D and hip curve E (Ill. 115) to fit between the legs. Long broken lines at 8 (Ill. 122A) indicate contour needed. Repeated snipping and fitting is necessary to make cloth go smoothly through legs and lie flat from crotch up the center-back seam (Ill. 122C).

Step 9   Insert pins through center-back seam from crotch up to waistline, then across waistline toward side-back seam but not yet *in* it. Draw connecting lines between pins. Trim excess cloth near pins (Ill. 122C).

Step 10   Remove pins from side-back seam and center-back leg seam (Ill. 122C). This is the cloth brought around from front and pinned in Steps 4 and 6.

Step 11   Smooth cloth from center-back seam over to side-back seam, pinning through seam from waistline down to hip gusset. Begin pinning again in center-back leg seam below hip gusset. Pin down to lower edge of leg (Ill. 122C). Draw lines between pins.

Step 12   Draw line around lower edge of leg (Ill. 122C). Remove all pins. Trim cloth along lines drawn. The torso pattern is now ready to "true-up." (See Ills. 123A & B and Ill. 124.)

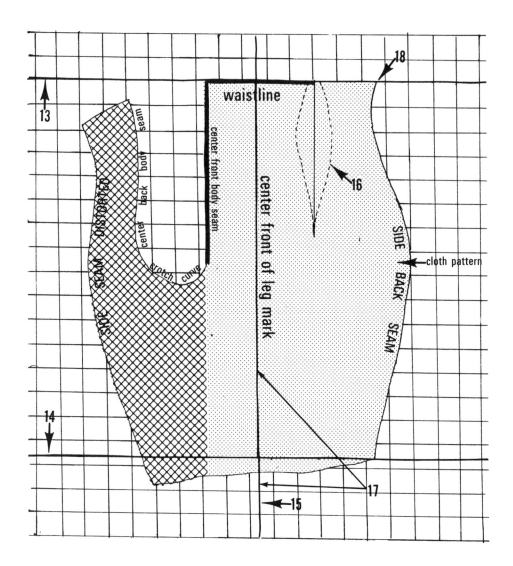

Ills. 123 A & B. These two drawings are keyed to Step 13 through Step 21. Note the distortion on left side of cloth pattern in 123A. Side-back and center-back seams will be deformed, to some extent, from any carelessness in snipping and fitting the cloth at the point where it goes between the legs and up the back (Step 8).

Step 13   Draw straight line across top of graph paper.

Step 14   Measure from *side* waistline of body down over side dart to lower scalloped edge. Transfer measurement to graph paper. If it was 9″, for example, measure 9″ down from top line and make second line.

Step 15   Find center of graph paper by measuring, or fold it in half, crease, open, and mark crease line with pencil.

Step 16   If side dart was basted together, open it.

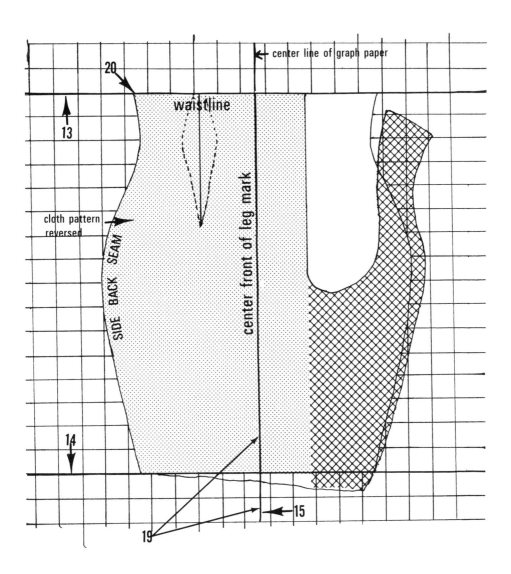

Step 17 Lay center front of leg mark (made on cloth pattern in Step 1 of Ill. 122A) on top of center line on graph paper, aligning waistline of cloth pattern with top line of graph paper. Center-front body seam must always be straight, down to the point where crotch curve begins. Mark seam (heavy black line) using cloth pattern as guide. Then mark straight waistline (heavy black line) from center-front body seam over to right side of cloth pattern, using upper graph line as guide.

Step 18 Draw side-back seam (along right side of cloth pattern) down to bottom line, then across, using that line to "true-up" lower leg. Draw left side of side-back seam along left edge of cloth pattern up to top line. Finish pattern by drawing waistline, center back, and crotch curve, following lines of cloth pattern. If left side of cloth is distorted, remove pattern and proceed to Step 19.

Step 19 Reverse cloth pattern. Lay center front of leg mark on top of center line on graph paper, aligning waistline of cloth pattern to top line on graph paper.

Step 20 Draw side-back seam down to line 14 (bottom line).

Step 21 Remove cloth pattern. The right and left side-back seam lines (18 and 20) are now identical. The width of pattern at waistline and lower leg are almost identical.

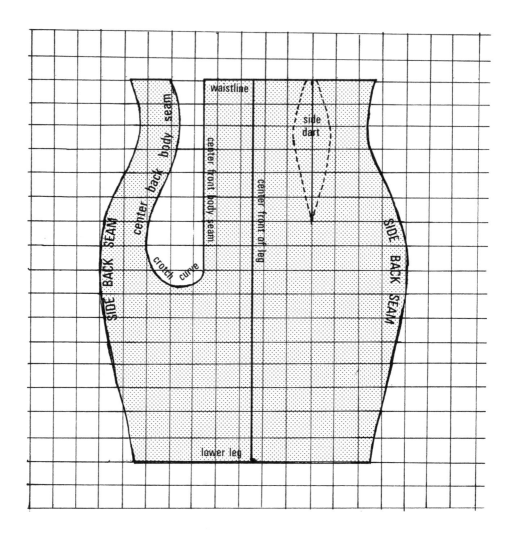

Ill. 124. Last two steps are explained by this drawing.

Step 22 Two methods may be used to draw crotch curve and center-back body seam. (1) Freehand, start crotch curve at end of center-front body seam and make curve of center-back body seam conform with curve of side-back seam, using pattern as guide. (2) Measure across body panel, beginning at waistline, and transfer mark to paper pattern. Drop down ½" on body, measure, and transfer to pattern; continue until crotch curve begins. It (crotch curve) must be drawn freehand.

Step 23 If the porcelain legs have same top circumference as those on body you copied, no adjustment need be made on lower leg line; if legs are different, measure circumference, then extend or reduce line 14 to accommodate them. Allow extra for seams.

13

Using a
Pantograph

Although a pantograph is the most valuable tool a pattern designer can own, it is priced within the range of a limited budget. Once a pattern is made, the pantograph enables you to copy the original pattern in many different sizes.

This indispensable instrument has four arms fastened together by movable joints so that it can travel freely over a pattern. It is so constructed that designs can be mechanically enlarged or reduced according to your needs. Pantographs are made in a variety of sizes and for many different types of work, but the one shown in Ill. 125A is ideally suited for doll pattern work. My wooden pantograph, made in West Germany and bought in an office supply store some years ago, is completely satisfactory. It would not be practical to buy a larger, more expensive one, but it is also not sensible to buy the cheapest. Buy a good one, for it represents a lifetime purchase and can be used in many other projects. Not only can you enlarge any pattern given in this chapter, but if you own the Colemans' *Collector's Book of Dolls' Clothes,* your pantograph can be used to enlarge the clothing patterns in that volume as well. (I mention this

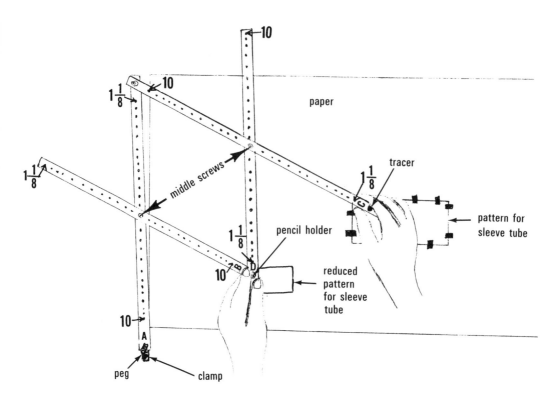

Ill. 125 A. Using a Pantograph. See description in text.

particular book because it is the only one I have found useful, though of course there may be other books where the patterns fit accurately.)

HOW TO USE THE PANTOGRAPH

The pantograph's metal clamp-and-peg (all one piece) is screwed to the left side of the work table. Your working surface should be no less than 36″ by 24″ in size. The hole in the wood at Side A (see Ill. 125A) of the pantograph fits over the metal peg, to hold the pantograph in place while it is in use. The tool can be lifted free of the peg for fast adjustments. Two of the arms measure 17⅞″; the other two measure 19¾″. Each arm has twenty-five holes, numbered from 1⅛ to 10.

The work table in Ill. 125A is covered with white paper, available by the roll. Regular typing paper can also be used if it is taped securely at strategic locations on top of the work surface. In this illustration a sleeve tube pattern was used; it is at the right under the hand holding the tracer. The left hand grips the pencil holder. The finished pattern reduction is depicted under the left hand.

Keep your eyes on the point of the tracer while your right hand guides it over the lines of the pattern. At the same time, exert slight pressure on the pencil holder with the left hand. Never *look* to see what the left hand is doing. If your hands are not steady in guiding the tracer and pencil holder, the image produced by the left hand will be shaky, but the lines can be firmed up by using rulers, templates, french curves, or simply by going over the lines already there. Any person who can pat his head with one hand and rub his belly with the other should have no problem in using the pantograph. Others may find the pantograph awkward to use at first, but not to a degree that cannot be overcome with practice.

Ill. 125A shows the position of the tracer and pencil holder in *reduction work*. For enlargement work they are reversed. Chances are, when you buy a pantograph, it will already be set for enlargements. If not, unscrew the tops and switch the tracer from *C* (under the right hand) to the holes at the junction of *B* and *D* (under the left hand); switch the pencil holder from the junction of *B* and *D* over to hole *C*. Because the pencil holder is now fitted through one hole instead of two (as it was where *B* and *D* overlapped), it is necessary to use the metal spacer that comes with the instrument. Stick the shank of the holder up through the hole, drop the spacer on top of the shank, and add the holding screw. Tighten securely.

The pantograph comes with a lead already inserted in the holder, plus a few extra ones; however, instructions for adjusting, removing, or replacing lead are nonexistent. In fact, the instructions that came with mine totaled six lines and were printed in five different languages. The leads, only $^{15}/_{16}''$ long when new, quickly wear down. A lead needs constant lowering for efficient operation. This is done by unscrewing the knurled/threaded nut *under* the *C* arm while the pantograph is on its peg and the tracer is resting on the work surface. When the lead drops down and touches the table, tighten the nut.

To insert a new lead, loosen the nut, let the short piece drop out, and insert the new one in its place.

To prepare the pantograph for an enlargement of the Bru Jne 8 pattern, place the two middle screws in the #2 hole. Then put the pattern under the tracer operated by the left hand, and the blank paper under the pencil holder operated by the right hand. When both the pattern piece and the paper are lined up, tape them in position so that they will not slip while you are working. Use drafting tape (indicated by the black rectangles on the illustration).

Enlarge the torso first. When that is finished—including all its markings—cut it out, fold it in half, and check to see that sides *F*

(Ill. 115) are identical. Then check the length. It should measure 8⅝″. The widest point of the hip curve should be 7¹¹⁄₁₆″. If your enlarged Bru Jne 8 torso pattern fits these measurements, you're in business. If not—if the pattern is lopsided or otherwise out of proportion—check the middle screws again. Both must be set in the #2 hole.

As progression is made from pattern to pattern, I will give directions for setting the middle screws for enlargements of each one, along with the size of the body that the enlargement will produce. Once the tracer and pencil holder are in place for enlargements, they need never be changed. It is a good idea, though, to check all the screws occasionally, for they tend to loosen a bit over even a brief period.

14

Working with Leather

Once upon a time—before the advent of plastics—the uses of leather were multitudinous. It was so much a part of our daily lives that we all took it for granted, not appreciating its beauty, versatility, and durability. Today I jealously hoard all the old leather items I can find, particularly the long, thin kid gloves. Sometimes, if I'm lucky, I accumulate enough matching pairs to create a fine replica of an antique leather doll body. But most of the time I have to rely on the leather that is available commercially.

Catalogs list it as "glove leather Cabretta skins." In 1978 it was selling at $2.00 per square foot, a cost that sounds high and is inflated, considering that Cabretta is a by-product from animals that are used mostly for food, and it is a split leather. I often suspect Cabretta is the one called a "fifth split," which means just what the words imply. The first split, Skiver, is used for book binding and similar purposes where appearance is more important than strength. The second cut is the true skin and the most valuable. The third cut is the main or No. 1 split; the fourth, the extra or No. 2 split, and so on down the line. The fifth split has been described as of uneven thickness (which is certainly true of the skin we dollmakers receive), and of a spongy texture; it is "used in cheap gloves and shoe tongues." Cabretta also contains holes and wrinkles, and has a rough texture and various other defects that are included in the "square-foot" price.

On the plus side, Cabretta does make beautiful doll bodies if you learn to work with its peculiarities. Also, the cost is not so prohibitive as it seems at first. Once you have stretched the skin properly, and dried it, you will have a much larger, thinner, and better skin than you received from the supplier. And one skin, the smallest amount you can buy, will furnish enough leather to last from one to five years, depending on how actively you collect and restore bodyless dolls.

A question debated among bodymakers is whether leather has a straight and a bias grain as fabric does. Most certainly leather has a grain, natural or embossed, but this must not be confused with the terms *straight* and *bias* as applied to woven materials. Every skin is different, and each has its thick and thin areas. Each also has areas with fine-grain texture as well as those with coarse-grain texture. Too, every skin has been damaged in some way before it reaches us—not by the supplier, but in the tanning and dyeing process. However, I have never found—or used—a skin with a so-called straight and bias grain.

There has been altogether too much mystery surrounding the making of leather bodies. The few experienced makers of such bodies whom I have met (at doll shows, conventions, and similar functions) seem to take a perverse pleasure in discouraging would-be students of the craft. So it's small wonder a defeatist attitude is so prevalent about this phase of doll work. Students take one look at an oval gusset of leather, and when told it must be stitched into a straight slit (gash) in the leather, they back off from trying. In print, the procedure admittedly seems formidable. In actuality, it is very easy.

If you can handle a needle and thread for basting; if you can operate a sewing machine, whether it's the latest model or an old treadle; if you have a bit of patience—you will soon be making lovely doll bodies. You will ruin some. Hang them up where everyone can see them. Have a few laughs over them. But let them serve as a reminder not to make the same mistake(s) twice.

HOW TO STRETCH A CABRETTA SKIN

You will need a 4″ × 8″ × ½″ plywood panel (or its equivalent), a good supply of thumbtacks, several heavy bath towels, and an aide. One person can work alone, but the job is much easier with a helper.

1. Soak the towels in water and wring them out as dry as possible.
2. Lay the skin flat on the board, wrong side up, and spread damp towels on the skin until its surface is covered.
3. Jelly-roll the leather and towels; then fold in the edges until the bundle is as small as you can get it. Wrap in another damp towel.
4. Cover the bundle with plastic, or put it in a plastic bag, and let it set overnight.
5. Remove the towels in the morning. The leather will be dampened through and through, and will be extremely pliable.
6. If you have a helper, now's the time to put him to work. Face each other with the leather between you. Each of you must grasp an end of the leather with both hands, and pull and flex it. Each shifts his grasp little by little until the skin has made a full circle between you. As the leather constantly is shifted in position, make sure that each part gets a thorough pulling and flexing. If you don't have a helper, go to step 7.
7. Fasten the leather to the board, pulling and stretching it in all directions as you thumbtack it around the edge. In this step, as in step 6, a much better job can be done if two people work together.

Put the board where it can remain undisturbed while the skin air dries. This may take as long as a week, but never try to speed up the process by exposing the leather to extreme heat.

After the skin is dry, remove it from the board and examine the *right* side for bad places—holes, skinned areas, damage of any kind. Then, on the *wrong* side, with a felt-tip marker, put a red circle around each damaged area. This precaution will save much time later when you mark out the pattern pieces. The red circles will warn you of the damaged areas to be avoided.

MARKING PATTERN PIECES ON LEATHER

I use two methods for marking around the body pattern pieces, depending on whether I'm terribly rushed or just moderately busy. If I'm rushed I use talcum powder; if not, I use my most reliable marker: an F-29 fine pt. Bic in *red*. It never bleeds through to the right side of the leather as some other markers do. Needless to say, it is downright discouraging to finish a leather body, stuff it, assemble the head, shoulder plate, arms, and legs, only to find—

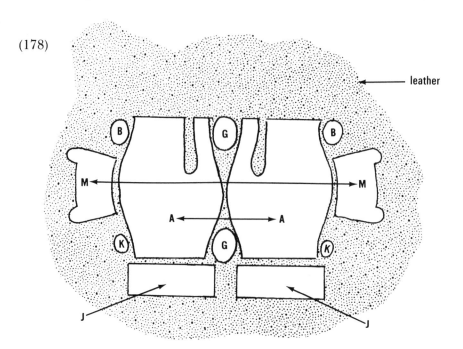

Ill. 125 B. Only six pattern pieces are used in this layout: *A* is the torso, the only pattern piece that must be reversed. Mark one side, reverse the torso, and mark the other; this will give right and left legs, hips, and waist. *B* is the knee gusset. *G* is the hip gusset. *J* is the sleeve tube. *K* is the elbow gusset. *M* is the lining cover.

WARNING: These pattern pieces were not reduced by a pantograph—they can *not* be enlarged to make a body.

perhaps a week later—ugly stains on the body caused by having used the wrong kind of marker.

Always mark the torso first. Since it is the largest of the pattern pieces that have to be cut in pairs, locate a spot in the leather where the grain texture is fine (as opposed to coarse). If you have cut many bodies from one skin and the coarse texture is all that's left, then match it up the same as you would the fine. Most of the coarse grain will disappear when the body is stuffed. Ill. 125B shows the layout of a Bru Jne 8 body. WARNING: A pantograph was not used to reduce these pattern pieces. This is not an actual pattern; therefore it cannot be enlarged and used. The lines in Ill. 125B are solid for illustrative purposes only. When you mark pattern pieces on leather, use broken or dotted lines. Pressing hard enough to draw solid lines will distort the leather; making broken lines or dots by using your pen with a mark-lift, mark-lift motion will not.

If you want to try marking the body with talcum powder, follow the general layout shown in Ill. 125B; however, as each piece is powdered, it must be cut out before marking the next one. Hold the torso pattern firmly against the wrong side of the leather. Generously coat the edge of a large powder puff with talcum. Run its edge all around the pattern edges, renewing the powder as often as necessary. This is not only the fastest method one can use; it is also the most accurate. There is never a problem of distortion when this method is used.

It may seem awkward to cut out each piece as it's marked, but each piece must be cut out separately anyway, regardless of which method is used.

SCISSORS, THREAD, NEEDLES, AND OTHER NECESSITIES

Sharp scissors are an absolute necessity in cutting out leather pattern pieces. The duller the scissors, the more distortion there will be because of their "chewing" action.

Electric scissors are best. Their cutting action creates very little distortion of the leather. Their only drawback is that you have to get used to working with them. Electric scissors cut much faster than regular ones, and this is a case when speed is not an advantage. Accuracy is the goal to strive for.

Any good sewing thread can be used for basting; however, most of it is inclined to tangle. Keep a supply of beeswax handy, to solve the tangling problems. (Beeswax can be found in most sewing departments.) When you cut off a length of basting thread, pull its entire length over the beeswax at least four times. This will not only prevent those aggravating tangles, but also strengthen the thread. For permanent stitching on the sewing machine, I highly recommend J & P Coats Dual Duty Plus, a mercerized cotton-covered polyester.

The type of needle used in basting leather is very important, and it is sometimes difficult to find unless you live in a large city. Look for "glover's needles" in sewing departments or fabric shops. If they are unavailable there, visit a Tandy Leather Store in your vicinity. What makes glover's needles different from regulars? Regulars are round and come to a sharp point. Glover's needles, above their sharp points, are three-sided. Regular needles small enough for basting leather are likely to break and need frequent replacement. Because of their unique shape, glover's needles penetrate the leather and slide easily through the double layers.

Force yourself to use a thimble. Get one that fits comfortably and use it to push the needle through the leather; otherwise you'll suffer from sore fingers before you've completed your first leather body.

Never use an overcasting stitch in basting. Many seamstresses hold raw edges together by taking slanted stitches over the two edges.

This is fine on fabrics, but bad on leather because of the problems created later, when you slide the leather under the presser foot and start sewing. The right sides of the leather are quite slippery, and instead of remaining aligned as they were when you overcast them together, the edges will roll and slide away from each other as you sew on the machine.

For lack of a better term, I refer to the basting stitch I use as a "stab stitch" because that describes it. With the edges of the leather aligned, "stab" the needle straight down through both layers and pull the thread through; straighten the edges again (always, before each stitch), then stab the needle through both layers again and pull the thread through. Repeat—completely around the part being basted. The smaller the stab stitches, the more securely they hold the edges together for machine stitching. This basting looks like a running stitch and, in fact, that's what it is. The only difference is that in basting leather you take one stitch at a time; in fabric, several. When you are ready to stitch the seam permanently, the leather edges *stay* together. They cannot roll or slide away from each other; so the extra time spent in basting with the stab stitch is not wasted.

Always keep basting stitches as near the *edge* of the leather as possible. All patterns given in this chapter were drafted so that the right edge of the presser foot (as you face it) can serve as a guide for the seam allowance (approximately ⅛"). All basting stitches, therefore, should be kept between the edge of the leather and the seam allowance.

If you followed the instructions on stretching skins, and the body or bodies that you have made still stretched more than you like, apply iron-on interfacing—the thinnest you can buy—to the wrong side of the leather. Follow the same procedure as if applying it to fabric (never use a steam iron setting). First, place all pattern pieces together as you plan on marking them out (see Ill. 125B). Take into consideration the fact that all body pattern pieces are cut in pairs; therefore, allow double the actual area the pieces take up. Cut out that much leather in one piece, apply the interfacing, and let it cool. Then draw around, mark, and cut out all pieces. In this case, use a soft lead pencil for marking, but do not put too much pressure on it. The interfacing will keep the pressure of the pencil from stretching the leather.

GET ACQUAINTED
WITH YOUR SEWING MACHINE

There is no earthly reason why women should not recognize the importance of ordinary, preventive maintenance of their sewing machines and be able to make simple adjustments on them. Too many women learn only how to turn on the machine and sew with it; they throw up their hands in despair when something goes wrong, having often been told that women are not mechanically inclined. That's a lot of hogwash. The mechanism of a sewing machine is basically very simple. Ordinary straight stitching has changed little since the days of the old treadle machines. Learn to do the simple things included in this chapter and you will save yourself a lot of headaches, money, and time wasted in waiting for the service man to "fix" your machine.

First, get out the instruction book and really study it, particularly the diagram or picture identifying the parts of your machine. You don't need to memorize the parts—those you will be concerned with in making adjustments can always be looked up; you *do* need to follow to the letter the instructions on cleaning and oiling the machine. The moving metal parts cannot work efficiently unless they are kept clean and well oiled. So the first thing to do preparatory to making a leather body is to clean and oil the machine. Don't neglect the bobbin mechanism. Take it apart and clean and oil it; then wipe off any excess oil with a lintfree cloth. Be sure to brush away all lint and thread fragments from the underside of the needle plate, the feed dog—all parts under the needle plate.

Has your machine ever "locked up"? When this happens, the flywheel either turns heavily or jams completely so that you cannot remove the article you were sewing on, much less get the machine to function. When you finally get a repairman, he is likely to tote the machine away to his shop, and later either you get an expensive repair bill for an unnecessary adjustment (that wasn't made but sounds important enough to justify the charges), or you find yourself being talked into buying a new machine. The only thing wrong may have been a piece of loose thread or a small ball of lint caught between the shuttle and the race. Such a little thing to start such a long chain of events, always resulting in needless dollars spent.

Ready two pieces of scrap leather for practice use during the machine adjustments. But, before doing *any* adjustments, make notes of all the settings on your machine prior to changing them as follows:

1. Attach a straight-stitch presser foot.
2. If the machine has a rotating needle plate, position it for straight stitching.
3. Set the stitch-length regulating knob on 3 or 4, which-ever setting gives the best results on two thicknesses of

leather. This, of necessity, you must try out. Rules that apply to fabric—such as "X" number of stitches per inch—do not apply to leather. Because of its nature, leather does not feed through as smoothly as woven materials. On fabric, a No. 4 setting is normally a machine basting stitch; on leather, it is sometimes the only stitch that permits the leather to feed properly.

4. The pressure on the leather is controlled by opening the face plate and adjusting the built-in presser-foot gauge knob. This is at the top of the face plate opening, and can be identified by the numbers stamped on it. Try a No. 7 setting first. Take a few stitches around a sharp corner, as you would have to do if you were stitching a gusset in. If the pressure seems too heavy, back the gauge to 6—or 5—or whatever position gives the best results. What you are adjusting for here is to get just enough pressure between the presser foot and the feed dog to feed the leather smoothly. If the pressure is too heavy, the feed dog may "chew" a hole in the leather; if too light, the stitches may be uneven.

Always be sure the presser foot is down *before making any adjustments to the upper-thread tension knob.* This is a most important rule to remember. Unless the presser foot is down, turning the knob all day will not change the tension of the upper (needle) thread.

5. When the tensions of the needle thread and the bobbin thread are nearly equal, the stitches on both sides of the leather will appear the same. This means that the two threads are locked in the center of the thicknesses of leather (Ill. 126A). The machine must be adjusted for this; otherwise, as the doll body is tightly packed with sawdust, the stitches will pop open. If the needle thread tension is too tight, the needle thread will lie flat, on top of the leather, and the bobbin thread will be pulled to the upper surface, where it will be visible in small knots (Ill. 126B). In this case, loosen the needle thread tension by turning the upper tension knob to a lower number.

   If the needle thread tension is too loose, the thread will lie flat but small knots will be visible on the underside of the leather (Ill. 126C). Then you must turn the tension knob to a higher number. Experiment with various tension settings until the stitches on your scrap leather are like those in Ill. 126A.

6. Insert a new #9 needle, or its equivalent. Contrary to what most servicemen will tell you, you do not need a heavy needle to sew soft Cabretta leather. In fact, I have never used the recommended needle size, even for regular sewing (#11).

7. Set your machine for its slowest speed.

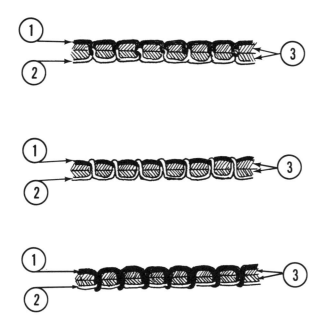

Ills. 126 A, B, & C. These three drawings show normal stitch tension and two adjustments. In all the drawings, the number 1 identifies the needle thread; the number 2 is the bobbin thread; and number 3 identifies the two layers of leather. DO NOT ATTEMPT ANY ADJUSTMENT OF THE UPPER TENSION WITHOUT LOWERING PRESSER FOOT.

If needle thread and bobbin thread tensions are nearly equal, the stitches on both sides of the leather will look alike because the two threads are locked in the center of the two layers of leather, as in A. In second drawing (B) needle thread tension is too tight. Needle thread lies on top of leather and bobbin thread has been pulled upward to the top surface. To correct this, turn tension knob to a lower number.

When needle thread tension is too loose, as in C, needle thread is pulled downward so that it lies flat on bottom layer of leather. To correct, turn tension knob to a higher number.

Cut a piece of leather from the edge of a skin where the grain is too coarse for use anywhere else. Then cut out an oval gusset. Cut a straight slit in the leather and, following the basting and stitching directions given under one of the following patterns, practice sewing a gusset into the slit.

If you have no trouble accomplishing this, then you are probably ready to make your first leather body. But if you have any problems, make your first body of cloth. Don't cut into your leather until you are confident of what you are doing.

15

Leather Body Patterns - Bru

It is possible—but highly improbable—that you possess a Bru Jne 8 antique head, shoulder plate, arms, and legs, but no body. It is more likely that you have acquired a Bru Jne 8 damaged head and nothing else. Thus, you would either have to locate the old parts or buy new reproduction parts. The only alternative would be to attach any kind of arms and legs you happen to have stashed away, whether they were originally on a German doll, a parian, or some other type. Without all the porcelain parts, there is no point in making this body. This applies not only to the Bru Jne 8 pattern that follows, but to the Bru Jne 9 as well.

Whether you are a skilled seamstress or a beginner, it is important that you understand the sewing terms as I use them in connection with the making of bodies. The following list defines them:

Back Stitch: A hand stitch used for strength. It comes closer to duplicating machine stitching than any other hand stitch. It is used in the corners of all gussets (each side of the corner). The only difficult part of machine stitching a gusset in place is at the corners where the gusset must be straightened out on the bed of the machine. This causes the leather (to the left of the presser foot) to form thick folds, which, in turn, would force the corners of the gusset out of alignment (edges not even) if back stitching were not used to secure them.

Bodkin: A blunt needle used to pass cording or heavy string through a casing (Chapter 14).

Clip: A short snip, in the seam allowance about halfway between the edge of the leather and the stitched seam; also used in reference to the extension of a slit to allow smooth fitting of a gusset (matching dots without having to "ease" the leather to do so).

Casing: Like a hem, but through which cording or wire is run.

Dart: A stitched fold, tapered at one or both ends, used in a leather body for contouring or custom fitting.

Ease: To fit together unequal seam lengths in order to accomplish a certain shape—like Bye-Lo bodies (Chapter 14). Leather is rarely "eased" together. To do so would create problems later—problems that cannot be rectified.

Gusset: A small oval, rectangle with rounded corners, or a circle set into a slash or seam to give humanlike appearance to joints in a fabric or leather body.

Layout: Diagram showing how to place pattern pieces most effectively for marking and cutting.

Lining: That part of a leather doll body made of cloth.

Notch: A tiny V-shaped mark or cut along seam edges to indicate where seams are to be matched.

Seam Allowance: The amount of fabric that extends beyond the stitching line.

Shaping Material (optional): Use lightweight commercial products such as Veriform-soft, Siri-soft, Capri soft, lightweight Interlon, Pellon and Keyback, Pelomite, Keybak Hot Iron. Apply the shaping material of your choice to the wrong side of the leather to keep it from stretching. Application is made before the pattern pieces are marked out. If it cannot be ironed onto the leather, buy Stitch Witchery yardage and use it between the leather and the shaping material. Iron it in place.

Slash: To cut into leather; a cut in the leather area that is longer than a clip or snip.

Trim: To cut away excess leather (or fabric) in seam allowance after stitching on the machine.

Stab-stitch Basting: The needle is pushed *straight down* through two layers of leather, the thread is pulled through, the needle is pushed *straight up* through two layers of leather in an ongoing seam. Each stitch should be about ⅛" long.

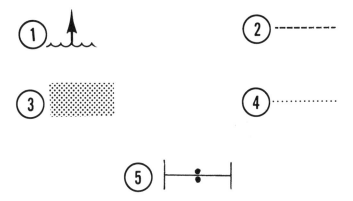

Ill. 127 A. What does it mean? Wavy line (1) accompanied by an arrow means that the edge to which arrow points should be scalloped, after adjustments are made but before basting. Medium-heavy broken line (2), used with symbol numbered 5, is guideline to follow when it is necessary to snip beyond the solid lines indicating the insertion of gussets. Shaded darts (3) are stitched in *as marked* on pattern. Unshaded darts are to be customized on each body, according to how leather stretches. Light dotted lines (4) need not be marked on all body pieces. They indicate center of a piece, if it is to be matched to another. In this chapter, the symbol marked 5 here always indicates position of a gusset. The dots in the center are to be matched to gusset-positioning dots.

Instructions for making a 23" to 24" Bru Jne 8 body are given first because sewing gussets into a large body is much easier than sewing them into a smaller one.

Ills. 134, 135, 136, and 137 provide a total of eight pattern pieces. Enlarge each of them. Set the middle screws on the pantograph at #2. As each piece is enlarged, transfer the gusset locations, darts, and other pertinent markings from the pattern piece you are copying. *Do not transfer the gusset-positioning dots.* They will only confuse you later.

Enlarge the torso first. Check its measurements. The length and width should be the same as those given in Ill. 134. Correct measurements are listed on each pattern piece. Be sure they coincide with the measurements of your enlargements.

If you have the porcelain parts, measure the circumference of the top of one leg (both will be the same) and adjust the right and the left torso pattern accordingly at line 8, Ill. 134.

Now measure the arm circumference and adjust the ends of pieces *J* (Ill. 136) to conform to that measurement.

Don't forget to add a ⅛" seam allowance to both sides of each piece that is adjusted.

CUTTING OUT THE BODY

Parts *A, B, G, J, K,* and *M* (Ills. 134, 135, 136, and 137) are cut of leather. They are also cut in pairs that must be identical, with the exception of *A,* the torso. It is the *only* pattern piece that must be *reversed* when the body is cut out. If it is not, you'll have either two right or two left legs. Otherwise they, too, are identical. Scallop the leg and arm edges where the porcelain limbs will later be glued in.

When the body is cut out, these six pieces will total twelve. There are six pieces to the right side of the body and six pieces to the left side of the body. When assembled, they comprise the entire torso that, on a Bru, encompasses the area from the knee to slightly above the waistline.

Note that the muslin lining, *I,* has the front and back marked as such. Obviously they have different shapes. This is because the Bru Jne 8 shoulder plate—in front—has definite projecting breasts; therefore, a separate pattern was drafted to accommodate them.

All pairs must be "trued up." This is another way of saying they must be identical, and if they are not, we must make them so.

Ill. 127B explains how this is done to a torso after it is cut out. All pairs are trued up the same way; otherwise the body is likely to have strange-looking lumps and bulges after it's stuffed with sawdust.

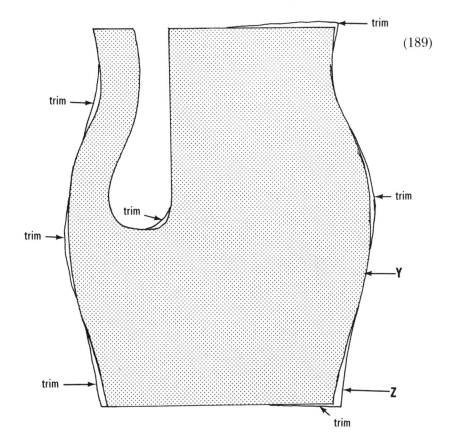

Ill. 127 B. Trueing-Up a Torso

Y is the right torso; *Z* is the left torso. *Y* and *Z* must match precisely. After torsos are cut out, put right (white) sides together, line them up, smooth out, and check to be sure they are identical. If any part of *Z* projects beyond *Y*, as shown here, trim off excess. Turn over and do same to other side. Use this procedure to true up all *parts* of a leather doll body.

Baste all parts together before machine-stitching them. When you've learned to handle leather, the only basting you need to continue doing is the small stab stitches holding the gussets in place.

Positioning dots on the gussets are marked *after* the gussets are cut out and trued. Fold each gusset lengthwise, right sides together. Crease the ends by exerting pressure with your fingernail. Place a dot at each end of the crease. Then, with the right sides still together but matching the dots you just marked, fold the gusset in half sidewise; crease the ends and mark a dot at each end. You now have four positioning dots. Their numbers will correspond to those used on the torso at points of insertion.

WARNING: Never crease the gusset by folding, then *pushing* the ends in opposite directions. This will stretch the leather beyond salvaging.

ASSEMBLING THE BODY

If you have never worked with leather before, it is advisable to make your first body of firmly woven cloth or muslin that has been interfaced to prevent "frazzling." Whichever you use, the steps in the assembly are the same.

Step 1   Baste the knee gussets in, following the instructions in Ills. 128 through 133. Machine stitch them in place.

Step 2   With right sides of the torso together, begin at 6 (Ill. 134) to baste the center front, the crotch, and the center-back seam together, ending at 7. Machine stitch. Clip the crotch curve.

Step 3   With right sides of the torso together, start at 8 and baste seam *F* up through 9, making sure the gusset lines match at points 10 and 12. Machine stitch. Repeat on the other leg.

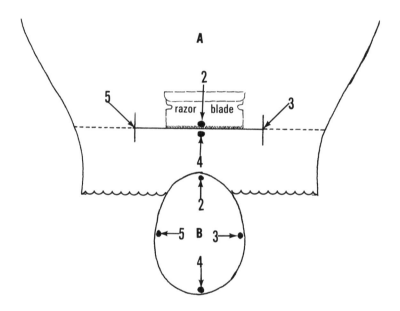

Ill. 128. Sewing a Gusset—Step 1. (*Do not use Ills. 128–133 as patterns.*)

Use a new single-edged razor blade to make the initial cut. Lay blade flat, as shown here, lining its edge up with the line between 3 and 5. Raise blade upright, making sure its sharp edge stays *on* the line. Push it down through the leather. Use sharp scissors to extend the slip to with ¼″ of each end of the line.

Broken lines extending beyond solid one are guidelines to use only if it becomes necessary to slash beyond points 3 and 5. Numbers on torso (*A*) correspond to numbers on gusset (*B*). Match them to one another in basting.

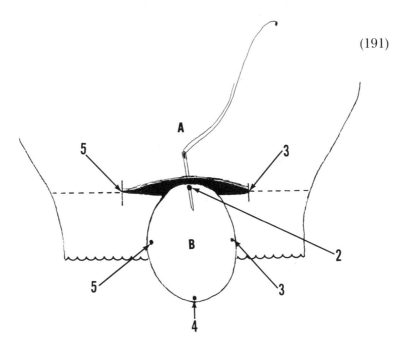

Ill. 129. Sewing a Gusset—Step 2.

With wrong side of leather torso and gusset facing you, insert needle through 2 dot on the torso (not shown), then through 2 dot on the gusset. Pull gusset and torso together. Then, taking one stab stitch at a time, baste the edges together, working toward side point #3. Keep the basting stitches between the edges of the leather and the seam allowance.

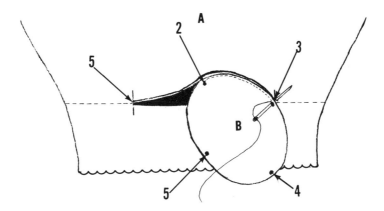

Ill. 130. Sewing a Gusset—Step 3.

As the oval gusset is stitched into the straight slit, the torso begins to assume curve of gusset. Once curve is established, if slit needed extending beyond 3 or 5, it would be impossible to cut straight out from these points without the guidelines.

When you reach corner 3, take a back stitch and another forward stitch through 3, to secure that corner when permanent stitching is done on the machine.

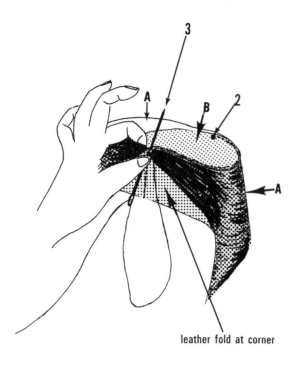

leather fold at corner

Ill. 131. Sewing a Gusset—Step 4.

White area marked *A* is right side of torso, where gusset has not yet been basted. Shaded area also marked *A* is wrong side of torso. Area marked *B* is wrong side of gusset. It shows where basting was begun at positioning dot 2.

Insert needle through corner dot 3 on torso and dot 3 on gusset. Work toward dot 4, which is hidden by the hand. Open the slash and fit gusset edges to it. This automatically makes torso form a triangular fold, as shown. Hold fold in place with thumb while you take a back stitch to secure that side of gusset. Now baste to dot 4, matching dots.

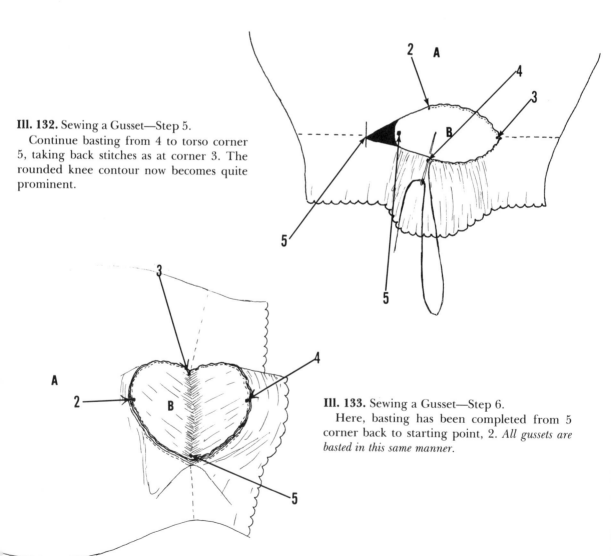

Ill. 132. Sewing a Gusset—Step 5.

Continue basting from 4 to torso corner 5, taking back stitches as at corner 3. The rounded knee contour now becomes quite prominent.

Ill. 133. Sewing a Gusset—Step 6.

Here, basting has been completed from 5 corner back to starting point, 2. *All gussets are basted in this same manner.*

Step 4 Cut a slit in each leg for the hip gussets. Lay the body against a heavy piece of cardboard (so that the razor blade will do no damage). Smooth out the leg next to the cardboard while keeping the other leg folded back out of the way. Position the sharp edge of the blade against the slit mark *G* and give the blade a sharp push. This will cut a straight slit about 1½″ long. Use a pair of sharp scissors (if necessary) to extend the slit to within ¼″ of marks 11 and 13. *Never* cut *all the way* to the numbered vertical mark.

A digression seems in order here. Perhaps the following explanation will make clear the reason behind that warning:

Once the positioning dots are marked on the gussets, they are never changed. In direct contrast, the corresponding numbered

Ill. 134. Pattern for enlarging Bru Jne 8 torso. Set middle screws of pantograph at 2. Enlarged measurements will be:
length 8⅝″
hip width 7⅝″

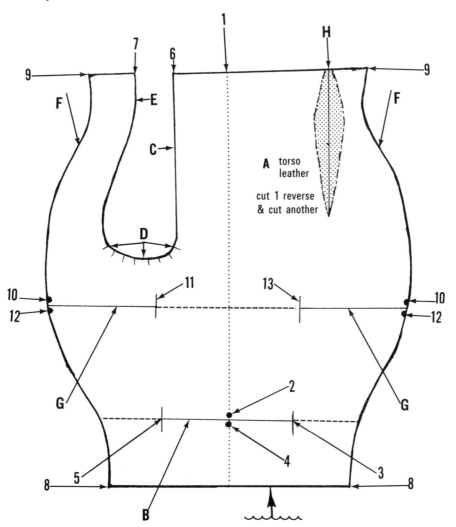

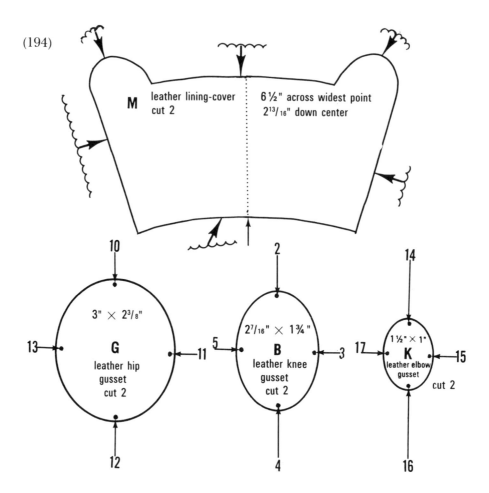

Ill. 135. Patterns for enlarging a leather lining-cover and gussets for a Bru Jne 8. Measurements after enlargement are noted on each pattern piece.

marks on the torso rarely stay as they are shown on the pattern pieces. They might accurately be called "mediating numbers." These little mediators—with the help of the broken lines marked in conjunction with and straight out from the gusset slash line—assure a perfectly fitted gusset every time. With one snip and one stitch at a time, as you near the corner of the gusset, you can always be sure that when your needle goes through the corner-positioning dot on the gusset, it will also go exactly through the corner of the gusset slash on the torso. It may fit short of the mark, or you may have to snip beyond the mark using the broken straight lines as a guide— but it *will* fit precisely.

And now, let's return to assembling the body.

Step 5 Baste the hip gussets in place, beginning at 10, stitching to 11, to 12, to 13, and back to 10. This is the same procedural sequence used in basting the knee gusset. Don't forget the back stitches at each corner. Machine stitch.

Step 6 Baste and stitch side dart *H*.

Step 7 Turn the body right side out.

Step 8 Stitch the side darts in *I* front (Ill. 137).

Step 9 With right sides together, match the center front of *I* (6) to the center front seam of the leather torso (*C* and 6). Run a straight pin through the very edge of the leather and the cloth to hold them together. Put another pin at the ⅛″ seam line on both sides of *I* front and insert the pins through the side dart seams on both sides. The folds of excess material to right and left of the center front form the custom-fitting waistline darts. Baste them in place; then machine stitch.

Step 10 With right sides together, match the center back of *I* (Ill. 136) to the center back seam of the torso (*E* and 7). Find the width of the waistline darts as you did the front ones in Step 9. Baste them in place; then machine stitch.

Ill. 136. Patterns for enlarging a muslin back lining and leather sleeve-tube for a Bru Jne 8.

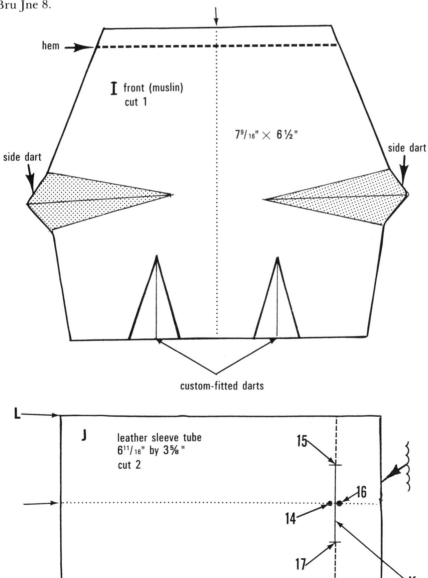

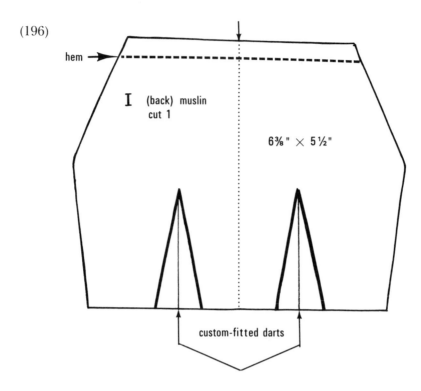

hem →

I (back) muslin
cut 1

6⅜" × 5½"

custom-fitted darts

Ill. 137. Pattern for enlarging a muslin front lining for a Bru Jne 8.

Step 11 With right sides together, stitch up the side seams of *I*—front (Ill. 137) and back (Ill. 136).

Step 12 Slip lining *I* down over the torso, right sides together, matching fronts and backs at center and side seams to side darts *H* in the torso. Baste the cloth lining *I* to the leather torso, *A*. Machine stitch.

Step 13 Glue the porcelain legs into place. Draw a pencil mark in the center back of each leg. Smear glue inside the leather leg tube, wipe off excess, stick the leg inside the tube, and line the pencil mark up with the center back leg seam. While the glue is drying, go to Step 14.

WARNING: Because it is very easy to glue a right leg into a left leg tube, and vice versa, it's a good idea to lay the body, front side up, on your work table and place each leg on its proper side. You will never get them mixed up if you take this precaution.

Step 14 Baste the elbow gussets, *K* (Ill. 135), into their slits as indicated on arm tubes *J* (Ill. 136). Begin at 14, baste to 15, to 16, to 17, and back to 14 (Ill. 135). Be sure to take back stitches at the corners. Machine stitch.

Step 15   Close arm tube seams *L* on both arm tubes *J* (Ill. 136). Begin your stitching at the scalloped end; otherwise, if the pressure of the presser foot is not adjusted to perfection, the leather next to the foot will be longer than that underneath when the seam is machine stitched. This would make the scalloped edge uneven.

Step 16   Place a pencil mark in the center of each porcelain arm, underneath (on the palm side). Glue each arm in place, matching the pencil mark to the sleeve seam *L* (Ill. 136). Let dry.

Voilà! You now have a beautiful doll body—ready for stuffing.

STUFFING THE BODY

In Chapter 11 instructions were given for making a sawdust sifter and for making three body stuffers from one wooden dowel rod. If you find you prefer permanent metal rods, as I do, visit a hardware store and have them made. Then you'll never have to worry about their breaking, nor about picking painful splinters out of your hands. You will need three metal rods with three diameters—½″, ⅜″, and ¼″. The length is not too important, so long as none of the three exceeds 18″. Anything longer than that would be awkward to handle. Have one end of each rod ground down to a point; then have the point blunted. These rods are quite inexpensive to have made.

Be sure the sawdust is bone dry and thoroughly sifted. If it is damp, what appears—at first—to be a lovely, firmly stuffed body will later become a sagging shapeless ruin as the sawdust dries inside the leather. And if the sawdust is not thoroughly sifted, small splinters may pierce the leather or lodge just inside it and make an ugly "bump."

There is an art to stuffing a doll body, simple though the procedure may sound. Take care not to shove the semipointed end of a body stuffer against the leather, so that you cause it to "pouch out" at the point of contact. This damage cannot be corrected. Use the flat end of the stuffer to push the gusset seams open and to pack sawdust firmly into the rounded contour of the "knee joint." Don't push so hard that you cause stitches to break, though.

Spoon sawdust into the body until it is level with the waistline seam. Then, using the longest body stuffer, punch the sawdust down into both legs, alternating between them. Repeat, adding sawdust and punching it down, until it reaches the knee-gusset area. Pack it as tightly as you can. Hold on to the top of the porcelain leg (where it's glued into the leather); then, with the semipointed end of the stuffer, punch a hole in the center of the sawdust. With hard, up-and-down pounding motions, using the flat and the semipointed ends of the stuffer alternately, pack sawdust into the hole you made. Repeat—time after time—until the semipointed end of the stuffer will not make a hole in the sawdust. That's how you know when it is packed hard enough.

Continue dumping sawdust into the body—packing, tamping, punching—until it is tightly packed to the bottom edge of the knee gusset. At this point, the body stuffer can no longer be used with an up-and-down movement. Use the flat end only, as you move the sawdust into—and press outward on—the rounded gusset seam. Follow the instructions given in Ills. 138 and 139. Precise hand positions are shown in the illustrations. These are the ones I use. They will get you started in packing gussets correctly. But when you learn what must be done—and how—the way in which you do it is not important. Other hand positions may be more comfortable for you.

Unless the bottom half of a gusset, no matter where it is located, is kept *flat* until the sawdust is hard packed; unless the top half of a gusset is held firmly against the hard-packed bottom half until it, too, is firmly packed—the gussets will hang open unattractively.

Once you get past the gussets, the rest of the body can be quickly stuffed. Before dumping in more sawdust, always make sure what you added previously is packed so hard that it is impenetrable.

When you have gone about halfway up between the side-front darts of the lining and the top edges, begin test-fitting the shoulder plate over the body. When the body has been packed sufficiently high so that the shoulder plate is a snug fit on top of the muslin lining, remove the shoulder plate and stuff two to three big handfuls of 100 percent Polyester Fluffy-Fill (or its equivalent) on top of the sawdust. Close the top by following the instructions in Ill. 140.

Stuffing the arms and the arm tubes does not require the sawdust to be packed rock hard, as in the rest of the body, but it should be packed firm to hold the shape. Work carefully around the elbow gussets. When you think the arm tubes have been stuffed high enough, hold them next to the body with the empty section across the top of the lining (where it will later be stitched). Ideally, the tips of the fingers should be on an imaginary line horizontal with the crotch seam. If more stuffing is needed, add it. When the arm tube is stuffed to the correct height, the arm will hang gracefully down the side of the body (and not stick out at an awkward angle). Hand stitch the top ends of the sleeve tubes to the muslin lining. Recheck to make sure both arms hang evenly.

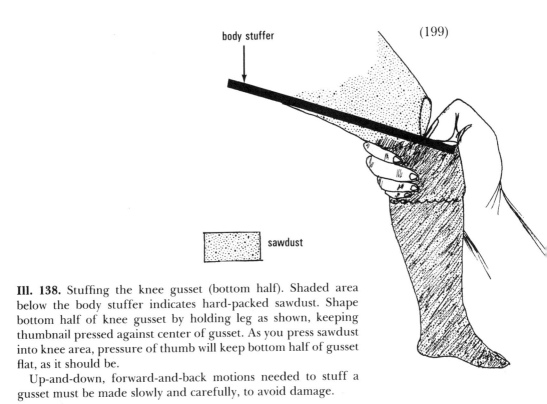

body stuffer

sawdust

Ill. 138. Stuffing the knee gusset (bottom half). Shaded area below the body stuffer indicates hard-packed sawdust. Shape bottom half of knee gusset by holding leg as shown, keeping thumbnail pressed against center of gusset. As you press sawdust into knee area, pressure of thumb will keep bottom half of gusset flat, as it should be.

Up-and-down, forward-and-back motions needed to stuff a gusset must be made slowly and carefully, to avoid damage.

body stuffer

hip gusset

knee gusset

Ill. 139. Stuffing the knee gusset (top half). Imagine you are seeing both the inside and outside of a leg being stuffed. One hand holds top half of knee gusset firmly against bottom half while you pack sawdust tightly in that area. Maintain gripping position with the hand until sawdust has been packed tightly to bottom half of *hip* gusset as indicated by heavy broken line. As long as procedures here and in Ill. 138 are followed, gussets will be beautifully shaped.

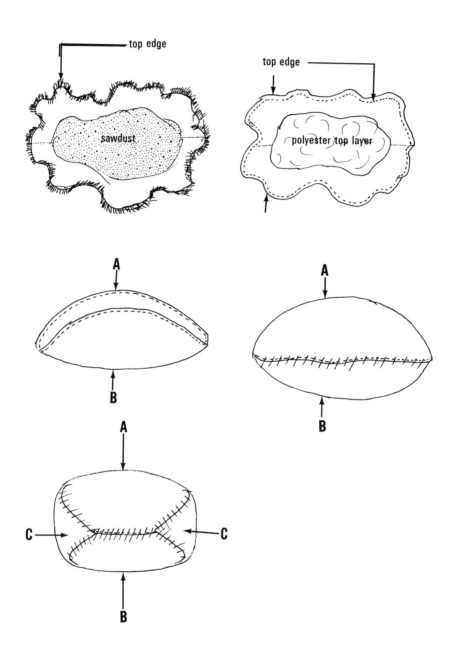

Ill. 140. Closing the lining top.
A. front of lining
B. back of lining
C. sides of lining
Overlap *A* over *B* as tightly as possible, and whip stitch together. Fold sides *C* toward center, and whip stitch in place.

AFFIXING THE HEAD TO THE SHOULDER PLATE

If the head and the shoulder plate are separate, you will need the four items shown, full size, in Ill. 141, plus a pair of needle-nose pliers. The items are:

W. cotter pin 1¾″ long
X. spring, no longer than 1⅜″; strong but not so heavy that it has no movement. If you can find only a longer one, cut it down to size with a wire cutter. If you can hold the spring between thumb and index or middle finger, and—in spite of its resistance—can compress it a great deal, it's all right to use.
Y. cotter pin 2½″ long
Z. faucet washer, commonly used to stop leaky faucets. These washers are dark brown plastic.

Ill. 141. Affixing the head to the shoulder plate.
T. shoulder plate
U. leather-lined shoulder plate socket
V. neck of doll

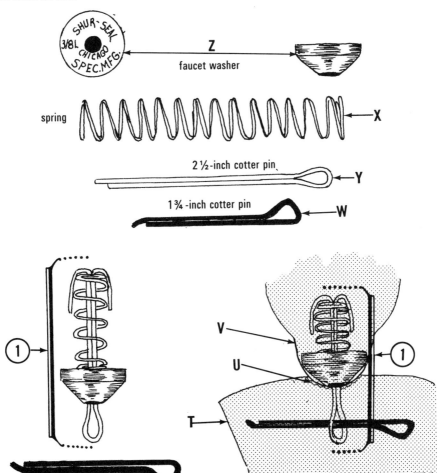

The above four items can be found at any hardware store and are quite inexpensive.

The neck of the doll head is indicated by *V* in Ill. 141. The arrow at *U* points to scallops that are barely visible. They indicate the presence of leather. The socket of the shoulder plate, *T,* should always be lined with leather, with the leather edges scalloped. Unless this is done, after the head and shoulder plate are assembled and the head is swiveled, the two porcelain parts will grate against each other, and make a thoroughly unpleasant sound.

Step 1   Insert *Y* through the hole (at the tapered end) of *Z*.

Step 2   Drop the spring *X* over *Y*.

Step 3   Without compressing the spring, use needle-nose pliers to bend the ends of *Y* down over spring *X*. This locks *X*, *Y*, and *Z* together as a unit, indicated by the circled 1.

Step 4   Drop the unit inside the neck of the doll head. Then place the loop end of the cotter pin in the hole in the shoulder plate socket.

Step 5   Put the thumb of one hand against the bent ends of the cotter pin (and the top end of the spring) and push downward, compressing the spring.

Step 6   As you compress the spring, the looped end of the cotter pin plunges downward far enough through the shoulder plate hole for the insertion of cotter pin *W*.

When you release the thumb pressure, the spring decompresses, cotter pin *W* moves up against the shoulder plate, and the assembly is complete.

GLUEING THE HEAD TO THE MUSLIN LINING

Step 1   If there are no sew holes (and there usually are not in a Bru shoulder plate), smear glue on the under side of the shoulder plate. Fit the shoulder plate down tightly against the muslin lining, and hold it in place with two heavy rubber bands until the glue dries. Slip a band around each leg, slide them up to the crotch, stretch one up and over the left arm onto the shoulder plate, and the other band onto the shoulder plate on the other side. Keep glue away from the cotter pin assembly. If any glue seeps between the shoulder plate and the neck, the doll head will not be free to swivel in its socket.

Step 2   The leather lining-cover *M* (Ill. 135)—like the muslin lining *I*—must be custom fitted to look right. *M* is the basic shape of the Bru Jne 8. Place one piece of the pair over the back lining. Arrange it so that its top edge overlaps the edge of the shoulder plate about ¼″, the rounded section fits partly on the porcelain and partly under the arm (crossing the lining side seam by about ¼″), and so that the sides cover the side seams of the lining. The lower edge should overlap the waistline seam about ¼″.

Step 3 When this piece is custom fitted to your satisfaction, remove it and scallop the edges all around. Then apply a thin, continuous string of glue within ⅛″ of the entire outer rim. Smear the glue all the way out to the edges and wipe off any excess.

Step 4 Press the leather lining cover into position over the muslin lining. Wipe off any glue that seeps out from under the edges. Let dry. Repeat for the front lining cover.

The remainder of this chapter, as well as chapters 16 and 17, will be devoted to body patterns and instructions for their assembly. The correct setting for the middle screws of the pantograph will always be given. The setting means that the body will be enlarged—by using the specified setting—to the original size, as stated; however, keep in mind that you are not limited to the original size. If you need a larger body, set the middle screws at #3 or #4.

Experiment with your pantograph. It can do wonders for you. It will enlarge or reduce pictures so that you can copy them in oils; it can reduce or enlarge any drawing, map, plan, blueprint, or diagram as much as ten times. But if you enlarged any of these body patterns that much, you'd need a baseball team to help stuff it.

This Bru Jne 9 body pattern will make a doll approximately 11″ to 13″ tall, not counting the head and shoulder plate. Taking them into account, the doll will measure between 18″ and 20″ in height. It consists of six pattern pieces.

PART	HOW MANY	MEASUREMENTS OF ENLARGEMENT
A. Leather torso Cut one, reverse and cut one	2	7¾″ x 6¼″
B. Leather knee gusset	2	1⅞″ x 1¼″
G. Leather hip gusset	2	2⁵⁄₁₆″ x 1⅞″
I. Muslin lining	2	4¾″ x 6⅛″
J. Leather sleeve tube	2	4½″ x 3⅝″
K. Leather elbow gusset	2	1⁵⁄₁₆″ x ¾″

You will have twelve pieces cut out, ten of leather, two of muslin. *All measurements in this and all other patterns are based on the widest or longest part.*

TIPS TO REMEMBER

As you finish each seam, tie off the threads, then trim off any unevenness between the two layers of leather. Usually the piece of leather against the presser foot will be longer, but it should never be more than ⅛″ longer. Trim and "customize" the body as you go.

Always use the straight-stitch presser foot. Its right prong (as you face the machine) can be used as a guide for the seam allowance.

To enlarge this pattern, set the two middle screws of your pantograph on 2. Enlarge the torso first. If its measurements agree with those listed, the instrument is set correctly. If not, recheck it. Enlarge the other five pattern pieces and check their measurements. Transfer all marks to the wrong side of the leather (except the positioning dots on the gussets).

Prepare the torso leg pattern for this doll as you did for the first pattern given (Bru Jne 8). When line 8 has been adjusted to fit the porcelain legs you plan on using, scallop the edges. Don't forget to take into consideration the ⅛″ seam allowance when you are making the adjustment.

Instructions for cutting out bodies, trueing them up, basting, marking positioning dots on gussets—everything given in the

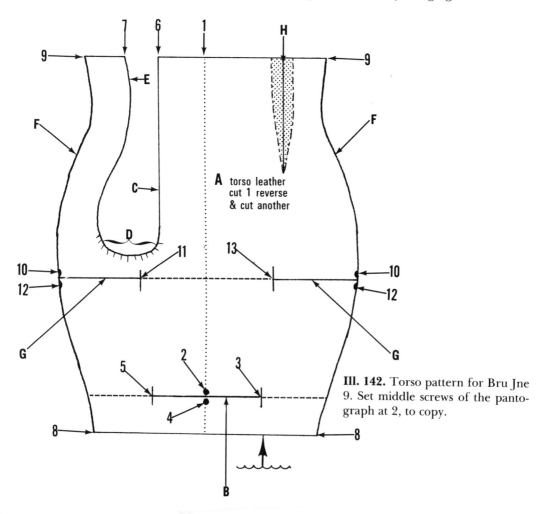

A torso leather
cut 1 reverse
& cut another

Ill. 142. Torso pattern for Bru Jne 9. Set middle screws of the pantograph at 2, to copy.

previous instructions relative to the Bru Jne 8 body—apply to *all* bodies made of leather.

ASSEMBLING THE BODY

Step 1   Baste the knee gussets *B* (Ill. 143) into the torso (Ill. 142), then machine stitch.

Step 2   With right sides of the torso together, begin at 6 and baste the center front, the crotch, and the center back seam together, ending at 7. Machine stitch. Clip the crotch curve. (See Ill. 142.)

Step 3   With right sides of the torso together, start at 8 and baste seam *F* up through 9, making sure the gusset lines at points 10 and 12 match. Machine stitch. Repeat on the other leg. (See Ill. 142.)

Ill. 143. Sleeve tube (*J*) and gussets (*G, B, K*) patterns for Bru Jne 9.

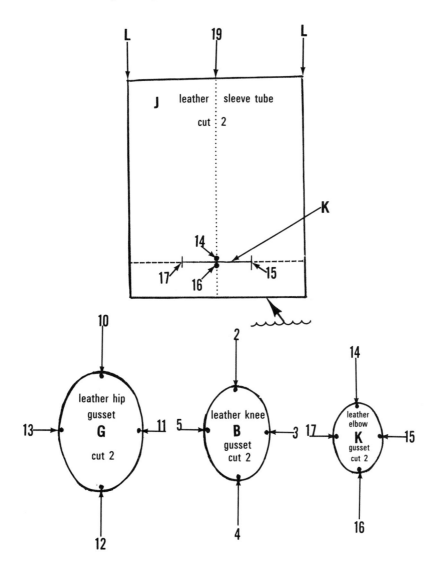

Step 4   Cut a slit in each leg for the hip gussets (as described in Bru Jne 8 instructions).

Step 5   Baste the hip gussets in place, beginning at 10, stitching to 11, to 12, to 13, and back to 10. Machine stitch.

Step 6   Baste and stitch side dart *H*.

Step 7   Turn the torso right side out.

Step 8   Stitch the waistline darts in *I* (Ill. 144). There are no side front darts in this pattern, and both front and back are cut alike. Only the darts will be different. Customize them to fit.

Ill. 144. Patterns for Bru Jne 9 muslin lining *(I)* and leather lining-cover *(M)*.

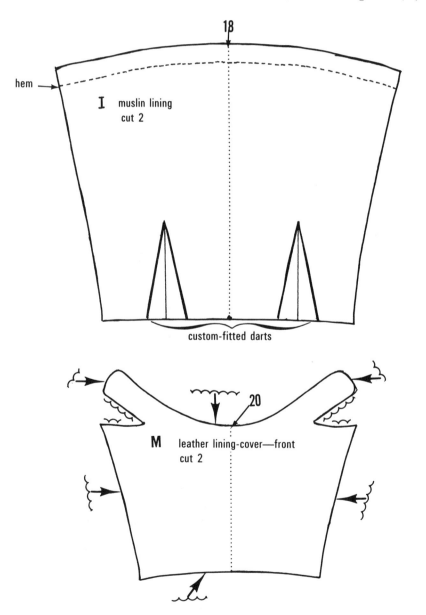

Step 9   With right sides together, match the center back of *I* (Ill. 144) to the center back seam of the torso *(E* and 7, Ill. 142). Find the width of the waistline (after darts are machine stitched). Place a mark on each side to indicate the line of stitching for the side seams. Do the same with the front.

Step 10   With right sides together, stitch up the side seams of *I* front and back. (Optional: hem the top.)

Step 11   Slip lining *I* down over the torso, right sides together, matching fronts and backs at center, and side seams to side darts *H* in the torso. Baste the cloth lining *I* to the leather torso *A* (Ill. 142). Machine stitch.

Step 12   Glue the porcelain legs into place. Draw a pencil mark in the center back of each leg. Smear glue inside the leather leg tube, wipe off excess, stick the leg inside the tube, and line the pencil mark up with the center back leg seam. While the glue is drying, go to Step 13.

Step 13   Baste the elbow gussets, *K* (Ill. 143), into their slits as indicated on arm tubes *J*. Begin at 14, baste to 15, to 16, to 17, and back to 14.

Step 14   Close sleeve seams *L* (Ill. 143) on both sleeve tubes *J*. *Always* begin the stitching at the scalloped end.

Step 15   Place a pencil mark in the center of each porcelain arm, on the palm side. Glue the arms in place, matching the pencil marks to the sleeve seam *L*. Let dry.

The body is ready to stuff. Follow directions given earlier, if necessary. Affixing the head to the shoulder plate and glueing the plate to the muslin lining are also done the same as with the Bru Jne 8.

16

Leather Body Patterns- French Fashion and Ne Plus Ultra Jointed

This French Fashion body pattern will make a doll approximately 15″ tall, not counting the head and shoulder plate. It consists of eleven pattern pieces.

PART		HOW MANY	MEASUREMENTS OF ENLARGEMENT
A.	Leather torso Cut one, reverse and cut one	2	8⅜″ x 5⁷⁄₁₆″
B.	Leather knee gusset	2	1⅝″ x ⅞″
G.	Leather hip gusset	2	2³⁄₁₆″ x 1¾″
H.	Leather insole	2	1⅜″ x 1⁹⁄₁₆″
HH.	Leather sole Cut one, reverse and cut one	2	2⅛″ x ⁶⁄₈″
I.	Muslin front lining	1	6¾″ x 5⅜″
II.	Muslin back lining	1	5⁹⁄₁₆″ x 4¹⁵⁄₁₆″

J.	Leather arm and hand *(Do not cut yet.* For now, cut two rectangles 9″ x 3¾″.)	2	
K.	Leather elbow gusset	2	1¼″ x ¾″
M.	Leather lining-cover—front (Scallop as indicated.)	1	5⅜″ x 5¹⁴⁄₁₆″
N.	Leather lining-cover—back (Scallop as indicated.)	1	3¹⁵⁄₁₆″ x 6⅛″

Out of the eighteen pieces you cut using the pattern, sixteen are of leather, two are of muslin.

TIPS TO REMEMBER

As you finish each seam, tie off the threads; then trim off any unevenness between the two layers of leather. This should never be more than ⅛″.

Always use the straight-stitch presser foot. Its right prong (as you face the machine) can be used as a guide for the seam allowance.

To enlarge this pattern, set the two middle screws of the pantograph on 2¼. Enlarge the torso first. If it measures 8⅜″ in length and 5⁷⁄₁₆″ at the widest part of the hips, the pantograph is set correctly. If not, recheck it. Enlarge the other ten pattern pieces and check their measurements. Transfer all marks (except gusset-positioning dots) to the wrong side of the leather.

MAKING THE TORSO

Slash the knee slit to within ¼″ of points 3 and 5 (Ill. 145). Baste in the knee gusset. Using stab stitches, begin at 2, baste to 3, to 4, to 5, and back to 2. Machine stitch knee gusset in place. Repeat on the other side.

Cut a slit from 6 (Ill. 145) straight down to a point between 7 and 8. Baste the insole *H* (Ill. 146) into this slit. With right sides together, stick your needle through dot 6 at the top of the insole, then through dot 6 on the torso. Keeping the edges of the leather as even as possible, use tiny stab stitches to baste from 6 through 7. Tie off. Again insert the needle through dot 6, and baste from that

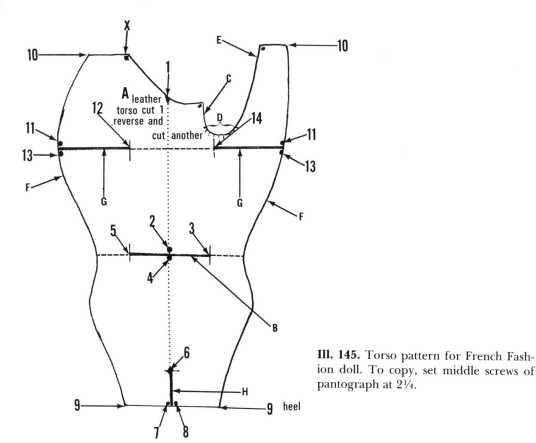

Ill. 145. Torso pattern for French Fashion doll. To copy, set middle screws of pantograph at 2¼.

Ill. 146. Patterns for gussets, insole, and sole of a French Fashion doll. Gussets are marked *G, B,* and *K.* Insole is *H;* sole is *HH.* (The hand points to the big toe.)

leather hip gusset
G
cut 2

leather knee gusset
B
cut 2

leather elbow gusset
K
cut 2

leather insole
H
cut 1 reverse and cut another

leather sole
cut 1 reverse and cut another
H H

point through 8. Tie off. Machine stitch, keeping the torso side *up* next to the presser foot.

Right sides together, close seam *F* beginning at 9 (Ill. 145, heel) and stitching through 10 (at the waist).

Slash the hip gusset line *G* (Ill. 145) to within ¼″ of points 12 and 14. Baste in the hip gusset beginning at 11, going to 12, to 13, to 14, and back to 11. Machine stitch the hip gusset in place. Repeat with the other hip gusset.

Match the right-hand sole (Ill. 146, *HH)* to the right-hand torso, and the left-hand sole to the left-hand torso by lining up the "big toe" (indicated by the pointing finger) with the center-front torso seam (Ill. 145, *C).* Baste one sole in place. Begin at the heel (Ill. 145, point 9), right sides together and matching back leg seam to the double dots, and use tiny stab stitches to baste to 8 (seam where insole is joined to torso), around the toes matching *Z*'s, on to 7 (seam where insole is joined to torso), and back to the heel (9). Machine stitch. Now sew in the other sole.

Baste the crotch seam together by turning one completed torso right side out and sticking it down inside the other torso, which is still wrong side out. Start sewing at center front seam *C* (Ill. 145) (match the dots), sew through the crotch seam *(D)* and on through the center back seam *(E).* Now turn the other half of the torso right side out.

MAKING THE TOP

With right sides together, baste leather front lining-cover (Ill. 147, *M)* to leather back lining-cover (Ill. 148, *N),* sides *x* to *y.* Machine stitch, starting at *y* and stitching down to *x* on both sides.

With right sides together, baste muslin front lining (Ill. 147, *I)* to muslin back lining (Ill. 148, *II)*—sides 15 to 16, both sides. Machine stitch, starting at 15 and stitching to 16. (Optional: Fold in a half-inch hem and machine stitch in place. This keeps the muslin from raveling and provides nonfraying edges to fold over for stitching the top closed.)

Turn the muslin lining right side out and slip it over the wrong side of the leather lining-cover, matching side seams, center fronts, and center backs. Machine stitch the waistline seam all around. Stitching the two together allows you to handle the lining and its cover as one piece of material at the waistline only, and leaves the two separate above the waistline seam.

Slip the upper body unit down over the torso (Ill. 145), right sides together (leather against leather), and—matching center front of *M* (Ill. 147) to the center front of torso *A* at seam *C*—baste the upper body to the torso, matching side seams *x* to torso *x,* and center back of leather lining-cover *N* (Ill. 148) to center back of torso seam *E.*

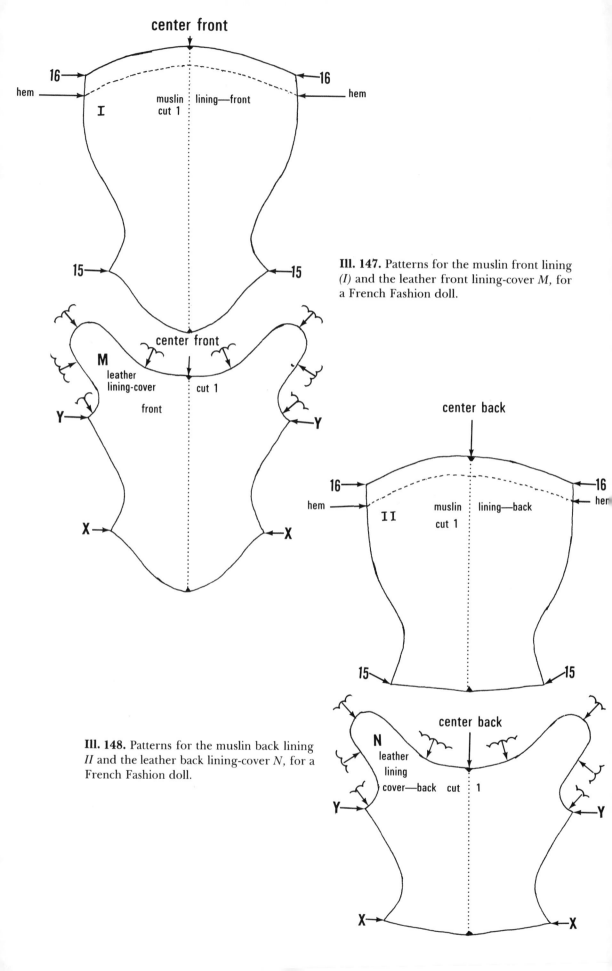

center front

16 → hem
← 16 hem

I muslin : lining—front
cut 1

15 → ← 15

M leather lining-cover
front
cut 1

center front

Y → ← Y

X → ← X

Ill. 147. Patterns for the muslin front lining *(I)* and the leather front lining-cover *M*, for a French Fashion doll.

center back

16 → hem
← 16 her

II muslin : lining—back
cut 1

15 → ← 15

N leather lining cover—back cut : 1
center back

Y → ← Y

X → ← X

Ill. 148. Patterns for the muslin back lining *II* and the leather back lining-cover *N*, for a French Fashion doll.

CONSTRUCTING THE LEATHER ARMS

Fold the leather rectangle lengthwise, right sides together. Line up the pattern on the fold and trace all around it. *Do not cut it out at this point.* Close arm seam *L* and stop with the needle in the leather at the outer edge of the little finger (Ill. 149). Turn the flywheel by hand as you round off the fingertips and stitch to the dots between the fingers. At each dot, before turning the leather all the way around to stitch up the other side of a finger, turn it at right angles to the line of stitching just finished, take one stitch forward, one stitch backward, and another stitch forward; *then* turn the leather into position for stitching up the side of the next finger.

Finish the hand by rounding off the top of the thumb to meet the fold and leave enough thread to tie a security knot. The space between the fingers is very small; therefore, a razor blade is a perfect tool to use in cutting between the fingers and, if great care is exercised, it can also be used in rounding off the fingers close to the line of stitching. Then trim away all leather to ⅛″ from the seam lines.

Cut slit *K* through seam *L* (Ill. 149) for insertion of the arm gusset. Baste the gusset in place; then machine stitch.

You will encounter no difficulty in turning the arm as far as the

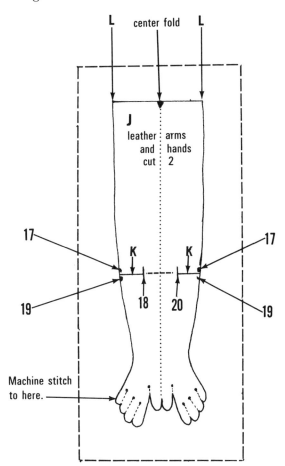

Ill. 149. Arms and hands for a French Fashion doll. Cut out two rectangles 9″ by 3¾″. The arm-and-hand combination should *not* be cut out until it has first been marked, then stitched, on the rectangle. (See text.)

hand. The hand itself, mainly the fingers, may present what appear to be insurmountable difficulties, but they really are not. The turning will be made easier if you sprinkle a generous amount of talcum powder into the arm and work it down inside the fingers. This makes the leather slick. Without it, the leather sticks together.

Thin plastic or rubber jar openers will make turning any part of a leather body easier (including the feet on a French Fashion body such as this): lock the hemostat jaws onto the very end of the thumb seam. Gently push it *inside* while, with the other hand holding the jar opener against the leather thumb, you push it toward the hemostat handles. This can be compared to the action of putting on a glove—one hand pushes into the glove (hemostat pushing inside the leather thumb) while the other hand pushes the glove onto the hand (jar opener gripping the leather and pushing it forward onto the hemostat). By keeping plenty of talc inside the fingers, this task can be accomplished, perhaps not as speedily as you'd like, but more easily than you expected.

If you cannot locate this type of jar opener, moistening the tips of your fingers on your tongue will somewhat prevent their sliding on the leather.

Now make the other arm.

STUFFING THE BODY

Stuff the toe area with small amounts of sifted sawdust, packing it carefully against all seams. Keep the sawdust between the leather body and the flat end of the body stuffer, and keep the sole as flat as possible.

Once the feet are stuffed, continue shaping and smoothing the contours of the body, alternately adding sawdust and packing it tightly. Make a special effort to keep the gussets as flat as possible— and held firmly together—as you progress in stuffing the body.

When the top of the body is filled high enough to fit the shoulder plate snugly, close it (see Ill. 140).

STUFFING THE HAND AND ARM

Slip several pipe cleaners into each finger, and when all the fingers have been stiffened with them, grasp the wrist (from the outside) and hold the cleaners in position while you twist them all together as much as you can.

Using cotton, lamb's wool, or Poly-Fill, pad each hand lightly, a wisp at a time. Do not pack the hand so full that it looks like a cow's udder. When the hand has been gracefully contoured, begin lightly packing sawdust around the twisted pipe cleaners, keeping them in the center of the arm. The arm packing should be on the light side, enough to be firm but not as hard as the body. When you have stuffed 1″ to 1½″ above the elbow gusset, start holding the arm against the body and checking it for correct fit. Sew the arms to the muslin lining; then recheck to be sure the fingers hang evenly on both sides.

FINISHING

Glue the shoulder plate to the muslin lining, using Elmer's Glue. Hold it in place with two heavy rubber bands. Let dry.

Smear glue into the wrong side of the back leather cover along the scalloped edges. Work it into the leather. Pull the shoulder pieces up over the shoulder plate, stretching as needed so that about ¼″ overlaps the lower edge of the shoulder plate in its center. Hold the straps in place until the glue *grabs*. If, when you turn the straps loose, they slide out of position, stretch them back into place and hold them there a bit longer.

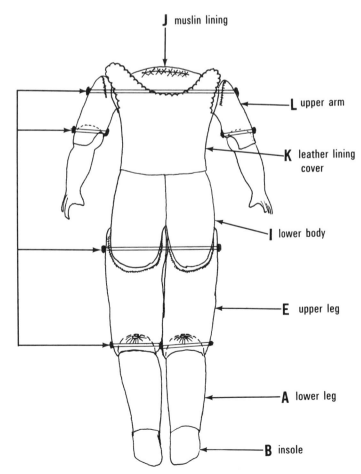

Ill. 150. Leather body with Ne Plus Ultra hip joints, Universal knee joints, and bisque forearms ball jointed at elbow. The four arrows at left of the drawing indicate points where the body parts are joined together by wire and metal buttons. The double lines represent the wires that are pushed through the leather and sawdust to anchor parts of the body together.

J muslin lining

L upper arm

K leather lining cover

I lower body

E upper leg

A lower leg

B insole

Repeat for the front, lapping the front shoulder straps over the back at least ½″, and holding them until the glue grabs.

Here is a fully articulated leather body (Ill. 150), made so by Ne Plus Ultra hip joints, Universal knee joints, and the jointed arms that consist of leather upper arm sections and porcelain ball-joint forearms with pierced holes. Although the pattern was drafted to provide full articulation, you may use non-ball-joint forearms and draft a simple sleeve tube pattern to accommodate them. Antique bodies were made both ways.

Although notches are shown on some of the pattern pieces, in actual practice it is best to *mark* the notch locations, not cut into the leather.

Set the middle pantograph screws at 2. The jointed leather body will then measure 21″ to 23″ when it is completed. If you want the body to be smaller or larger than this, vary the setting of the middle pantograph screws accordingly.

The same body pattern can be used to make a cloth body—fully articulated—for some china dolls and other types. When made in cloth, the body parts are joined together with threads instead of wires, as their leather counterparts are.

This pattern consists of fourteen pieces. Nine are cut of leather, two of muslin and three of thin cardboard.

PART	HOW MANY	SPECIAL INSTRUCTIONS
A. Lower leg (leather)	2	None
B. Insole (leather)	2	Cut one; reverse pattern and cut a second one (for right and left feet).
C. Sole (leather)	2	Cut one; reverse pattern and cut a second one (for right and left feet).
D. Knee inner liner (cardboard 3x5 file cards are ideal)	2	None
E. Upper leg (leather)	2	None
F. Knee facing (leather)	2	None
G. Top of upper leg (leather)	2	None

H. Upper leg liner (cardboard)	2	None
I. Lower body (leather)	2	Cut one; reverse pattern and cut a second.
J. Lining (muslin)	2	None
K. Lining cover (leather)	2	Scallop edges as indicated in Ill. 158.
L. Upper arm (leather)	2	Cut one; reverse pattern and cut second.
M. Upper arm liner (cardboard)	2	None
N. Upper arm liner (muslin)	2	None

When all pieces have been cut out, there should be a total of twenty-eight—eighteen of leather, four of muslin, and six of thin cardboard.

TIPS TO REMEMBER

As each seam is finished, tie off the threads, using security knots. Trim off any unevenness between the two layers of leather, muslin, or cardboard.

Use the straight-stitch presser foot. Its right side (as you face it) serves as a guide for the seam allowance.

Verify the measurements of the enlarged pieces: lower legs *(A)* 5½″; upper leg *(E)* 5″; lower body *(I)* 4¾″. If these are correct, the other pieces will be, too.

The instructions for cutting out bodies, trueing them up, basting, and marking notches (there are no gussets in this body), along with all other information presented earlier, are applicable to this body as well.

In addition to the enlarged pattern pieces, to make this body you will need:

Leather (or firmly woven cloth)	Cotton (or its equivalent)
Thin cardboard such as 3x5 file cards	Wire cutters
	Ice pick
Metal buttons (see list of suppliers)	Bisque ball-joint forearms with pierced holes
Needle-nose pliers	Sifted sawdust

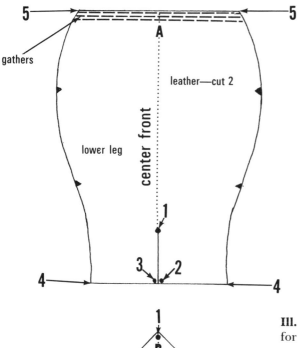

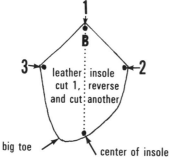

Ill. 151. Jointed leather body. Patterns for lower leg *(A)* and insole *(B)*.

ASSEMBLING THE LOWER LEG AND FOOT

Step 1 Slit the lower leg from point 1 straight down between 2 and 3. With right sides together, baste insole *(B)* into the slit, starting at 1 and basting to 2. Again, start at 1 and baste to 3 (Ill. 151). Machine stitch. Repeat for other lower leg.

Step 2 With right sides together, baste leg seam together from 4 through 5, matching notches (Ill. 151). Machine stitch. Repeat for other lower leg.

Step 3 With right sides together, baste sole *C* (Ill. 152) in place, taking care that there *are* right and left soles (not two rights or two lefts). It may be necessary to trim sole *C* down a bit at front (toe) edge, in order to customize its fit. Baste from heel point 4 over to point 6, and tie off threads with a security knot. Begin again at heel point 4 and baste over to point 7. Again tie off threads with a safety knot. Check between points 6 and 7, matching centers and dots; if sole is a bit too long, trim it to fit the opening. Baste trimmed part of sole into place. Machine stitch. Repeat for other lower leg. The two lower legs are now assembled. Turn them both right side out.

Step 4 Run three rows of machine-gathering stitches (longest stitch the machine will make) at the extreme *top edge* of lower leg

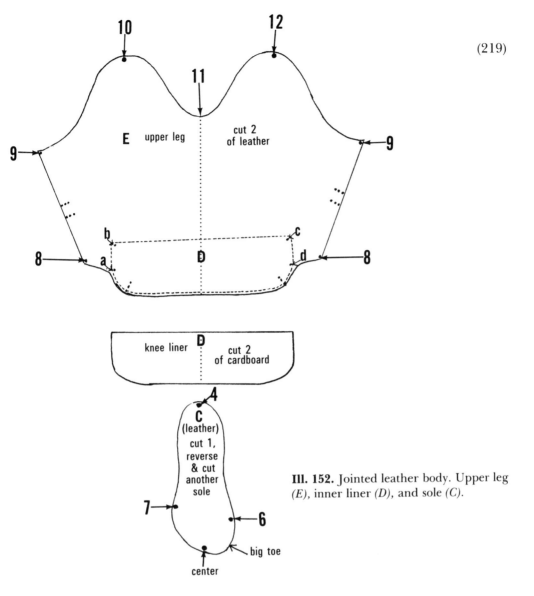

Ill. 152. Jointed leather body. Upper leg (E), inner liner (D), and sole (C).

piece A (Ill. 151). Use the strongest thread you can find; space the rows of gathers about ¼″ apart. Tie security knots at one end of the gathering stitches; leave threads loose at other end. Repeat for other leg.

Step 5 Stuff both legs firmly, keeping the soles as flat as possible. Pack the stuffing to just below the third row of gathering stitches. Cover the sawdust with a generous layer of cotton or its equivalent. Now close the top by pulling gently but firmly on the loose gathering threads. As the gathers form, push them toward the tied ends of thread. When the gathers have entirely closed the top of lower leg (A), tie the thread ends in a double security knot. Tuck the raw edges to the inside. Lower legs are now finished.

ASSEMBLING THE UPPER LEG

Step 1   Glue cardboard knee inner liner *D* to wrong side of leather upper leg *E,* as indicated by broken lines (Ill. 152). Position it just *inside* the seam line. Let glue dry.

Step 2   With right sides together, baste leather knee facing *F* (Ill. 153) to bottom edge of upper leg E, starting at 8 and ending at the opposite 8, and matching center front and triple dots. Stitch along the *edge* of the card inner liner, but *not into* the card.

Step 3   Open facing *F.* Set the machine for a #2 stitch. With wrong side of leather up, stitch around the three straight edges of the cardboard inner liner *D,* starting at *a,* on to *b,* to *c,* and through *d* (Ill. 152).

Step 4   With right sides together, baste upper leg seam and the leather knee facing seam together in one long continuous seam. Machine stitch. Repeat for other upper leg piece.

Step 5   Set machine on its longest (gathering) stitch. Sew three rows of gathering stitches across the loose edge of the facing. Repeat on other facing.

Step 6   Turn facing to inside. Reset the machine for a #2 stitch. Top stitch all around the lower edges (8 to 8), this time catching the lower edge of the cardboard inner liner *D* along its length.

Step 7   With right sides together, baste the top *(G)* of the upper leg (Ill. 153) to upper leg *E* (Ill. 152). Begin at point 9 (center back leg seam) and stitch to 10, to 11, to 12, then back to 9. Machine stitch. Repeat on other leg. Both upper legs will then be shaped like a "saddle." The four parts of those legs that are longest (two on each leg) are called "lugs" (see Ill. 154).

Step 8   Draw the gathering threads tightly together until there is only a tiny hole visible in the center. Tie off the thread ends, using a double security knot (two separate knots, one on top of the other).

Step 9   Cut lengthwise slit (Ill. 154) in the top of the upper leg *G.* Turn the leg right side out through the slit. Repeat on other upper leg piece.

Step 10   Fit the knee end (8) of upper leg *E* over a round object—such as a marble—and hold it there while you pack sawdust as tightly as possible around leg bottom. Here you are actually forming a leather socket. The more solidly you hold the knee end over the marble, and the tighter you pack sawdust, the more perfect the socket will be. Put a thick layer of cotton or its equivalent over the top of the sawdust.

Step 11   Insert upper leg cardboard liner *H* through the slit in the top of the upper leg *G.* Wiggle it around until it is seated properly into position; then close the slit, using neat hand stitches (Ill. 155).

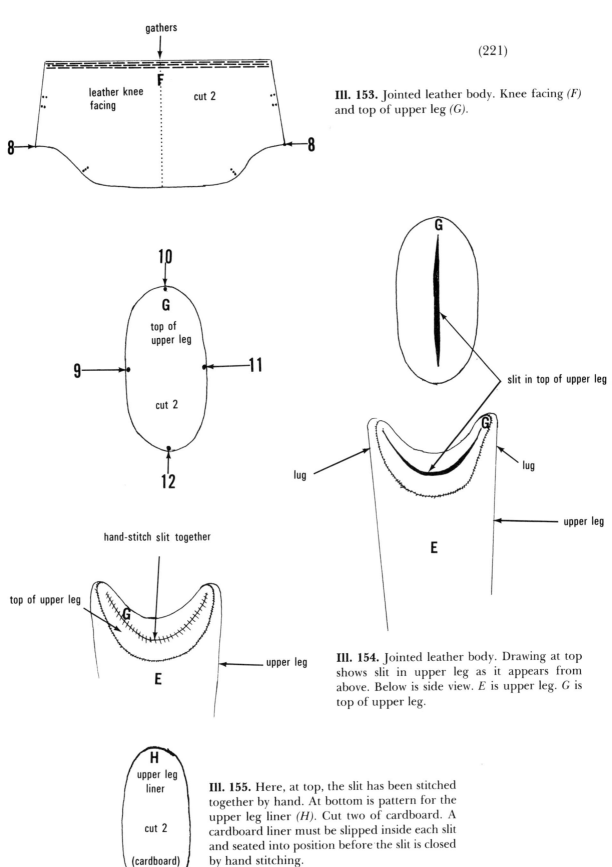

gathers

F

leather knee facing

cut 2

8   8

Ill. 153. Jointed leather body. Knee facing (F) and top of upper leg (G).

10

G

top of upper leg

9   11

cut 2

12

G

slit in top of upper leg

G

lug   lug

upper leg

E

hand-stitch slit together

top of upper leg

G

E   upper leg

Ill. 154. Jointed leather body. Drawing at top shows slit in upper leg as it appears from above. Below is side view. E is upper leg. G is top of upper leg.

H

upper leg liner

cut 2

(cardboard)

Ill. 155. Here, at top, the slit has been stitched together by hand. At bottom is pattern for the upper leg liner (H). Cut two of cardboard. A cardboard liner must be slipped inside each slit and seated into position before the slit is closed by hand stitching.

ASSEMBLING THE LOWER BODY

NOTE: Contrary to the usual warning against easing one part of a leather body to fit another, in this particular case you must do so during construction of lower body *I,* to give that portion the proper contours.

Step 1 With right sides together, insert needle through dot at 13, then through dot 14. Pull the pieces together. Baste around the curve formed when the pieces were pulled together, and through dot 15. Tie off threads. Machine stitch.

Step 2 With right sides together, insert needle through dot at 16, then through dot 14. Pull the pieces together. Baste around the curve that was formed, from 14 to 16 through dot 17. Tie off threads. Machine stitch. Tie off threads again.

Step 3 Set the machine on long stitch (basting); lower presser foot and reset the upper-thread tension knob at its highest number. Raise presser foot and run a line of stitches between 18 and 16 (Ill. 156) as near the edge of the leather as possible. This will provide the necessary easement for stitching that section to the opposite side, 18 and 13. (Don't forget to lower the presser foot, return the upper-thread tension knob to normal, and raise the presser foot.) Insert needle through dots 18, draw them together, and baste around the curve from 18 to 13/16. Machine stitch.

Follow the same procedures in constructing the other side of the lower body.

Step 4 With right sides together, baste seam from center front through center back, matching notches and crotch seams (Ill. 157). Machine stitch.

Step 5 Turn lower body right side out.

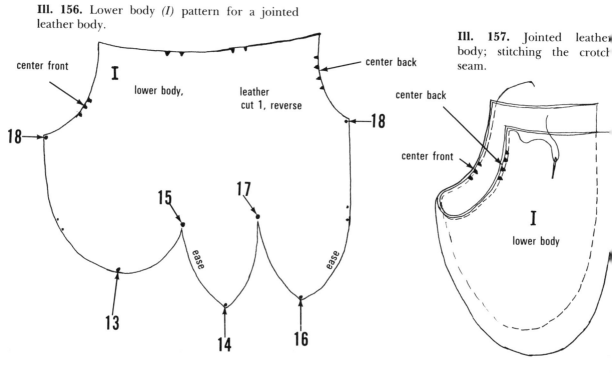

Ill. 156. Lower body *(I)* pattern for a jointed leather body.

center front

I

lower body,

leather
cut 1, reverse

center back

18

18

15

17

13

14

16

ease

ease

Ill. 157. Jointed leather body; stitching the crotch seam.

center back

center front

I

lower body

ASSEMBLING THE MUSLIN LINING
AND LEATHER LINING-COVER

First, prepare the leather lining-cover *K* by scalloping around the edges as indicated in Ill. 158 (if you haven't already done so).

Step 1 Baste, then stitch, muslin lining *J* together along both sides, from 19 to 20. Turn right side out.

Step 2 Baste, then stitch, leather lining-cover *K* together along both sides, from 21 to 22. Turn right side out.

Step 3 Insert muslin lining *J* inside lining-cover *K*, matching notch locations at waistline, and matching side seams. Baste together at waistline. Machine stitch. This completes the upper body unit.

Step 4 With right sides together, slip upper body unit over lower body *I*, and baste the two together at waistline, matching center fronts, center backs, and side seams. Machine stitch. Turn right side out.

Stuff the body "rock hard" with sifted sawdust. Cap off the sawdust with several handfuls of cotton or its equivalent. Turn under raw edges of the muslin and close the top with small, neat hand stitches (Ill. 162).

Ill. 158. Leather lining-cover *(K)* for jointed leather body. Note the edges to be scalloped.

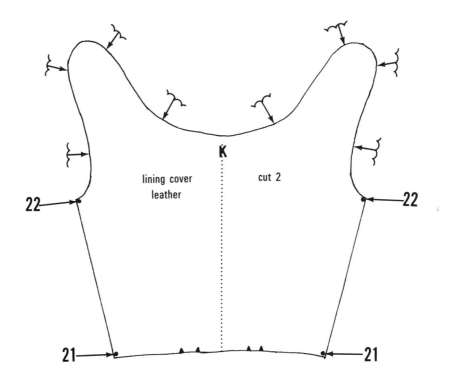

lining cover
leather

K

cut 2

22

22

21

21

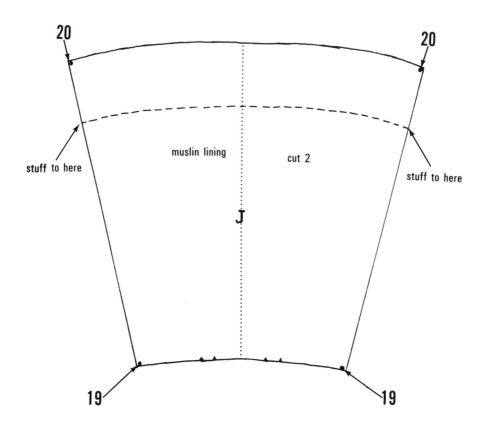

Ill. 159. Muslin lining (*J*) for jointed leather body.

ASSEMBLING THE THREE-PIECE UPPER ARMS

Step 1 Glue upper-arm card liner *M* to wrong side of upper arm *L,* as indicated in Ill. 160. Repeat for other arm. Let glue dry thoroughly.

Step 2 Top stitch around three sides of card liner *M*, leaving its bottom edge free of stitching.

Step 3 Clip curves across from 23 to center, as indicated (Ill. 160).

Step 4 Smear glue along lower edge of card liner, and wipe off excess. When the glue begins to feel sticky, fold the lower straight edge and the clipped curved edges of the arm up *onto* the cardboard liner *M*. Repeat for other arm. Let glue dry.

Step 5 With wrong sides together, baste upper arm seams together from 23 to 24. Machine stitch. Repeat on other arm.

Step 6 Baste upper arm muslin liner *N* from 25 to 26. Machine stitch. Repeat for other arm.

Step 7 Turn upper arm muslin lining *N* up along fold line (Ill. 161) and, with a hot iron, press in place. Set machine for long basting stitches. Run three rows of gathering stitches along the lower, folded edge of muslin, the first row along its very edge. (See detail, Ill. 161.) Repeat for other arm.

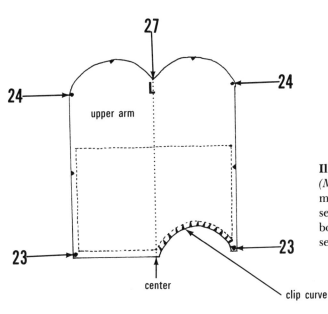

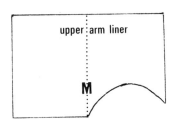

Ill. 160. Upper arm *(L)* and upper arm liner *(M)* for jointed leather body. Upper arm is made of leather. Cut one, reverse, and cut a second one. The liner is made of thin cardboard. Again, cut one, reverse, and cut a second one.

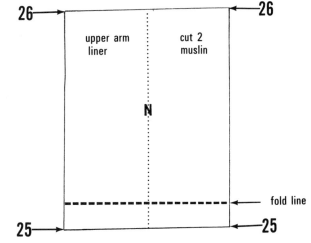

Ill. 161. Upper arm muslin liner *(N)* for a jointed leather body. Detail at bottom shows three rows of gathering stitches.

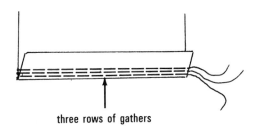

Step 8   Insert lining down into leather upper arm *L*, with seams facing the same direction. Baste across the upper arm curve from 24 to 27. Machine stitch. Trim muslin close to the seam line. Turn right side out. Repeat for other arm.

STUFFING AND FINISHING THE ARM

Step 1   Tightly pack upper section of the arm with cotton or its equivalent; stuff rest of arm with sawdust, being careful to pack it tightly in the card liner area. Cap sawdust with cotton or its equivalent. Draw the three gathering threads up tightly, until only a tiny hole can be seen in the center. Tie off threads with a double security knot. Stuff the gathered edge inside the leather arm tube. This forms the socket for the bisque ball-joint lower arm.

ASSEMBLING THE BODY

Regular two-hole buttons can be used (if they're strong enough), but metal buttons made for this purpose are best. If those you order have sharp points attached to their sides, cut them off. They serve no purpose in the construction of this body; in fact, if you don't cut them off, they'll damage the leather at the point of penetration.

Ill. 162 depicts the left bisque forearm (1) and the lower leg and foot (2) fastened to the body.

The tops of the upper arms (3) are ready to be fastened to the body. The left upper leg lug and lower body (4) are held together with wire here, and the wire is ready to be pushed through the right side of the lower body as soon as the right upper leg (5) is pushed up into place.

Right lower leg (6) is ready to be pushed inside its socket and fastened.

The inset shows the enlargement of the button *B* and wire *W*. Before wire is shoved through any part of the body, insert one end of it through a hole in the button. Use needle-nose pliers to bend the wire into a hook, with the end of the hook ready to go through the other hole in the button when the wire is pulled tight from the opposite side. This hook anchors the wire and button solidly in place. When the other end of the wire emerges from the opposite side of the body, slip a metal button onto it and push the button down tightly against the body. Cut off the excess wire, leaving only enough to bend into another hook that is pushed through the other hole in that button. (Refer to Ill. 162 when in doubt about the part being assembled.)

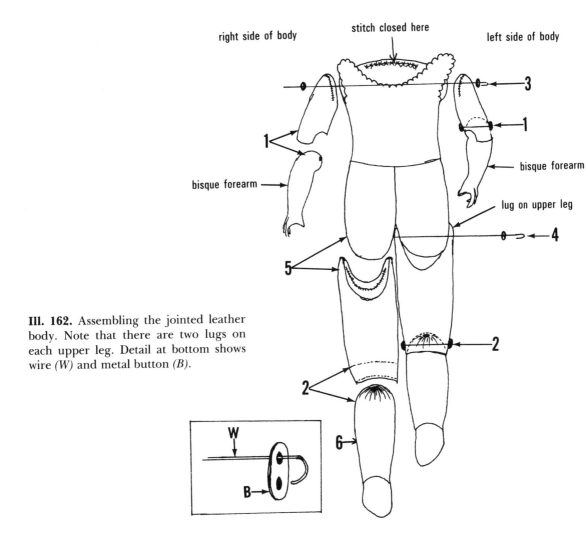

right side of body stitch closed here left side of body

bisque forearm

bisque forearm

lug on upper leg

Ill. 162. Assembling the jointed leather body. Note that there are two lugs on each upper leg. Detail at bottom shows wire *(W)* and metal button *(B)*.

W

B

Step 1   Insert the ball portion of the bisque forearm into its socket (1). While holding it there, place light pencil marks on the outside of the leather, opposite the holes in the porcelain ball. Notice the position of the bisque arms and leather upper arms in relation to the body. Pay close attention to this, so that there will be no mixup in getting the arms where they belong—i.e., right arm on right side, left arm on left side.

Step 2   Remove the bisque forearm. Using an ice pick, insert its point at one pencil mark and shove it through the leather and sawdust, guiding it carefully so that its point will emerge through the opposite pencil mark.

Step 3   Cut a piece of wire long enough to go through the channel you made with the ice pick.

Step 4   Slip a metal button onto the wire; then bend that end of the wire into a hook, as described earlier. Position the bisque forearm back into its socket, matching its holes to the holes in the leather. Push the wire through the leather, the holes in the bisque forearm, and through the opposite side of the leather. Anchor that end of the wire with a metal button. Now fasten the other leather/bisque arm (1) together the same way.

Step 5 Attach the lower leg to the upper leg (2) in the same manner. Be very careful in guiding the ice pick through the sawdust. Make sure its point emerges through the pencil mark on the opposite side. Anchor it as you did the arm. Assemble the other leg to the upper leg (2) in the same way.

Step 6 Cut a piece of wire long enough to go through both hips and all four leg lugs.

Step 7 Do not use pencil marks in preparation for joining the hip "stumps" to the upper legs. Instead, fit the two lugs of one leg over the "stump" at the hip. Holding the position securely (as you want it to be when finished), insert the ice pick through the *center* of the outside lug and, aiming for a similar location on the opposite side of the stump, shove the ice pick through the stump, the inside lug, and a short distance into the other hip stump. Your aim will never be precise, but close enough, up to this point. Remove the ice pick and the leg.

Step 8 Repeat the procedure in Step 7 on the other side of the body, this time aiming the ice pick toward the hole you made in Step 7. Back off the ice pick enough to allow the first leg lugs to be placed into position over the stump. Then carefully insert the point of the ice pick through the lug hole in the crotch area. Wiggle the ice pick, as though you were feeling for the first channel you made through the sawdust. You can tell when you hit it. Push the ice pick the rest of the way through the hip stump, and through the outside hole of the leg lug. Be sure its point emerges through that first hole you made. This part of the body is now being held together by the ice pick alone.

Step 9 Slip a metal button onto the wire you prepared in Step 6; then bend the wire into a hook. Start removing the ice pick and, as you back it off, insert the wire to follow it. Continue withdrawing the ice pick and pushing the wire against the point of the pick until finally the ice pick is completely clear of the body and the wire has emerged from the opposite side. Anchor the wire in place with a metal button.

Step 10 Fasten the upper arms to the shoulders, following the same procedure used in attaching the leg lugs to the hip stumps.

The body is now complete and fully articulated. Its arms are bent; it can be "walked" across the floor; it can even "set and rest a spell."

17

Making Cloth Bodies for China and Bisque Dolls

Antique chinas, parians, and bisques—dolls originally made with cloth bodies—often need parts of their bodies repaired or replaced. You may find one with its body pinned together with small, rusty safety pins, or covered with patches, or its rips held together by old adhesive tape. Sometimes a lone head may be found, waiting for someone to make a body for it, and supply it with new limbs and a shoulder plate.

Cloth bodies were made of many fabrics, of solid colors, even of printed materials. It is not the intent of this chapter to furnish the reader with an extensive background of where, when, how, or by whom those soft bodies were made. Other books on the market cover that subject. Nor will this chapter present a course in basic sewing techniques, since most collectors have at least a nodding acquaintance with these already. It will, however, point out any peculiarities in body construction, as well as describe the techniques needed for creating a lovely doll body from a simple piece of cloth.

One of the most common mistakes made in constructing cloth doll bodies is not allowing sufficient width for the arm or leg tube.

Keep in mind that the leg and arm tubes for the bodies in this chapter will have to be customized to fit the arms and legs you may wish to use. Stick to the curved shape of the Bye-Lo arm, but adjust its width to accommodate the hands you use. This rule applies not only to *all* patterns in this and the preceding chapter, but to any pattern you may buy or borrow.

Keep the doll as authentic as possible. Even though a cloth body is stained, mildewed, or badly decomposed, and the musty odor is almost unbearable, save it if you can—by whatever means available. The same thing applies to the clothes the doll may be wearing.

If you must make a new body, see whether there is enough of the old one left to copy. Take it apart—stitch by stitch—and transfer its lines to paper. Remember, the old body stretched when it was stuffed, and stretched more through years of handling. Make allowance for this when you true up the paper pattern.

If you're copying a rather complicated cloth body, keep a pencil and a sheet of paper handy to write down—or sketch—any instructions or diagrams that may be needed later. Without such instructions, once the body is taken apart you may forget how the pattern pieces fit together, particularly if you are the same kind of person as I am—a "hopper" who has many projects going at the same time.

If you collect soft-bodied dolls (another name for cloth-body dolls), you know that many had voice boxes, sometimes called squeakers. Some of the dolls were simply called Mama dolls. Most old voice boxes are now worn out and will no longer work, but replacing a voice box is not difficult. Dollspart (see list of suppliers) carries two types of these. I much prefer the one labeled "Mama Voices."

To install a new sound box, locate the point where the top of the body was tied, or wired, over the flanged neck. Don't try to save this thread or wire—it's probably too old and unsafe to reuse. Keep a firm grip on the head while you cut the wire or thread to release the flange. Put the head aside in a safe place. Carefully pull out the body stuffing and remove the old voice box. Insert a new one in the same location. Put the stuffing back as it was, being careful not to disturb the position of the new voice box. It must be seated in the tummy so that, when the body is supine, the mechanism will reset itself and be ready to cry "Mama" when the body is tilted forward. Do not attach the head until—with the stuffing in place and the top of the body held closed with one hand—the baby "cries" each time you tilt it backward and bring it forward.

If the flanged neck was held in place originally with wire, use new wire and attach it the same way. You may have to cover with masking tape the end first inserted in the casing so that, in threading it through, the end will not puncture the cloth. Twist the two ends together, using needle-nose pliers. If heavy cord was used originally, use cording as nearly like the old as you can find.

MAKING THE BYE-LO BODY

There are only three pieces to this pattern. Suitable cloth is unbleached muslin, if you want the body to resemble the old ones. Even more authentic looking is that fabric called (in our midwest area) turkey cloth. I have seen it only once—in 1977 while browsing in a Tri-State fabric shop. It was like finding buried treasure, and I bought the whole piece, almost 30 yards. I suspect it will be enough to last me until Gabriel blows his horn or I stop working with dolls, whichever comes first. I had never heard of this material before, nor have I seen it since. Ask for it in your area because it is perfect for making old-looking cloth bodies.

The Bye-Lo body pattern, in the size presented here, will fit a 1″ porcelain head. The overall measurement—when the doll is finished—is a tiny 4½″. When costumed in a dainty christening dress and bonnet, with bootees to match, the doll is adorable. If you're lucky enough to have a miniature antique Bye-Lo head but lack the hands, they can be ordered. Make a body from this pattern, attach the old head and the repro hands, and you will have a delightful "pocket-sized" baby doll. (Of course, you can always buy a small kit to use.)

Set the middle screws of the pantograph on #4. The enlargement made with this setting is for a life-size Bye-Lo baby with a head circumference of 14″. Smaller sizes can be made, of course, by changing the position of the middle screws of the pantograph to any point lower than 4.

To make the body you will need, in addition to the porcelain parts:

> Cloth
> Sharp, straight pins
> Heavy cardboard
> Cotton or its equivalent
> Needle and thread
> Scissors
> Cord or wire for fastening
>   cloth to the flanged neck

Before cutting out the body, cut circles of heavy cardboard to fit the head and hand openings. Glue them in place. They will keep the body stuffing from going into the hollow head or the hands. By the time the body is cut out and ready to assemble, the glue will be dry.

ASSEMBLING FRONT *B* AND BACK *A*

Step 1 Set the machine for its longest stitch (for basting and gathering). With presser foot *down,* change the upper-thread tension knob from normal to its highest number—i.e., 2½ (normal) to 6, 7, or higher. The combination of long stitches and tight thread tension usually produces the necessary easement on the longer sections of the body. While the presser foot is down, run a line of stitches along both sides of the body back *A* and in the crotch area, as indicated by the long broken seam lines in Ill. 163. As each stitching line is finished, tie off the threads at one end and leave those on the other end free, in case more gathering must be done later.

Ill. 163. Bye-Lo body, back pattern.

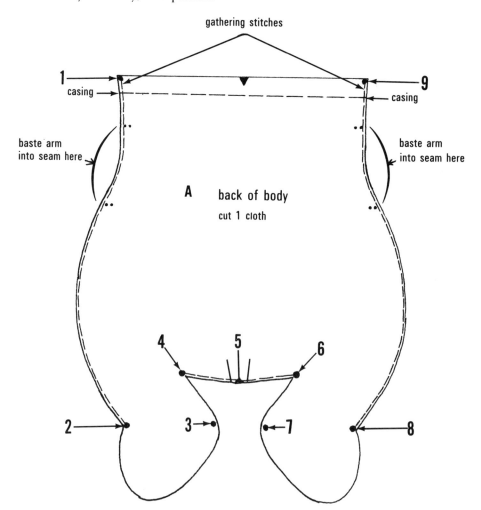

Step 2 *Lower* the presser foot, turn the upper-thread tension knob back to normal, and raise the presser foot. Now adjust the stitch length to 1½. Always use extremely short stitches (giving more stitches per inch) when sewing *cloth* bodies. Normal stitches may pop open when you stuff the body. These short stitches will hold.

Step 3 With right sides together, pin the front and back together *only at the numbered dots*—i.e., 1 to 1, 2 to 2, and so on, around to dot 9.

Step 4 Baste front and back together, leaving the space between the double dots open (Ill. 163). (The arms will later be basted into these spaces before the body is stitched on the machine.) After the numbers are pinned together in Step 3, front and back will look as if they do not belong together, the back being much larger than the front. This is as it should be. The long basting lines made in Step 1 should have minimized the differences, but if still more adjustment is needed, pull the loose ends of those threads tighter, and distribute the gathers that form so that they are not visible as gathers, simply as easement.

At *TG* (Ill. 164), two or three tucks can be made, or that area (on the back) can be gathered to fit at this point. This will provide the

Ill. 164. Bye-Lo body, front and arm pattern.

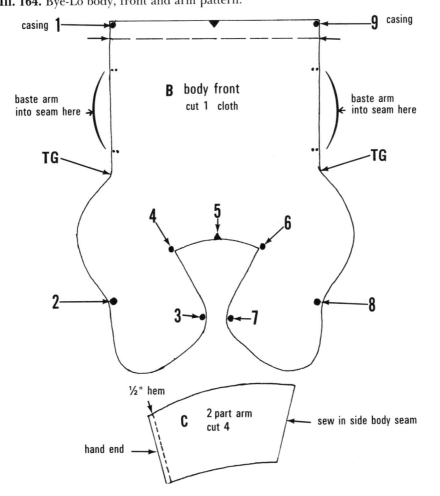

sit-down bottom for the Bye-Lo. If you're in doubt as to how much cloth should be worked into tucks or gathers, baste from 1 to *TG* and stop; then baste from 2 up to *TG*. You will know the excess fold of cloth at that point must be tucked or gathered in that specific area. Do the left side of the body the same way. Follow the same procedure in the crotch area, forming either tucks or gathers in the center. *Do not machine stitch yet.*

Step 5   Each arm *(C)* has two cloth parts. Baste both seams, right sides together. The longer seam is the cloth *upper seam;* the shorter, the cloth *under seam.* Machine stitch. At the hand end (Ill. 164), turn the arm tube up and into a ½″ hem. This will prevent the edges from fraying when the hand is attached (tied in).

Step 6   Mark approximate center of the bisque hand (palm side) with pencil. With arm tube wrong side out, slip the hand inside. Push it up toward the hemmed edge of the tube until the end (where the cardboard is glued) is even with hemmed edge of the cloth. Work the hand around until the pencil mark is lined up with the cloth under-seam. Hold the seam against the pencil mark so that

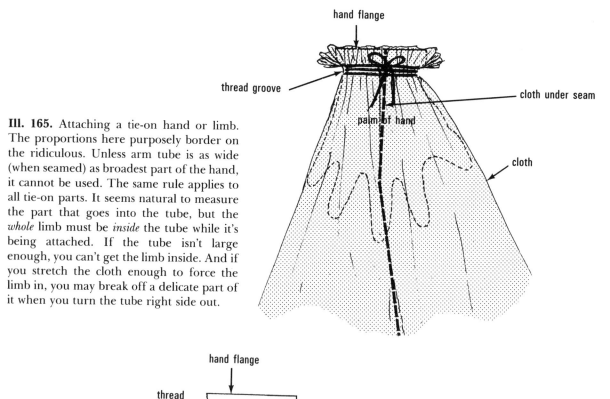

Ill. 165. Attaching a tie-on hand or limb. The proportions here purposely border on the ridiculous. Unless arm tube is as wide (when seamed) as broadest part of the hand, it cannot be used. The same rule applies to all tie-on parts. It seems natural to measure the part that goes into the tube, but the *whole* limb must be *inside* the tube while it's being attached. If the tube isn't large enough, you can't get the limb inside. And if you stretch the cloth enough to force the limb in, you may break off a delicate part of it when you turn the tube right side out.

it can't slip. Now—unless you have a helper—hold a piece of strong thread between your teeth and, with free hand, wrap the thread around and around in the thread groove (Ill. 165). When you're sure it won't slip while you tie a double security knot, do so. If thread ends are too long, clip them, but not right down to the knots. Spread Elmer's Glue sparingly along the wound threads, and with a toothpick work it down into them. Let glue dry while attaching other hand to its sleeve tube. Turn arms right side out.

At this point, take time to check both arms and hands to make sure they will not come apart when you stuff them. Hold the bisque limb in one hand, the sleeve tube in the other, and pull in opposite directions. If they cannot be pulled apart, they are ready to be stuffed with cotton or its equivalent. Stop packing when you are within a half-inch of the top of the arm tube. Close the top with machine stitching.

Step 7 Baste the arms into the body seam at indicated positions in Ill. 164. Doublecheck to make sure you get the right hand on the right side, the left on the left side. An easy way to do this is to turn the body right side out, put the left arm in place (and put the right one completely away from the work area so there'll be no chance of a mixup). Turn the body wrong side out again and baste the left arm into place. Be sure you get the upper seam toward the head. Machine stitch around the body, then turn it right side out.

Step 8 Stitch ½″ hem (casing) at the neckline, starting at one shoulder and ending back there, leaving a small opening for insertion of wire or heavy thread.

Step 9 If heavy thread is used, attach it to a bodkin or a safety pin and run it through the casing. Slip the flanged neck of the Bye-Lo head inside the neck opening. Pull both ends of the thread, making the casing fit as tightly as possible around the flange. Distribute the gathers evenly. Tie off the thread ends with a double safety knot. Put a small drop of glue on the knots and work it into the fibers. Let dry. Push the loose ends of the threads inside the casing.

Your Bye-Lo baby is now ready to be costumed.

This four-piece pattern was drafted from a 10″ "American Schoolboy" doll. In larger sizes, however, I have seen it used on parian and china lady dolls with tiny wasp waists. On lady dolls, two waistline darts are taken in the front (Ill. 169).

Set the two middle screws of the pantograph on 2½. The enlargement made will be for a 24″ to 25″ doll. For a doll this size, the head should measure about 3″ from the chin to the top of the forehead. Each arm should measure 12″ (combining the porcelain arm and the muslin sleeve tube to which it is attached). Each leg should measure about 13½″ (combining the porcelain leg and the muslin leg tube to which it is attached).

In addition to the porcelain parts you will need:

Cloth
Finely sifted sawdust
Electric iron
Strong thread for tying on
  the parts
Needle and thread
Scissors
Elmer's Glue

This body goes together so easily and quickly that you may not need to do any basting, unless perhaps across seam 3-1-4 (Ill. 168). It is the contour of this 3-1-4 seam that gives the body its beautifully shaped derrière. You will probably find that it takes longer to read the directions than to make the body. Chances are, the whole thing is so simple that once you have made one, you will never need to read the instructions again.

Always remember to measure the circumference of the upper leg and arm, and "customize" that portion of the cloth body into which they go. Also, in making cloth bodies where tie-on parts are used, compare the upper leg and arm circumferences with the length of the foot, and the distance around the broadest portion of the hand. If any part of the limbs are larger than the tie-on end, use the largest number to customize the matching body part. Otherwise, when the part is tied on, you will not be able to turn it right side out.

Step 1   With right sides together, stitch upper backs *A* together, 1 to 2 (Ill. 166). Press seam open.

Step 2   Press down and machine stitch ½″ hem at top of upper back *A* (Ill. 166).

Step 3   With right sides together, baste lower back leg and seat *B* (Ill. 167) to center back seam of upper back *A* (3-1-4; Ill. 168), matching notch 1 (Ills. 167 and 168) to the seam at 1 (Ill. 166). Machine stitch. Press seam toward waist.

Step 4   Press, then machine stitch, ½″ hem at top of body front *C* (Ill. 169).

Step 5   If the body is for a lady doll, stitch the waistline darts in place as marked (Ill. 169).

Step 6   With right sides together, baste assembled back *(A and B)* to body front *C* (Ill. 169) from 5 to 6, on both sides.

Step 7   With right sides still together, baste the inside leg seam, beginning at 7, stitching to dot 8 and down to dot 9. Now go back

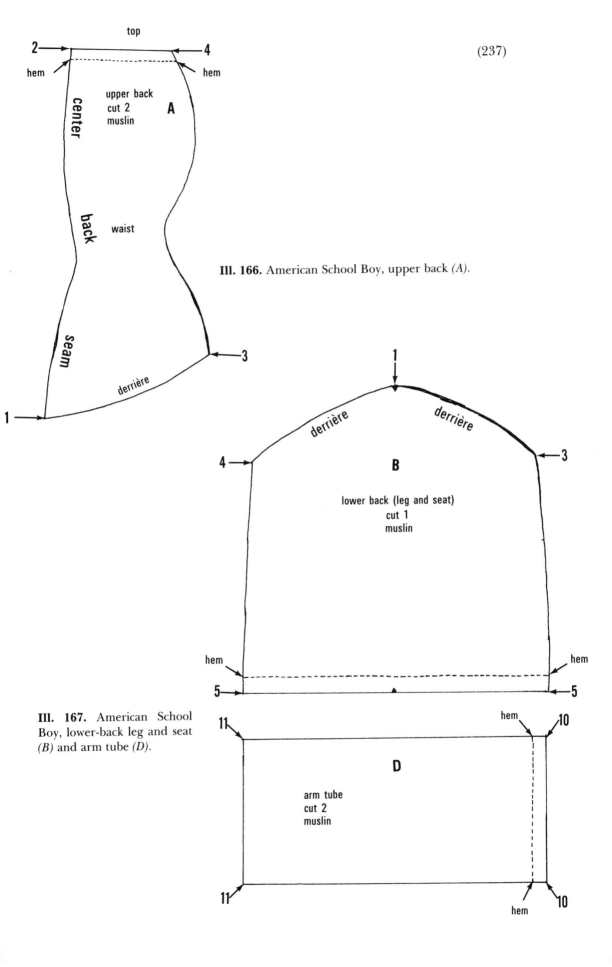

(237)

top

2 → | ← 4

hem ← | ↑ → hem

upper back
cut 2
muslin

A

center

back   waist

Seam

derrière

→ 3

1 →

Ill. 166. American School Boy, upper back *(A)*.

1
↓

derrière   derrière

4 →

← 3

B

lower back (leg and seat)
cut 1
muslin

hem ←   → hem

5 →   ← 5

Ill. 167. American School
Boy, lower-back leg and seat
(B) and arm tube *(D)*.

11 ↗   hem ↙ 10

D

arm tube
cut 2
muslin

11 ↗   ↓ ↘ 10

hem

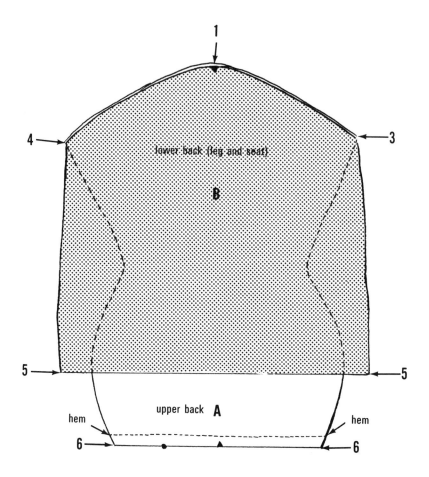

Ill. 168. Sewing upper back to lower back. *(This is not a pattern.)*

and stitch another continuous seam over the first one, starting ½″ below dot 8 on one side, stitching through dot 8, then stitching another ½″ below dot 8 on the opposite side. This is to reinforce the crotch. Cut through both layers of cloth from a point between 7 and 9, up to dot 8 (Ill. 169). Do *not* cut into the stitching. Trim seams down to ⅛″ if necessary.

Step 8   Mark the center back of each china or bisque leg.

Step 9   Find the center back of each cloth leg tube by folding the leg seams together, toward the front, and creasing them in the middle. Mark the crease location.

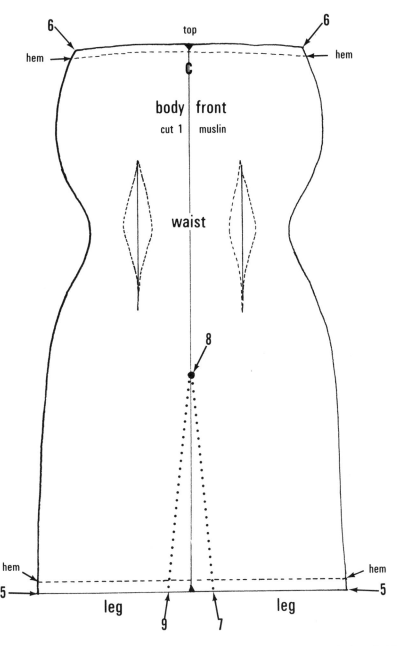

Ill. 169. American School Boy front *(C)*. Reinforce the crotch area (8) by stitching over the first seam ½″ down each side from 8.

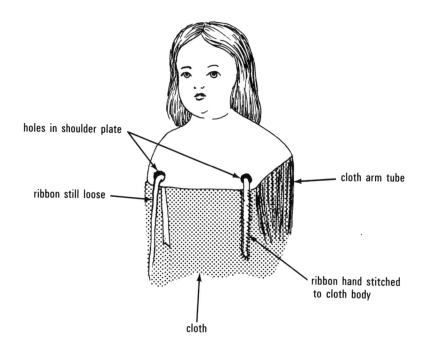

holes in shoulder plate

ribbon still loose

cloth arm tube

ribbon hand stitched
to cloth body

cloth

Ill. 170. Attaching the shoulder plate with ribbon.

Step 10 Check to make sure you're ready to attach the right leg to the right leg tube, and the left leg to the left leg tube. If in doubt, turn the body right side out and hold the left leg to the left side (put the right leg away from the work area so there will be no mixup). Turn the body wrong side out again and tie in the left leg. This is done by slipping the china or bisque leg, top first, through the body top opening, and working it downward until its heel is to the back, and the center back pencil mark on the leg is aligned to the center back mark on the cloth body tube. Hold it there while you wrap thread around and around in the groove. Tie a double security knot, and clip the thread ends if they're longer than ½″. Run a thin string of glue on top of the threads, working it into the fibers with a toothpick; let dry. Repeat on the other leg. Turn body.

Step 11 Hem one end of the arm tubes *D,* as indicated in Ill. 167. Stitch both arm tube seams, 10 through 11.

Step 12 Mark the center of each arm (palm side). Slip the arm inside its arm tube, matching the pencil mark to the seam, and tie it on as you did the legs in Step 10. Turn right side out.

Step 13 Stuff the body rock hard with sifted sawdust, and close its top with hand stitching. Stuff the arms; check them against the body, pin them in place, and recheck them. Then hand stitch the arm tubes in position across the body top. The rechecking is done to make sure one arm does not hang longer than the other, and that both are correctly positioned in relation to the widest part of the hips; also, to make sure each arm is on the correct side of the body.

Step 14 Glue the head to the body. If there are holes in the corner of the shoulder plate, it can be glued *and* stitched to the body, using a curved needle; or, before applying glue to the under side of the shoulder plate, run narrow ribbon or bias tape through the holes and leave the two ends loose, to be stitched later to the cloth body (Ill. 170).

There is a mystery that plagues beginners—sometimes even veteran doll collectors, or dollmakers—one I propose to clear up in this last part of Chapter 17. The mystery is how one goes about proportioning a doll body so that it will have attractive lines that are compatible with its head and limbs.

The market is glutted with cloth body patterns—some excellent, some fair, and others pretty bad. Some are marked, for instance, "Makes 21″ doll," or they carry similar markings denoting the finished size. Good ones are correctly labeled; some, when made up, make a person wonder if the pattern designer just pulled a figure out of thin air—the measurements are so far off.

Whether you want to draft your own patterns, learn how to figure correct body proportions, or simply check patterns you have bought or borrowed, Ill. 171 will provide a solid basis for understanding the elements that go into the making of a well-proportioned doll body. If you are drafting a body pattern for a lady doll, it should have more delicate lines than that of a male. Shoulders should be a bit narrower; arms should be shorter; the waist is smaller, and the hips are wider than those of a male.

If the body pattern is for a child doll you want to appear as perhaps three to four years of age, the height should be about half that of a full-grown male. If you want the body to represent a doll in the early teen years—thirteen to fifteen, for instance—the height should be about three-quarters that of an adult male.

Let's apply these general rules to the drafting of a body pattern, or checking one you already have. Measure the length of the doll's face from the chin to the top of its forehead. For example, let's assume the face is 1″ long. Multiply that by eight. The length of the doll, then—completely assembled—would be 8″.

Here are some other examples:
If the head is 1½″, the finished doll should be 12″.
If head is 2″, the finished doll should be 16″.
If head is 2½″, the finished doll should be 20″.

If the head is 3″, the finished doll should be 24″.

If the oval (head) in Ill. 171 measures 1″, and you count the ovals, eight of them comprise the body length (or height). Pursuing the process a bit further, you can also figure the length of the arms and legs. Ill. 171 shows that an ideally proportioned body has arms that measure four ovals each (four times the chin-to-forehead measurement), starting from the center of the chest and extending to the fingertips. Add the lengths of *two* arms—four ovals each—and they equal the *length* of the body, or *eight* ovals.

The widest part of the hip is four ovals *up* from the feet, four ovals *down* from the top of the head.

The leg separation begins approximately three and a half ovals *up* from the feet.

The table of *general* measurements given here—based on the *general* proportions in Ill. 171—will help you get started. Use it merely as a guide, not as an exact rule to follow. Dolls were never proportioned like humans—at least, very few of them were. Old French bodies came closest.

A study of doll bodies makes one wonder if the oldtimers used any kind of guide in making *some* of them. I have known many contemporary dollmakers whose philosophy is that "a body is just something to hang clothes on. It doesn't show; therefore it doesn't matter what it looks like." I happen to believe otherwise.

The method I worked out many years ago is condensed into the chart below. Measurements are given in inches. The column heading abbreviations are:

C-T-F: chin to forehead   T-L: torso length
    L-L: leg length   A-L: arm length
        F-D: finished doll

C-T-F	T-L	L-L	A-L	F-D
1	3½	3½	4	8
1½	5¼	5¼	6	12
2	7	7	8	16
2½	8¾	8¾	10	20
3	10½	10½	12	24
3½	12¼	12¼	14	28
4	14	14	16	32

Do not add allowances for seams. If you wish, add 2″ to 3″ to the top of the torso (Ill. 172).

If you order tie-on parts, when you receive them examine the grooves at the tops of the arms and the legs. Dollmakers who are more interested in quantity production than they are in quality

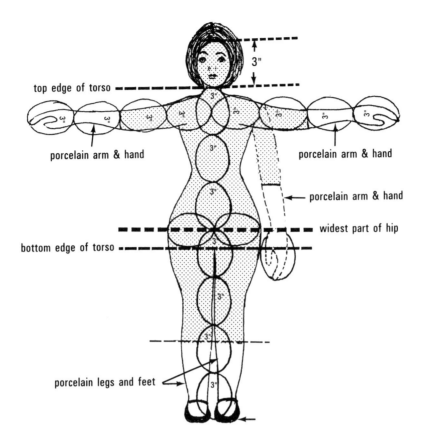

top edge of torso

porcelain arm & hand

porcelain arm & hand

porcelain arm & hand

widest part of hip

bottom edge of torso

porcelain legs and feet

Ill. 171. You can proportion a body by using the chin-to-forehead measurement. The length of the body here is 24″ (eight ovals multiplied by the chin-to-forehead measurement of 3″).

rarely take the time to deepen the grooves while the limbs are in the greenware state. They don't have to struggle with them; you do— once you buy the parts, it's your problem. Unless the grooves *are* deepened evenly before they are fired to bisque, that is, carved deep enough so the wound threads will seat firmly in the groove, it is impossible to tie/glue the porcelain and cloth together so that they will not separate, either while the doll is being stuffed or after it is finished.

If you receive arms and legs with shallow, or nonexistent, grooves, return them with a letter explaining why you refuse to accept them. If enough collectors will do this, dollmakers will be forced to take the few necessary extra minutes to deepen the grooves before firing them to bisque.

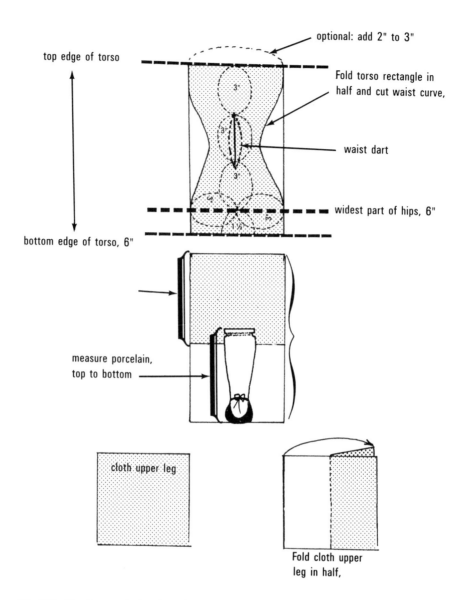

optional: add 2" to 3"

top edge of torso

Fold torso rectangle in
half and cut waist curve,

waist dart

widest part of hips, 6"

bottom edge of torso, 6"

measure porcelain,
top to bottom

cloth upper leg

Fold cloth upper
leg in half,

Ill. 172. Cutting and shaping the torso and leg tube. The length of the torso is 10½", finished (3½ ovals multiplied by chin-to-forehead measurement of 3"). Finished length of the leg is 10½" (3½ ovals multipled by chin-to-forehead measurement of 3"). Find the length of the cloth upper leg by subtracting the length of the porcelain from 10½".

The same thing applies to examining tie-on arms and legs in a shop. Don't buy them unless the grooves are carved properly.

To proportion an arm tube, multiply chin-to-forehead measurement—for instance, 3" times four ovals; 3 x 4 = 12. This is the total length of one arm. (Part of the tube is stitched to the top of the torso [body] to hold the arm in place.) Measure the length of the china arm, fingertips to end. If, for example, that measurement is 5", subtract 5" from the total length, 12". Your cloth arm tubes, then, would be 7". They are not tapered as are the legs (Ill. 173).

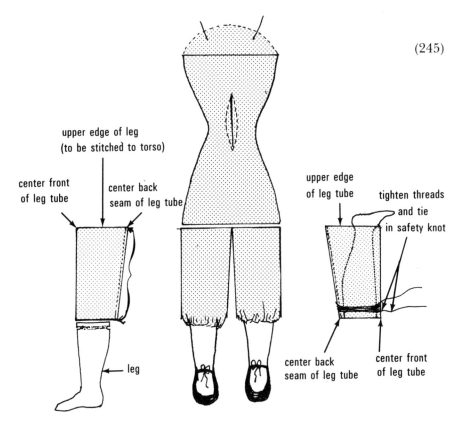

Ill. 173. Making the leg tube and tying in the leg. Slip the porcelain leg inside the leg tube, wrap thread several times around the groove, and tie it off. Apply glue on top of the thread and let dry. When the legs are turned right side out, they will look as shown here. Legs are stuffed before being stitched to the torso.

The arm is attached to its arm tube just as the legs were attached to theirs. The back leg seam is matched to the center back of the china leg. The arm seam is matched to the center of the under side of the arm (palm side).

The size of the arm tube is found by measuring the circumference of the *broadest* part, whether it be the hand, spread fingers, *or* the tie-on end. If you don't allow enough cloth to go around the broadest area, you cannot turn it right side out.

Before stuffing, and after turning the legs and arms right side out, check to make sure the parts are securely connected by string and glue. Hold the porcelain limb in one hand, its cloth tube in the other, and pull them in opposite directions. If you cannot pull them apart, they're ready for stuffing.

Always stuff the hollow limbs with sawdust, or glue heavy cardboard circles on top of the hollow end so that the stuffing will not work down into the empty parts of the limbs. This will prevent the stuffing from sifting into the limbs, leaving the tubes limp and unattractive.

18

General Instructions for Wax and Composition Dolls

The surface (skin) of an antique wax doll is susceptible to damage from anything that touches it, and from some things that don't. Excessive heat will soften or melt it; extreme cold will cause it to crack; sunlight will fade the colors. Fingernails, hangnails, friction against another object—even a rough cloth used to clean the surface—can also mar it. Beginners should never attempt major jobs of restoration on an old wax doll.

In fact, before you attempt even the simplest kind of repair with wax, it is essential that you learn to handle wax by familiarizing yourself with its behavior. Experiment with various waxes, such as paraffin, melted candles, Posmoulage, and beeswax. Learn to carve wax, mold it, pour it, deliberately damage it and then repair it, color it with crayons—learn everything you can about wax, and *then* make use of this knowledge in repairing or restoring an old doll.

The two most common types of true wax dolls are those with solid head and limbs formed by carving a block of wax or by hand molding warm wax, and those with poured-wax head and limbs. The second type was made by heating wax to a fluid state, pouring it into a mold, allowing the walls to set to the desired thickness, and then pouring the remaining still fluid wax back into its container. Because of the fragility of the poured waxes, the shells were usually reinforced on the inside with more substantial materials.

A third kind, referred to as dolls with dipped heads and limbs, are actually wax-coated compositions, papier-mâchés, woodens, metals, sometimes even plaster dolls. Base materials used for the dipped heads and limbs could be anything that would hold the shapes.

I strongly suspect that many antique dipped dolls began as "opposite" types in the doll world, but because of some production accident or error ended up as beautiful wax-dipped dolls—still of top-notch quality but quite different from what they started out to be. Many times, on opening the kiln and discovering minor flaws that went unnoticed during a prefiring inspection, I have "saved" a doll by painting and dipping it. Most dolls that have undergone this treatment have turned out to be delicate beauties that would not have been made otherwise. Minor flaws are rendered invisible by the wax coating.

CLEANING A WAX DOLL

Most waxes, because of their very nature, have accumulated a heavy coating of dust, dirt, and fumes over the years. Sometimes the only product that will clean them well is turpentine. Unfortunately it also removes the paint if the features were painted on the surface of the wax.

First, try a solution of cold water and Woolite. Saturate a cotton ball, then squeeze out part of the solution. Using very light pressure, try cleaning a small area. The heaviest accumulation will be in the low places—around the nose, the eyes, inside the ears—so work carefully in just one of these areas to see how the wax is going to respond to the cleaning. If the cold water/Woolite solution has no effect on the dirt, let the spot air dry; then dab on a small amount of cold cream (the same cream you would use on your face) and spread it out a little. Lightly swab a piece of silk, stretched taut over your fingertip, or a Q-Tip, across the cold-creamed area. If that does not clean it to your satisfaction, try a cotton ball soaked in denatured alcohol. And if none of these things works, use turpentine as a last resort. As the cotton gets dirty, switch to a clean area. Turpentine tends to soften the wax slightly if too much is used or if too much pressure is put on the area being cleaned. Keep this in mind as you work, and watch the wax carefully.

Think twice before you alter a wax doll, for alter it you most certainly will in any procedure you use on it. It is worth far more dirty than it would be with repainted or altered features. If you opt for cleaning an all-wax doll, know that the paint was probably applied directly to the surface. If so, the turpentine will most surely remove it. In this case you will have to repaint the features.

Dipped heads and limbs are cleaned in the same manner; however, the paint was usually applied to the base material—that is, to the porcelain, composition, or whatever was used. In this case no repainting will be necessary.

REPAIRING CRACKS

A careful cleaning precedes making crack repairs. It doesn't matter if there is just one crack to deal with or a dozen small ones, the method is the same. Each is done very carefully using the lighest touch possible, whether you're using the warmed bowl of a spoon, the rounded surface of a large nail, or whatever the tool may be. The biggest problem is getting the tool warm enough to smooth the wax, but not hot enough to melt it. Quite often a hair dryer will provide enough heat to accomplish the job. Set the dryer as high as it will go, then hold the tool in front of it, to absorb warmth. Hold the tool against your cheek. If it feels slightly warm, try swirling it against the back of the doll head. Do not exert much pressure, only enough to move the old wax into and over the smallest cracks.

A large crack cannot be mended in this fashion. It must, of course, be thoroughly cleaned. Then remove old wax from an inconspicuous location, to use for filling in where it's most needed. If the head has large cracks in several places, you probably will not be able to get enough old wax to fill them all—so fill only those most apparent. Cracks that appear where hair, clothing, or the body will cover them can be filled in with paraffin colored to match the old tint.

Hold the head in front of the hair dryer until the wax becomes quite warm. At the same time, hold the extra wax closer to the heat and allow it to soften. When you can work it with your fingers, act quickly and, with a delicate touch, fill in the crack. The area can be smoothed by the same warmed tool you used to repair small cracks.

REPAIRING THE NOSE

Often the tip of the nose is broken or worn away; the nose may even be completely gone. Hold the wax head in front of and fairly close to the *hot* air flow from a portable hair dryer. When the wax reaches a malleable state, remold the end of the nose, or construct a new one by pulling the surrounding wax toward the nose end. This will make the doll look different, of course; but if you must repair it, this is one way of handling the problem.

Trying to match the old wax and its color is an ambitious project that requires much patience and fortitude. It can be done, but the basic material I have found best is quite expensive. A 1979 catalog lists it at around $6.00 a pound, plus shipping (see list of suppliers). That material is Posmoulage. It is the only wax I have used since I first discovered it six years ago. A solid-wax head made from it at that time has withstood temperatures as low as 10° and as high as 98° without cracking or melting. Special coloring media can be ordered from this San Francisco company, but color crayons work quite well.

REPLACING MISSING HAIR

If hair was attached to the scalp by means of a slit in the wax, and if, over the years, that hair has become quite sparse, it is easy to replace. Find hair that matches the hair remaining on the doll. This will maintain as much of the doll's originality as it's possible to do.

Again, use a hair dryer. With the setting on high, direct the air flow to the slit. When the wax softens, gently tug on the remaining hair until it pulls loose. This will leave a damaged spot. Warm the bowl of a spoon and use it to smooth over the area until its contour has been restored. Then recut the slit, using a warmed paring knife. Mix the old hair with the new, and insert a bit at a time into the slit, sealing each section with a heated blade as you go.

Wax dolls that had "tufts" of hair applied in small areas all over the head may be restored in a similar manner, following these directions.

STRIPPING WAX FROM A DIPPED HEAD

If you acquire a dipped wax head and limbs so badly damaged that they are hopeless, remove the old wax and replace it with new. It can be removed by scraping or by dipping in hot wax. If you scrape it off, take care not to damage the color applied to the base part. Or melt paraffin to a clear liquid state in a coffee can—no more than three-quarters full. Make a "dipping tool" from a heavy coat hanger wire, one for each part of the doll. In succession, dunk each piece repeatedly in hot paraffin. This will strip off the old wax and will probably leave the base color undamaged. If you wish to use paraffin to recoat the base units, allow it to cool until it begins to look slightly opaque.

At this point, each doll must be judged according to its individual appearance. For example, after you have stripped the wax, if you find that the base unit had features painted against a *white* skin but that the *original* wax was pink, color your dipping wax. If the base unit is already a gaudy color with features applied heavy-handedly, then dipping it repeatedly in the white paraffin will soften the colors.

If the wax doll's features were painted on the surface of the wax, restore them the same way. Artists' oil paints, applied with a light hand to eyelashes, eyebrows, and lips, are satisfactory. Color the cheeks with your fingertips, much as you would apply rouge to your own face. In fact, creamy rouge will sometimes prove an ideal coloring agent to use on the cheeks of a wax doll. I prefer using powdered china paints ground in light balsam of copaiba because of its easy-flowing manageability (see Chapter 3).

In Chapter 9, instructions were given for repairing ball-jointed bodies. Many of those same techniques are applicable for use on composition or papier-mâché heads. The rest of this chapter will deal with one head in particular—that of an old Campbell Kid. The methods described may be used on any doll heads made of similar materials.

Step 1 Make descriptive notes about the doll head you are working on. For example: Campbell Kid; hair, dark brown in center back fading to light brownish tan around hairline; decal eyes looking to left side; eyelashes dark gray, nine on upper left lid, ten on upper right lid; no eyelashes below; two red dots, one in each nostril; watermelon mouth; eyebrows a single thin reddish brown curved line across center of each molded eyebrow.

Comment: Barely enough "flesh" clings to the 10mm. thickness of this composition head to distinguish the colors. The eyes appear to have been painted on paper, then glued to the sockets. Very little paper remains, only the black pupil. The surfaces of the eye sockets are the only parts of the doll head that are not cracked, badly crazed, or damaged in some way. Along both sides of the mold line the head gapes open. Underneath, where the head comes in contact with the shoulders, the composition is so crumbly that it falls off when touched.

If possible, take a closeup photograph of the doll head before you start work on it. (If the doll head is wigged and has glass eyes, of course they must both be removed before starting repair work.)

Step 2   Peel off all surface covering where the doll head gapes open along the mold line. As you do this, hold the head over a paper so that you can save all pieces. These will later be recycled. Do not use sandpaper on the head until directed to do so.

Step 3   Cut a 2″ wide strip of cloth long enough to circle the head and tie in a security knot.

Step 4   From the inside, apply plastic wood generously and force it into the crack along both sides of the head (down the mold line). Squeeze the front and the back of the head together, to force out excess plastic wood; quickly clean off any that seeps to the outside, then tie the cloth around the head. Pull it tight enough to hold the front and back of the head together while the plastic wood dries. Do not disturb for at least 24 hours.

Step 5   Remove the cloth. A crack will be visible on the outside along the mold line. Using an Exacto knife, scrape away all flakes or chips of paint that could fall into the crack as you fill it (from the outside) with plastic wood. Use a palette knife to spread the plastic wood and force it into the crack. Keep it smoothed out by dipping the knife blade into plastic wood solvent and running the blade over the applied wood. If any thin or weak spots are apparent inside the head, repair them now with plastic wood. Leave undisturbed for another 24 hours, or until the seam line is thoroughly dried out.

Step 6   Now that the head is strong enough for work to proceed, examine it all over, on the outside. If there are holes or cracks that need patching, do them now. Always build an outside repair a little higher than the surfaces around it, and feather the repair out onto the old surface so that there will be no lines of demarcation. At any point where filler needs to be applied, scrape off the old surface but save it for recycling later.

Step 7   Examine the neck hole. Scrape off crumbly areas and save them. The crumbs, too, will be recycled.

Step 8   Cut a cardboard circle of wide enough diameter that its edges, when glued to the remaining surface, will rest solidly on the surface. Cut an opening in the center of the cardboard. Glue cardboard over neck hole. Let dry thoroughly.

Step 9   Put the crumbs you saved into a mortar and, with a pestle, grind them to powder. Add a wad of plastic wood and enough plastic-wood solvent so that, when mixed, the filler is spreadable but not runny. From the outside, apply this mixture to the cardboard. Build it higher than the surrounding areas and smooth it over onto the old surface, so that you cannot tell where one ends and the other begins.

You have to use your "inner vision" here, for as you work on the head you must see (and anticipate) the problems that will face you later in sanding and painting the repairs. The smoother the repair, the less sanding you'll have to do.

Step 10   Smooth the hole edges of the repair by dipping your index finger into the solvent as often as necessary, and running it around the hole. If the surface of the repair is somewhat "ridgey," do the same thing to that. Make it as smooth as possible. Put the head aside to dry, this time for at least 48 hours.

Step 11   Sand all repaired areas, being careful not to rub off any more of the crazed and flaked surface than necessary.

Step 12   Now you will need rubber gloves, Formby's Furniture Refinisher, and steel wool #00.

Into a small bowl put all the flakes of the painted surface that you saved or that fell off the doll head. Add a very small amount of Formby's. Use a pestle to grind and mix the old surface flakes with Formby's. Dip a small piece of steel wool into this and, without squeezing it, apply to a bare spot on the head. Dip and dab the mixture from the bowl to the head several times. It takes only seconds for the solution to begin softening the old finish. Go over the entire head, applying the wet steel wool and rubbing in a constant circular motion, one small area at a time. As the old crazed surface "melts down" under this treatment, it is reconstituted. The circular motion carries the reconstituted finish onto other areas, until usually the old surface has been completely spread out— thinner than it was originally but still there, a part of the doll.

All features will have been dissolved by Formby's; therefore they will have to be repainted. If there are splotches of uneven coloration on the head after you go over it the first time, use fresh steel wool, fresh Formby's, and go over it a second time, to even the color. Discard the used steel wool and pour the solution into a separate metal can that can be capped tightly. The sediment will settle to the bottom and the liquid can be used again and again.

Almost all crazing will have disappeared during this treatment. All loose flakes will have "melted" down and once again become a part of the doll's surface. Naturally the colors of the doll's features will also have become a part of the "flesh," but quite often, if you have worked at the head until the reconstituted color is perfectly even, the doll's flesh need not be repainted. Only the features need be added.

Refer to Chapter 3, the section on Grinding China Paints, and follow the instructions given there for painting the face with a china paint/balsam of copaiba mixture.

19

Detecting a Repaired Antique Doll

Years of experimentation, followed by specializing in making invisible repairs myself and in the reconstruction of parian, china, and bisque dolls, have taught me ways to detect the presence of such work even when it is superbly done. Moreover, because of my expertise at reconstruction work, I have often been approached by dealers and pickers—usually by telephone—with offers to "go into business" with them. Their business? Cheating doll collectors and honest dealers by representing repaired dolls as being in mint condition.

This chapter will explain many of the deceptions that are practiced, and explain the methods you can use to detect a repaired doll head. Of course there is nothing wrong with buying a doll with such a head IF you know about the repair and the price is right. But the larger and more extensive the repair, the lower the price should be.

When a dealer or picker misrepresents a doll a crime is perpetrated. Experienced but too avid collectors are often the victims; dealers who do not specialize in dolls (and even some who do) are often hoodwinked too. Outnumbering the combined total of these, however, are the beginners. They are easily deceived because they usually enter the world of doll collecting without either knowledge or experience (as most of us did). Research, studying dolls in collections, visiting museum displays, asking questions of knowledgeable collectors—these will all help, not only the beginner but everyone involved in collecting antique dolls, for no one can ever know all there is to know about them.

Everyone is familiar with the term *dealer*. Antique dealers' shops abound in villages, towns, and cities all over the country. Most dealers are honest. They have to be if they want to keep the respect of their friends, neighbors, and customers.

The term *picker* is not so commonly known. A picker is—in a sense—a traveling salesman (or woman). He is on the move coast to coast if he's big time; in a limited area, if he's just starting out. The professional picker of dolls (or any other collectible) knows which ones are rare; he knows the going prices, and he knows his customers. He knows, for example, that Jane Doe in California will pay any price for a rare A.T. not in her collection. That Mary Smith in Florida is searching for a rare Bru she does not have. The picker also knows the price limits (if there are any) that most collectors will pay, and so he begins to search. Along his route he buys damaged dolls as well as old doll bodies, odd arms, legs, wigs, doll clothes. If an item is associated with dolls, he knows he can sell it somewhere. There is nothing wrong with this method of doing business if the picker is honest with his buyers. Unfortunately, though, the very nature of his activities leads him into temptation; it is so easy to cheat!

How does he start? He cannot work alone. Because of the time involved in repairing, he must have at least one person to do the actual repair work while he peddles the repaired dolls. A trusted friend or acquaintance, talented in such work and suspected of being receptive to such an arrangement, is taken into the picker's confidence. They reach a satisfactory financial agreement, and together they undertake this extremely profitable but hazardous venture.

The picker may already know several dealers not averse to turning a fast buck. He probably knows others who are "iffy"; they need a bit a of assurance that they won't get caught. But he gets in touch with still a third group, who will not handle repaired dolls themselves, but will tip him off (for a kickback) to individual collectors with unlimited funds to spend. This third group is not as profitable for the picker to work with. It takes more time, and personal contact with the buyer, and his chance of getting caught is far greater. He knows his dealers, but he cannot know just what kind of "foxy" lady he's going to face. *He* usually avoids the male collector, leaving him for the sharp-looking female picker to "take to the cleaners."

The collector who deals directly with a picker who works this last way is, indeed, to be pitied. Even if the deception is discovered right away, the chance of locating the slippery picker is slim. What about the dealer who sent the picker to the collector? When questioned (if he is), he will simply deny having done so. Who can prove otherwise?

What happens when a collector buys a "mint" doll from a dealer and discovers it has been repaired? Some collectors keep quiet about the deception because they don't want to admit being fooled. Others go back to the dealer and complain. Often the dealer tells them a sad story of how he himself was "rooked" by a picker. The story may well be true, but an honest dealer will refund the money and take back the doll, or will make a price adjustment.

There is also the combination "dealer-picker." Somewhere he has an antique shop, but he doesn't stay in it. Another person runs it for him while he travels around the country, displaying at shows. Occasionally a dealer-picker will confide in another person in the same business, given the right circumstances.

Recently, at a major antique show in one of the larger cities, Mr. X became quite friendly with Mrs. Z, who had the adjoining booth. Business was slow the second day, and their conversation centered around dolls, since both specialized in them. Mrs. Z was suspicious of several he had on display, but she played it cool in an attempt to draw him out. She had met his type before. By closing time she knew many of his "secrets" because she had won his confidence. He thought she might become one of his "contacts."

"We can both make a hunk of dough on 'em," he bragged.

But Mrs. Z, who believed the words once penned by La Fontaine, "It is a double pleasure to deceive the deceiver," led him on. She discovered that of the approximately seventy-two dolls Mr. X had for sale, only forty-two were in mint condition. None of the forty-two was rare, but all had high price tags.

Laughingly, Mr. X told her his motto was "Let the buyer beware." Then he added: "If collectors weren't so greedy, people like me would starve to death!"

Sad to admit, his statement is true. Collectors and some dealers unknowingly encourage the Mr. X's to ply their fraudulent trade. In their greed to acquire rarities, such doll people are ready to believe any story.

A longtime collector and an enthusiastic reader of doll books (I'll call her Mrs. R) spent nearly $9,000 not long ago on one rare doll. A picker had brought it to her home, saying that a "mutual friend and business acquaintance" had sent him there. He told her about the doll and offered to bring it from the car for inspection.

Mrs. R's excitement knew no bounds when she saw it. The doll was "mint," just as he had said. The wig and pate were loose and she inspected the inside of the head. Perfect!

The seller explained that he had bought the estate of a woman who had collected dolls for more than fifty years, and because his "friend" told him that Mrs. R. bought only the rarest dolls, he had personally selected this, the rarest of them all, to bring to her. But he had more at home, if she cared to see them some day.

Mrs. R. was flattered that the picker was giving her first chance at this rare beauty. Needless to say, he cashed her check that same day and left for parts unknown.

The collector suspected nothing when she showed the doll to me. My cursory examination of it revealed a superbly reconstructed head. During the examination, Mrs. R. bubbled on about the nice gentleman she had bought the doll from. "He's going to bring some more next week to show me." No, she couldn't remember his name, but it was on a receipt "somewhere"; no, she hadn't asked where he was from; no, the "mutual friend" wasn't someone she actually knew, but his name sounded familiar.

When I told her the doll had been extensively repaired, at first she became indignant. "I examined it, all over, inside the head, outside, everywhere, and it's in perfect condition," she sputtered. "Look inside the head. You can tell the plaster around the eyes is old. And look at all that dirt inside the head!" She went on to point out the dirt in and around the nostrils, the ears, the eyes. Dirt smudged the face too, but it did not have the soft patina of ancient soil.

There was no point in arguing. Whoever did the repairs was truly a master at his trade, and there was simply no way a quick visual check could reveal the restoration to the unpracticed eye. The average person sees what he is *told* to see; the *professional* does not assume a doll head is mint just because he's told it is. He's a doubting Thomas, and his examination is conducted accordingly.

Mrs. R. should have been suspicious even before checking the doll because it was such a rare one and she knew it. And she should have been dubious when she was told it was in mint condition. But her behavior is understandable to those who love dolls. Most "doll people" I know are sensitive, enthusiastic, gullible—confused because of so many contradictory things said about doll history; unsure of what they read in books. When confronted by a professional con man who seems to know all there is to know about dolls, they are easily intimidated, easily convinced that what he says is the gospel truth.

This is not written to categorize all dealers and pickers as crooks because only a very small percentage engage in such corrupt schemes. Nor is it meant, in any way, to cast aspersions on the personalities of doll collectors. As a whole, they are among the nicest, most interesting people in the world.

It was easy to prove to my collector-friend that she had been ripped off. (The methods I used will work equally well for you.) A lighted flashlight inserted inside the head of the doll revealed five repaired cracks, several chips, and a large area extending from above the left eyebrow, over the left ear, to part of the back of the head, an area that had been missing and was filled in.

This test is 95 percent successful. Why? Porcelain is translucent; that is, it allows the passage of light, but diffuses it. Nontranslucent repair materials are glaringly obvious as darker spots (chips), streaks (cracks), and large opaque areas (where missing sections have been replaced). See Plates 7–10.) Since light rays cannot penetrate through such repair materials, you will know in seconds if any repairs have been made on a head. This simple test can be done at home, if you're examining dolls with an eye to buying; carry a flashlight and a magnifying glass if you're going on a buying trip. Most dealers have no objection to a close examination of dolls they're offering for sale. Many leave the wig and pate loose so that the customer can see inside the head. And, quite often, the *dealer* is honestly shocked when your flashlight reveals repairs on a doll he bought as mint. If you do find such repairs, chances are that you and the dealer can come to a mutual agreement on the price, which should be far below what you would pay for a doll in mint condition.

If the doll seems dirtier than you think it should be, moisten the tip of a finger with your tongue and draw the finger across a particularly grimy area. New dirt readily comes off. Old dirt has combined with fumes over the years, and is harder to remove. After doing this test on my friend's doll, my fingertip was black. And I could smell the strong odor of tobacco, indicating that the doll had been recently "dirtied." Cigarette ashes are one of the most popular substances used to add the "old look" to dolls. I'm sure that was what had been used on hers.

The obvious question at this point is, what if the pate and wig are not loose? When the flashlight cannot be used inside the head, try pulling the wig as high as possible and holding the flashlight *against* the back of the head while you view it from different angles, starting with the face. Move the flashlight to one side of the head while you examine the other side. Repairs are more difficult to see this way because the light rays must penetrate two layers of porcelain, so be sure you have good batteries in the flashlight. Most doll heads are thin, so if the flashlight beam is powerful enough you will be able to detect repaired areas, unless they are under the wig.

This method can also be used for examining parian or china heads when they are glued onto a body. It is not completely infallible, but well worth a try.

Another simple test, difficult to explain but readily understandable once it's tried, is what I call the "sound test." Undamaged porcelain produces a clear sound when tapped with a fingernail. If the head is on a body, the sound is naturally a bit muffled, but it's there. You can develop an ear for this sound by trying it on dolls you own. Tap near the eyes, then tap on the cheeks. Listen to the difference in the sounds. The plaster holding glass eyes in place causes the porcelain to have a dull thunk, but when you tap on the cheeks, which are hollow, you will hear a clear tone. Train your ears to pick up these variations. Do this test on doll heads you know are repaired, and listen to the clear sound of the undamaged part compared to the dull thunk when you tap directly on the repaired part.

Always be suspicious if you're offered one or more rare dolls claimed to be mint. Invisible repairs are quite expensive, not in materials used but in the equipment and time required for perfect work. The con artist and his cohort(s) cannot afford this time expenditure unless the doll is of sufficient value to warrant the expense. If you're considering the purchase of a doll priced under $200, it's still a good idea to do the flashlight test, if possible. A professional crook would not go to the expense of having such a modestly priced doll repaired, but dolls are constantly coming on the market when an owner dies who *might* have had them repaired for sentimental reasons. (Often the expense of having a less costly doll repaired far exceeds the actual value of the doll.)

Don't be a sucker for a romantic tale concerning a doll's history. An acquaintance, now deceased, owned a so-called Biedermeier, a bald china shoulder head with a black circle on top of the head. The doll was authentic and in mint condition, but was not worth the $350 my acquaintance paid for it more than ten years ago. The picker (who claimed it was a family heirloom) had spun a yarn about one of her ancestors who was given the doll about 1864. The Andersons were quite wealthy, as the story went. The mother owned many pieces of jewelry containing valuable diamonds. When the family saw they were going to be stripped of their possessions by marauding soldiers (during the Civil War), the mother, to save her favorite diamond ring, ripped open the cloth body, hid the ring inside, and stitched the body together again. The young owner carried the doll (and the ring) to safety.

My acquaintance bought the story and the doll. She was so enthralled with this romantic tale that she did not ask the picker what happened to the mother, why she didn't remove the ring, how it could have passed down through the generations without at least one heir being curious enough to look for the ring. The picker said it was, to her knowledge, still in the doll. Nothing about this romantic tale rings true. Yet as long as this lady lived, she proudly related this "sad Civil War story" to all who would listen. And she claimed she had never tried to find the diamond.

Although this incident has nothing to do with detecting repaired dolls, it is included here to alert you to another ploy used to line sellers' pockets with your dollars. Be wary of anyone who finds it necessary to spin yarns to sell dolls. Ask logical questions, and don't be satisfied with less than logical answers. Even if everything seems to fit—don't neglect a close inspection of the doll. Romantic tales encourage "dollers" to pay far more than a doll is worth.

As stated earlier in this chapter, the flashlight test, the "dirty finger" test, and the ring test show up repaired doll heads 95 percent of the time. What about the other 5 percent? It is possible (though very few possess the knowledge) to do kiln repairs. Materials similar to those used when the dolls were made are utilized in this type of repair work. When fired in a kiln, such materials become translucent to a certain degree. Here, the ring test is worthless as a test, but if you know what to look for, the flashlight test will reveal these repairs, not as stark black, but as shadows. (See Color Plate 7). Such repairs are more difficult to expose because even though one complains about the suspicious shadows, he may be told that the old porcelain was thinner in some parts than in others. This *could* be true. In such cases, the only advice I can give is this: if the price is right and you want the doll, buy it. You can be suspicious, you can challenge the dealer or picker, but in many cases you cannot prove your suspicions.

Repaired arms, hands, legs, and feet are usually easy to detect because those who mend them spend as little time as possible on them. Use a good magnifying glass for examining the extremities. Look first at the mold lines. If a break occurred there, you will find the mold line ends and a smooth (sanded-down) surface takes over. The most common breakage on a hand or foot is damage to or the loss of finger(s) or toe(s). Such repairs are rarely invisible; most can be seen with the naked eye.

What about "marriages"—the common practice of assembling heads and bodies not originally part of the same doll? This is a difficult area to explore, for only through doing research, visiting museums, and examining dolls known to be original can you develop a talent for discerning this practice. On composition bodies, check the fit of the head in its socket. Check also to see if all parts fit snugly. Usually such dolls are fully costumed, making it difficult to examine them without removing the clothes. If possible, take time to remove them, with the owner's permission, of course. Be doubly suspicious of clothes that are sewed on (without snaps, buttons, or ties).

Dolls (heads, arms, and legs) made in different periods of time had, incorporated into their designs, the characteristics of that period. What causes a great deal of confusion is the practice of continuing the production of a popular doll well into another time period. Too, many factories made heads only; the bodies were made elsewhere. Therefore, in doll bodies, there will be wide variations in body styles and materials. This resulted in many composites—French heads on German bodies, German heads on French bodies. Until about 1879, the facial features and the bodies were in better proportion than in the period from 1870 to 1900. Many dolls produced during this thirty-year period were made with unusually fat arms and legs, ending in small, delicate hands and feet. In determining whether the extremities are original or have been replaced, one of the finest books to study is *The Collector's Encyclopedia of Dolls* by the Colemans. Their *Collector's Book of Dolls' Clothes* provides much valuable information, too. There is no substitute for experience, but much can be learned through study and research.

The world of dolls is a breeding ground for corrupt dealers and pickers, some of whom even advertise in national publications. Even though an ad may say "return privileges" or words to that effect, this is no guarantee that the advertiser will live up to that promise. I was the victim of such an advertisement in 1969. It was my first and last time to order a doll by mail. When it arrived, it was not the antique K*R 114 at all. It was an unmarked reproduction of an A.M. 390. I immediately returned it, with a covering letter demanding a refund. By return mail the woman replied that the doll was broken "into a thousand pieces" when she received it, and that she had no intention of issuing a refund. A letter to the Postmaster General in Washington, D.C., describing the incident and containing copies of the ad, the letters, and proof of insurance resulted in a phone call from a young lady employed in that department. She explained that they could not act unless at least twenty persons complained of similar incidents. After a lengthy discussion, somewhat heated on my end of the line, I dropped the matter, having decided I was fighting a losing battle. Later I wrote the advertising manager of the publication, and he apparently canceled this woman's advertising. I have never seen her ad in that particular paper, but I often see it in other papers and magazines.

In every field of collecting where big money is involved, there will always be swindlers. What has been described here is only the tip of the iceberg, but perhaps it will make the reader more cautious. No one person can be aware of every scheme being used to bilk the consumer, any more than a so-called expert can know all there is to know about dolls. The best procedure to protect yourself in investing in dolls is to develop a show-me attitude toward any doll offered for sale. Before any money changes hands, prove to yourself—and the seller—that the doll is exactly as represented.

20

Distinguishing Replicas and Fakes

A replica is an honest copy of an antique or collectible doll. It is signed and dated. This is the law.

A fake is an unsigned, undated replica of an antique or collectible doll, deliberately planned from the beginning to be sold as such. This is, of course, against the law.

But there is an in-between doll—one that was signed and dated when it was made. It was sold as an honest copy. If it is an excellent replica of a rare and valuable antique doll, and if it falls into the wrong hands, the signature and date may disappear, by way of a grinder (if they were incised in the porcelain before it was fired), or if they were china painted, eaten away by acid. An experienced collector has no difficulty in recognizing the marks of an electric grinder, but acid usually leaves no trace of china paint. Fortunately for collectors, very few doll artists use china painting to identify their work.

Always make a close examination of any doll you're thinking of buying. Never take the word of even a good friend; she too can be fooled. And don't ever rely entirely on what a dealer tells you, not because you suspect she's dishonest but because she also can be victimized. Of course, she could also be dishonest.

Where, then, can you start, and whom *can* you depend on? Perhaps the following anecdote will give you some ideas.

Once upon a time Junie Marooney (fictitious name, of course) came down with a case of "smart-itis." Fortunately it lasted only a short time and it never surfaced as obnoxious behavior. Smart-itis is a disease that often infects doll collectors, at one time or another. Most of them get over it quickly; some never do.

As for Junie—she read a doll book written by that famous author Mr. I. M. Smart. She had heard that Mr. Smart knew all there was to know about dolls. She was a beginner. She believed!

Junie located a museum with a doll section. Although the dolls were behind glass, each one had a card attached giving its history and description. She took many notes. She was learning. And she believed!

She attended a two-day doll auction. She found the opportunity of examining so many dolls and talking with experienced collectors highly thrilling. The affair added much to Junie's education; however, she heard a few things that confused her a bit, although her belief in Mr. Smart was still unshaken.

Finally came the big event she had looked forward to for weeks— the annual "Razzle-Dazzle Doll Show." Dealers from everywhere would be there. Junie was ecstatic. She felt that she could hold her own in any doll discussion. All those hours spent reading and studying and making notes and talking with others were going to pay off. She knew all the things to look for in distinguishing fakes from the real thing. For example, a certain doll (it will not be named here) must have fifteen lashes on the upper lid, thirteen on the lower—count them. Unless this was so, the doll was a fake. That same unnamed doll, in addition to having delicately feathered eyebrows, must have eyebrows that almost come together in the center; otherwise it was a fake. The artist painted the mouths of *all* J.D.K. babies by holding a stencil in place and applying china paint through it, making *all* the mouths identical. If china dolls didn't have red lines above their eyes, they were fakes; if they didn't have red dots in each nostril, they were fakes. Yes, Junie Marooney had memorized all these things, and more.

Junie Marooney was now suffering from a full-blown case of smart-itis, and it had to get worse before it began to get better. The treatment that finally checked its progress came in the form of a present from her husband, another book on dolls, this one by another famous author and doll expert, Mrs. C. A. Light. As Junie read through the first part of the book, something didn't "feel right." Finally, it occurred to her that Mrs. Light had, in several places, contradicted Mr. Smart, and her pictures gave proof of what she wrote. And Junie began to doubt.

That was the beginning of her practical education and the end of her smart-itis. The moral of the story is, of course, to regard everything you read and hear with a grain of salt. *Think* about what you read, hear, and see. And depend on yourself when it comes time to render the final judgment on a doll that's captured your fancy.

If you read fifteen books by fifteen different authors, you will find many contradictions, yet each author may be correct. The dolls themselves are contradictions, and this is something every collector should understand. There are no substitutes for good books. Every careful writer has something important to say, and I like to believe most of them write to share their knowledge with others, and that they believe what they write to be true.

Counting eyelashes or judging a doll by such trivial variations as "X" number of lines in feathered brows; believing that only one type of body was ever used on certain dolls; denouncing a beautiful china doll as a fake because it does *not* have a red line above the upper lid—these are simply wasted efforts in detection. They should have no place in your judgment of dolls. Why? The doll faces were hand painted, and human beings are not now—and never were—so completely mechanical that they could duplicate their *own* work, line for line, feature for feature, with 100 percent exactness. It *is* true that very few dollmakers today can duplicate the delicate brows and lashes painted on old dolls, but when this type of work is done clumsily and heavy-handedly, it would not fool even a beginner.

Many doll collectors believe that one of the surest ways of distinguishing between a replica and a fake is that a replica is smaller than the original. Although this is true, it is also false—and this is another confusing statement. In Plate 11, my replica Dusky Bru Jne 9 has the *same* incised markings on the back of its neck as does the real antique Bru Jne 9. Note the difference in their sizes. The replica stands 22½" tall, the antique 18". The logical explanation for this is that, in the beginning, when the doll was sculpted, it was large. A mold was made from it. A porcelain doll was made from that mold, and the doll head was fired. Porcelains of today shrink as much as 18 percent during the firing. We do not know for sure the percentage of shrinkage that occurred in the old porcelains, but we do know that there was some. So the first head poured in the first mold and fired *did* come out of the kiln smaller than its original.

Another mold was made from that fired head. Again the same detailed procedures were gone through. *That* head, during its firing, shrank. And there were more molds made, more heads poured and fired, and more shrinkage. Therefore, when you think about this particular method of distinguishing a replica from a fake, ask yourself the question, "What can I compare it to?" You can be sure the mold from which a particular doll was made was copied from a larger one. But without the known original—whatever its size may have been—you cannot judge any doll you're examining on size alone. This applies to *every* antique doll that was a commercial success. The more popular the doll, the more sizes it was made in—this was a matter of economics. The large dolls were purchased by the affluent; but since it has always been man's bent to "keep up with the Joneses," doll manufacturers were happy to make dolls in all sizes to fit all pocketbooks.

The Dusky Bru Jne (Plate 12) is another replica poured in a mold having the same back-of-the-neck incised letters as the antique Bru Jne dressed in blue silk (Plate 13). When my replica was taken from the mold—while it was still quite wet—the eyes were cut slightly larger and the features were "water carved" a bit more prominently to match the appearance of the antique doll I was copying. The replica, just 14″ tall, *might* have been made from a mold used to copy an original such as this one. The antique doll stands 16″ tall. See Plate 13.

"F. G." in a scroll is incised on the back of both doll heads in Plate 16. Again we encounter a replica taller than a similar antique doll, yet both have the same markings. The replica stands 24½″ tall, the antique doll 22″; yet a close examination reveals that the mold I used to make the replica was almost certainly copied from a doll head in this series. Note here the difference in the parts of the composition bodies that show. The old body is much darker than the new replica composition body.

Which is the real Bye-Lo, which the replica? In Plate 17, is the one on the left real? No. It has an *original* tag on its tummy, but that's the only real thing about it. If you look closely at the Bye-Lo on the right—the one with the tuft of hair—you will see a spot where, with the owner's permission, I removed the original label and placed it on my replica. This was done to show how easy it is to fool many collectors. Never base your judgment on something so easy to change.

When I first began making replicas, my dolls were always signed behind or below the left ear with red china paint, fired on. At that time I didn't know it could be removed with acid. Also, at that time, my 15″ Bye-Lo was a best seller. (This was back in the days when I made my own molds, before there *were* any doll mold companies.)

Mrs. J., one of my most ardent customers, called one night from Utah. She was on a buying trip, and she *thought* a Bye-Lo she had found was one of my replica heads on an old, authentic cloth body. The doll had celluloid hands, like the old ones. "But something about it doesn't feel right," she said, "and when I looked under the left ear, I could see faint lines that looked like a red *M* and a *Y*." The owner of the doll, a lady in her late 70s, had paid $950 for it, Mrs. J. said. This was an outrageous price at that time.

The story, fortunately, had a happy ending. In addition to my signature and the date in china paint, there was another identifying mark on the doll (one I use to this day on all my replicas). We were able, quite easily, to trace the man who had sold the doll. He wasn't a bit reluctant to cough up the money and take the doll back. It was following this incident that I began incising my name in the porcelain greenware, not only under the left ear but also on the left foot, if it is made of bisque. As for my "secret mark"—that shall remain my secret. Only one other person knows it.

At the start of this chapter, I defined a replica, a fake, and the "in-between" doll. There is still a fourth doll to consider. Commercial establishments and individual dollmakers advertise doll kits for sale. These contain the shoulder head (or head and shoulder plate if the doll is swivel necked), a pair of arms, a pair of legs, and instructions for making a body of cloth or leather. The hobbyist puts the doll together and costumes it. Later, what started out as a signed and dated doll head along with related parts in a kit—if it happens to be an *excellent* piece of work—is often sold as the real thing. It may be years before the buyer undresses the doll. When she does, if the maker's name and date are visible, she either realizes she's been swindled or is so naive she believes she owns a rarity, particularly if the date is incomplete, for example "'78" or the like. Some new collectors interpret this as 1778 or 1878, when in reality it was meant as *1978*. And the dollmaker's name leads her to believe she has acquired a rare artist-signed doll.

To protect yourself from this sort of skulduggery, ask the seller to remove the top of the costume, or to allow you the privilege. Examine the shoulder plate, and if its bottom edge is covered by cloth, leather, ribbon, or something else, run the tip of your index finger over the edge from shoulder to shoulder. Often names and dates are incised deeply enough so that you can feel them through the covering. Almost all the dollmakers I know sign and date their dolls in this area.

Some time ago Mrs. A, who delivers products to my studio, called to ask a favor. Her friend, Mrs. B, had just bought two large antique china dolls said to be twins. Mrs. A thought her friend had been cheated. Could they bring the dolls out for me to check?

The dolls were not only *fakes;* they were what is referred to in the trade today as "ceramic china" dolls, on which the glaze was already badly crazed (cracked). These dolls would have fooled *no one* except a beginner who had not "done her homework." It was as though this young lady, upon arising that morning, had decided today was the day to go out and buy antique dolls, and she just happened to come into contact first with a dishonest antique dealer.

As for Mrs. A, she had no interest in doll collecting but had done some costuming for me and had "grown up" with my dolls. Although she had never read a book on dolls or owned any, exposure to them over the years had taught her, subliminally, to recognize a fake.

Fortunately, when the young lady took the dolls back, the dealer gave her a refund of what she had paid—$500.

In Chapter 1 you learned the differences between china dolls, bisque dolls, and parian dolls. But you also learned they were *all* made of *porcelain* clay or slip. China dolls were glazed; bisque dolls had delicate flesh tones painted onto white bisque, and parians were left white and had features painted on.

Now you have been introduced to another term, which, at this point, may be confusing unless you have worked in modern ceramics. What are "ceramic chinas"? And what makes them so different from "porcelain chinas"?

"Ceramic chinas" imitate the *surface* of antique china dolls—to some extent. They are actually made of earthenware, and are just as worthy of respect as porcelain as long as they are sold for what they are and priced accordingly.

Earthenware is usually made from natural clay, and that used in today's ceramic industry requires firing over a period of approximately 6 hours, maturing at 1,859° F. The *body* of earthenware is soft and porous; it will not hold liquids unless it is glazed, and the glaze requires a second firing. Each company that produces "ceramic slip" has its special formula, combining different kinds of clays and sometimes adding other ingredients to achieve special properties. But there are also some *individuals* who have made a study of the properties of clay, who have some knowledge of chemistry, and who persevere in their experiments until they can produce a ceramic slip far superior to any sold commercially—and they often turn their talents in the wrong direction. This same type of individual may also formulate glazes to fit the body of the ware she or he has created. And so we meet up with "ceramic china" dolls.

The antique dolls—china, bisque, or parian—began as porcelain clay or, later, porcelain slip (a thick fluid product). Porcelain requires the highest fire of all ceramic pottery wares. In the greenware state it requires extremely delicate handling. The shrinkage is so great that it cannot be fired quickly, as can ceramic/earthenware. Without giving an exact timetable, I will say that my dolls are fired more than 20 hours, as compared to the suggested firing time (in manuals that come with kilns) of a mere 7 to 8 hours. My porcelains reach maturity at approximately 2,400° F.

Porcelain dolls have always held a special place in the hearts of doll collectors who want the real thing. But doll collecting today has reached such gigantic proportions that there is not enough of the *real* thing to go around, and what is available is so expensive that it is out of the reach of many collectors. This situation has proved to be a fertile—and extremely lucrative—breeding ground for swindlers.

When I first began making replica dolls and displaying them at doll shows, elitists would sail by my tables with their noses in the air. In those days, reproductions were frowned upon. Today, because of the shortage of the *real* thing, they are now sought after. It is far more sensible to buy a fine porcelain replica, sold and priced for what it is, than to scour the countryside for antique dolls if you lack the knowledge to tell the difference between a fake and the real thing.

Real china dolls do not change color, nor does their glaze crack. You can usually tell the difference between "ceramic china" and the old porcelain china by a simple comparison test. Carry a small china chip or perhaps a china salt shaker with you. Hold it near a china doll, and if the doll has an off-white or yellowish cast, look closely at the glaze. In all probability—if your vision is good—you will see crazing to some degree. Look at the glaze through a magnifying glass. (You should always carry a small one in your purse.) If you don't see crazing but still feel uneasy about the doll, try this surefire test: dampen the tip of a finger, draw it across a dusty surface (you can always find dust), then run the finger over the doll's cheek. Your finger must be quite damp to do this successfully. If the doll head is a real "porcelain" china, the dirt will smudge and wipe off easily; but if it's a modern "ceramic china" doll, the dirt will immediately outline any fine crazing that's there. And once the dust from your finger goes into the crazing to outline it, it cannot be cleaned out. Any attempt to do so will cause the dust to penetrate deeper (remember, earthenware/ceramic is very porous). If you're reluctant to carry out such a "dirty trick," keep in mind that you're not only protecting yourself; if the doll is not authentic, you will have marked it for what it is and also be protecting those who come after you. Of course, you may not be welcome in that particular shop again, but it would be foolish to buy *any* dolls from such a dealer. He's either an out-and-out swindler or so uninformed about dolls that you couldn't trust anything he told you anyway.

If the head proves authentic after this test, check the arms and legs the same way. Often they have been replaced. Old china dolls are usually whiter than today's whitest porcelains, so even if the arms and legs pass the test, see if they match the head in color. Any kind of replacement decreases the value of the doll.

The flashlight test, as described in Chapter 19, can also be used. A "ceramic china" doll is opaque. Light rays cannot pass through it as they do through all the old translucent porcelains.

If you hold the china chip against a china doll and the doll has a pinkish cast to it, it could be a rare pink lustre, and very valuable. Or it could be a fake pink lustre. If the pinkish cast is rather dull, "muddy looking" as opposed to clear, it probably *is* a fake. Do the "dirty trick" test and find out.

If you collect parians, it's easy to tell whether the head is a modern ceramic or old porcelain bisque. Parians are not glazed. Wet the tip of your index finger and place a drop of water on the surface of the doll head. If it disappears immediately, the head is not porcelain bisque. Modern ceramic bisque is porous (unless it has been sealed). Water disappears right before your eyes. Porcelain is completely vitrified. Water will remain on the surface until it evaporates, or run off if the surface is tilted. It cannot be absorbed because porcelain, like glass, is not porous.

The biggest danger in today's doll market is in buying medium to rare bisques. They are the ones now being faked most often. The A.T.'s, the A. Marques, the Brus—if they're valuable, somewhere they are being faked. Let some writer point out that only a few such-and-such dolls were made, or only thirteen examples of so-and-so are known, and the demand is created. Not only do some doll artists have the ability to simulate the style of the oldtimers, they can also deal with today's highly refined porcelains, knowing just the right ingredients to add to make them resemble the old.

I advise all doll collectors to follow this checklist (of course it is assumed they already know *something* about antique dolls):

1. Are the eyelashes and eyebrows delicately painted, with eyelashes slanted outward and eyebrows feathered? And are the rims of the eyes dark? To recognize the fakes, you must study the old. Often an inspection will begin and end here, for very few doll artists today have taken the time—weeks and months, actually—to practice the brush strokes necessary to copy the old masters.

2. Are the lips a soft red with a hint of rust in them? Many shades of red china paints are available in today's market. In the beginning, I bought a vial of every red, brown-red, and yellow-red available. Many weeks and experimental firings later, I realized that none of them matched the lips or cheeks of any *old* doll I tried them against. Finally, by mixing several together, keeping careful records of the proportions and varying the thickness of application, I discovered an ideal combination. If I can do it, others can. So, on bisque dolls, look for a translucent rusty red. If the color is very dark red, almost red-black, and looks opaque, the doll has either been repainted or is probably not authentic. Also look for tiny crescents of darker lip red outlining the two curves of the upper lips, and often two on the lower lip; sometimes there is only one on the lower lip.

(*Do not* base your judgment entirely on *1* and *2* above. Although these comparisons are important, they are not conclusive.)

3. Examine the skin tone by eye and by feel. A close examination of an antique doll's "skin" will almost always reveal white splotches somewhere on its head. After the doll was originally fired, it was white. Color had to be applied over the white to create the skin tones. For this purpose, china paints were mixed with oils (to hold colors on the bisque until heat fused them to it). When a worker handled the doll before the second firing, some of this oil/paint mixture would stick to his fingers wherever he touched the head, no matter how careful he was. This left all-white or smudged pink-and-white spots on the head. Unfortunately, these are easy for a money-hungry doll artist to duplicate.

What *is* hard to imitate is the patina, but to recognize the difference, one must touch and feel as many antique dolls as possible. Draw the index finger along the cheek of as many antique dolls as you can manage; while you do so, look away from the doll and concentrate on what you're feeling. (For some reason, your fingertip is more sensitive if you are not *looking* at the doll.) The old ones feel a bit like the extrafine sandpaper used in refinishing antique furniture, almost smooth yet almost grainy—a paradox. Today's porcelain is refined to such a degree that, when it's polished, it feels like satin. The difference between the two surfaces is one of the surest ways of distinguishing between a fake and the real thing.

4. Look *inside* the head. A knowledgeable dealer will never glue the pate and wig in place unless he has something to hide, particularly if

he deals in rare dolls costing hundreds of dollars, even thousands. Anyone experienced in the sale of such dolls knows that the customer, before spending a small fortune on a rare doll, will want to examine it, head to foot. This cannot be done unless the wig and its pate are loose. Examine the inside of the head for repaired areas; also check for a white interior. Look at the plaster holding the eyes in place. It should be quite soiled and grainy looking, as opposed to the fine-grained plaster most often used now to set eyes in place.

While you're at it, examine the eyes themselves. The beautiful antique glass eyes were made by artisans highly skilled in their trade; the eyes had a depth not seen in today's glass eyes. The colored iris and the black pupils sat deep within the clear glass domes that imparted such realism. These are the type often referred to as "paperweight eyes." When you view them from the side, you can see the clear glass domes projecting out beyond the upper and lower lids. New glass eyes—all those I have seen—either have a very shallow covering of clear glass over the iris and pupil, or none at all.

While you're examining the inside of the head, try to determine if the mechanism holding the head to the body, or the head to the shoulder plate, is old. You may see a wooden neck button and metal S-hook (if the head is on a composition body), a wooden button with a spring on top of it, the arms of a cotter pin bent down over the top of the spring—whatever assembly holds the head in place should *look* old, if the doll is claimed to be in original condition.

If the doll has an open mouth with teeth and tongue, check to be sure the teeth are porcelain and not plastic. Before I started making my own porcelain teeth for replacements in the old dolls, I once ordered teeth in twelve assorted sizes, advertised as unglazed porcelain—"just like the old ones." When they came, they were as plastic as a credit card, and as shiny as glass. These are easy to spot if you're looking for them, but easy to miss if you're not.

5. Inspect the pate and the wig, looking for cork, thick brown molded cardboard, papier-mâché, and the like used for the pates (crowns). As for the hair, if it's human it will have a heavy feel to it. This is a combination of accumulated fumes and dust. If you pull against a curl or wave, it will not spring back in place as quickly as will Dynel or other modern-day materials disguised to look like old human hair.

The "odor" test is, as far as I'm concerned, the most reliable. To my knowledge, no one has yet been able to impart the odious musty smell that emanates from old pates and wigs. Unfortunately, the ability to recognize the difference must be developed from an association with antique dolls.

If the wig is mohair, or any of the other materials used in olden days, it will have a disagreeable odor much like old human hair; and even though the wig may have been cleaned and refurbished, it is impossible to completely smooth any but the top layer of hair. Look beneath it. If the hair that lies beneath the top layer is tangled and rough looking, it's probably an old wig.

6. Remember that old chinas are much whiter than those made today. So are parians. The biggest difference between the old chinas and parians is that one is glazed and the other is not. Look for signs of wear on the back of a china's molded hair and on that of a parian. If either type of doll was looked at more than it was played with, you will find no wear marks. The color will be as good today as it was when the doll was first purchased; but if it was handled a great deal, not only will the color be worn away on the back of the head (where the doll lay), but the nose will often show wear to some degree, the glaze being worn off by friction and sometimes, if the nose was very sharp to begin with, the end of it will be chipped.

The cheek and lip colors were—in my opinion—the same on parians and chinas. That opinion is based on experiments in making both types of dolls. On parians, the color appears softer, more delicate, because there is no applied glaze to heighten and brighten it. On chinas, after glazing and firing, the same mixture of colors used on parians produces a brilliant red, one that could be defined as "apple red."

7. Wherever there are booths displaying dolls, stand several feet away from each booth and let your eyes wander over the exhibit. Be slow and lazy about it, not examining an individual doll, but absorbing what your eyes see as they travel over the dolls as a group. If your eyes tell you there is a "sameness" about *all* the dolls, chances are you're viewing a display of reproductions. Each may have been made from a different mold, but there is still that sameness. It resulted from the dollmaker's pouring them all of the same brand of colored porcelain slip, and also because the dolls were fired in the same way, for the same length of time, and china painted with the same colors. Any alert, sensitive collector who owns several dolls made by the same doll artist can recognize that artist's work, even if she finds it hundreds of miles from where it was produced.

A booth of authentic antique dolls, when observed by the same lazy method, shows no evidence of such "sameness." Even if, for instance, there are two K*R 100s, there will be a difference in skin tone. Because most of the antique dolls were first fired to white bisque, the skin tone painted on, and the doll refired, no two came out of the kiln exactly alike. That slight difference is observable.

You may not understand why you "feel" a difference, but you will know it's there.

Another booth with a mixture of reproductions—whether honestly represented as such or dishonestly represented—and true antique dolls can be confusing to the viewer. Then it is time to step up to the booth—as close as you can get to the dolls—and check them over, beginning with their skin tone.

If you are still suffering from smart-itis to some degree, hide it until the attack passes. At a doll show held recently, Mrs. M was asked to exhibit some of her rarest dolls. Because the show was for a cancer benefit, she agreed, and there she encountered a collector with the most advanced case of "the smarts" she had ever met. The episode developed quickly, to the astonishment of most and the embarrassment of Mr. and Mrs. M.

The collector, well known in the area, chuffed up to Mrs. M's booth and, for some reason, singled out a very rare doll she claimed to be interested in; in a loud voice she declared that it was a fake. She based her claim on one of the facts mentioned earlier in this chapter—the doll did not have the correct number of eyelashes. Going to the manager, she demanded that Mrs. M and her husband be "thrown out" of the show for being dishonest. This collector created such an uproar that, in order to pacify her, the show manager asked a visiting professor to examine the doll, with the permission of Mr. and Mrs. M. Even after the professor had made his judgment—that the doll was authentic—the irate collector was adamant in her accusation.

I was made aware of all this by way of a phone call late that night from the lady who had created the scene at the show. Having met her only once, I was totally unprepared for her obviously irrational behavior. At first, I didn't understand what she was talking about, but eventually I got the gist of it, enough so that I could ask pertinent questions. What she wanted from me was my agreement about the "eyelash" question—not that I am the world's greatest authority on antique dolls, which of course I'm not, but because she knew I had done a good deal of research and experimentation to make my replica dolls as much like the old ones as I could.

To this day that collector believes that what she read in an "authoritative" book is the unmitigated truth, instead of only the truth as "that author saw it," in describing one doll out of thousands.

This chapter could be endless because there is so much territory left unexplored—the bodies, the clothes, the accessories. The omission of comments on these subjects is deliberate. Most antique dolls offered for sale are fully costumed. You can hike up the dress and underskirts, but usually pantaloons hide most of the body. However, don't *buy* a doll unless you *can* examine it all over, body and limbs. This advice is not meant to encourage you to grab an antique doll and immediately undress it. You have no right to do that. Ask the owner to do it for you, but not unless you are truly interested in buying it. To do so otherwise would make *you* dishonest, and waste the dealer's time.

If you will remember that, when made, some of the beautiful old heads and limbs were classified as seconds and often sold as such, or carried home by workers for their own children, you will realize how so many confusing and contradictory statements can be made today about this or that particular type of doll. For example, suppose an A. Thullier doll head with a small flaw was carried home by a worker, and turned over to his wife. And suppose a composition body—if that was what the factory attached the head to—was not available to her. She might devise a shoulder plate that the head would fit, make a cloth or leather body, stuff it with whatever she had on hand, and costume it beautifully. Today, the A.T. in this case, with its limbs and body made of the same material, would be just as old, just as authentically dressed (in a costume of the period), and just as valuable as her factory sister. Would it, then, not be ridiculous for a writer or collector today to state positively that unless this *type* of A.T. was on, for instance, a fifteen-piece ball-jointed body, it was a fake?

However, an author cannot always be held responsible for the rumors and half-truths that arise from something he or she has written. The reader studies a picture caption describing one particular doll, and believes the caption applies to all dolls of that type. Then, too, there are a few writers who publish their own books and are thus free to make any—and as many—positive statements as they wish, whether these be true or not. Generally no one edits their texts, and all too often their research and experience are both inadequate. Still, there is something to be learned from almost any book, particularly from those that deal with a subject in depth; but don't be so gullible that you accept everything written, without question. Perhaps a hundred years from now some writer will do research on "Marty dolls." Unless that writer has access to my records (providing they survive the years), he will be able to write only in generalities. And if he *does* have my records of experiments and formulas and a day-to-day diary, he would still need a similar background knowledge in order to interpret the technical notes before he could write accurately about them.

Without a doubt, doll collectors in the year 2079 will be as confused about dolls being produced today as we are about those made a hundred years ago.

As a final, honest statement, I must end this chapter on what may be a discouraging note. There are teams operating today who are such fine artists and accomplished "con" persons that they can fool even the most knowledgeable collector or authority on dolls. I know of no 100 percent guaranteed way you can protect yourself from such teams other than to go along with your own intuition—a most unscientific method, perhaps, but one every experienced doll collector will understand. Just as some very sensitive people *feel* the telephone is going to ring, and it does—or know who is going to call, and it's that person—most experienced doll collectors *feel* something is not right when they view a doll that is not what it's claimed to be. If you have such feelings, don't ever ignore them.

The study of dolls is no standstill affair. You have to keep working at it, remembering that what seems to be an absolute truth today may be a half-truth tomorrow, and a discovery may be made tomorrow that will make the first absolute worth nothing at all. You will learn from day to day, by being eternally curious about everything related to dolls.

List of Suppliers

Animal Veterinary Products, Inc.
  P.O. Box 1267
  Galesburg, Ill. 61401
    Twinco slicker brush and comb.
  Ph: (309) 342-9511

B E C Doll Molds
  4048 W. Compton Blvd.
  Lawndale, Calif. 90260
    Doll molds and composition bodies.
  Ph: (213) 679-3013

Dick Blick
  P.O. Box 1267
  Galesburg, Ill. 61401
    Art and educational materials.
  Ph: (309) 343-6181

Brookstone Company
  127 Vose Farm Road
  Peterborough, N.H. 03458
    *Hard-to-find tools and accessories (pantographs, hemostats, magnifiers,
    jeweler's saws).*
  Ph: (603) 924-9511

Con-Ferro Paint & Varnish Division
  The Valspar Corporation
  St. Louis, Mo.
    Eze-Ply Spray Enamel—baby pink.

DeMeo Brothers
Importers, Manufacturers & Distributors
  73 Fifth Avenue
  New York, N.Y. 10003
    Hair goods supplies.
    Ph: (212) 243-8512, 13, or 14

Dollhouse Molds
  207 McAlpine St.
  Duryea, Pa. 18642
    Molds, composition bodies.

(276)

Dollspart Supply Company
  46-13 11th St.
  Long Island City, N.Y. 11101
  Wigs, glass eyes, Flo Paque paints, wax (Sticky and Pink), metal buttons, composition bodies, cloth bodies, complete equipment, and accessories for dolls.
  Ph: (212) 784-0400

Donald Durham Company
  Des Moines, Iowa 50304
  Durham's water putty.

Formby's Fine Old Furniture Refinisher
  P.O. Box 788
  Olive Branch, Miss. 38654

General Beauty Products Company
  1741 North Western Avenue
  Chicago, Ill. 60647
  Complete supply of products and equipment for working on doll wigs (hairpins, combs, scissors, curlers, etc.).

House of Ceramics
  1011 N. Hollywood St.
  Memphis, Tenn. 38108
  Complete line of ceramic supplies and molds.
  Ph: (901) 324-3851

Meyer Jacoby & Son, Inc.
  32 West 20th St.
  New York, New York 10011
  Hair goods and supplies.
  Ph: (212) 243-8340

A. Ludwig Klein & Son
  P.O. Box 245
  Harleysville, Pa. 19438
  Nonfiring repair materials for china, glass, wood. (William Karl Klein wrote book on using their products: Repairing and Restoring China and Glass—The Klein Method.)
  Ph: (215) 256-9004

Leiber-Standard Leather Company
  3415 South Grand
  St. Louis, Mo. 63118
  This company does not sell Cabretta skins for making bodies. Their leather, sold by the pound, is called "patching"; it includes all colors and is ideal for making doll shoes and other accessories.
  Ph: (314) 772-4466

Magi-Dyes Company
  Division of Magix Corp.
  Central Islip, N.Y. 11722
  Magix Leather Preparer and Magix Shoe Color Spray. Color spray available in many colors as well as white. Products excellent also for stripping and redyeing real leather shoes and purses.

Peak Doll Enterprises
  P.O. Box 757
  Colorado Springs, Col. 80901
  Compo doll bodies, compo doll body parts, clothing, books.
  Ph: (303) 392-6548

Reinhold Lesch
  Glas und Plastikaugen Fabrik
  D 8633 Rodental
  Coburger Strasse 47
  Postfach 17
  West Germany
  Tel. (09563)222
  Round and flat glass eyes for dolls. (It helps if you speak and write German when dealing with this firm. When you write, ask for "Preisliste Nr. 11/79 für Puppenaugen," and when the price list arrives, order from the section marked: "Runde Puppenaugen hohl—NR 201—lieferbar in den Farben braun und blau-grau.")

Rynne China Company
  222 W. 8 Mile Road
  Hazel Park, Mich. 48030
  Imported German Dresden overglaze china paints in powder form. Imported oils, fine brushes.
  Ph: (313) 542-9400

Schoepfer Eyes
  138 West 31st St.
  New York, N.Y. 10001
  Oval and round glass doll's eyes.
  Ph: (212) 736-6934

Seeley's Ceramic Service, Inc.
  9 River St.
  Oneonta, N.Y. 13820
  Doll molds, composition bodies, complete ceramic supplies. Home of the Doll Artisan Guild.
  Ph: (607) 432-3812

Yesteryear Products
  P.O. Drawer 4415
  Scottsdale, Ariz. 85258
  Doll molds and composition bodies.

Index